Praise for Katherine A. Dettwyler's

DANCING SKELETONS

"The chapters contain moving stories and precious vignettes on the relationships established between the anthropologist, her assistants, and Malian households. They recount frustrations, arguments, humorous conversations, and offer penetrating accounts of local views on death, disease, well-being, and social proprieties. In summary, the book has two main advantages. First, it engages the reader because it is well written. Second, it offers a broad scope for discussion of academic and practical issues."
— *Journal of Biosocial Sciences*

"An outstanding, well-written book that should be read by students preparing to work in anthropology. It reflects what I would like to think is anthropology at its best."
— Mark Cohen, Distinguished Professor, *SUNY Plattsburgh*

"The ongoing critique of ethnography has, happily, changed the genre, and today real people walk the pages of the best ethnographies. Dettwyler's *Dancing Skeletons* is surely one of the best. The text emerges as an extended meditation on applied fieldwork as a gradual melding of people and meaning. No student will leave this ethnography without both objective data and better subjective awareness of the 'is-ness' of suffering. None will go away gushing over the romance of fieldwork; yet, many will be attracted to the humanity of the applied research process."
— *American Journal of Human Biology*

"Dettwyler has used the reflexive style that our students love to read and that our colleagues in public health or international development would be well advised to hear."
— *American Anthropologist*

". . . a gem of a book on anthropological fieldwork. . . . This is a very personal journey that Dettwyler tells us about. Almost every page shows her interacting with her subjects, primarily interviewing mothers about infant feeding and child health, measuring children's growth, and gaining entrance to rural village society. The author never launches into abstract theories or generalizations, but lets the informants speak for themselves."
— *Academic Library Book Review*

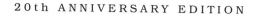

20th ANNIVERSARY EDITION

DANCING
SKELETONS
LIFE AND DEATH IN WEST AFRICA

KATHERINE A. DETTWYLER

University of Delaware

WAVELAND
PRESS, INC.

Long Grove, Illinois

For information about this book, contact:
    Waveland Press, Inc.
    4180 IL Route 83, Suite 101
    Long Grove, IL 60047-9580
    (847) 634-0081
    info@waveland.com
    www.waveland.com

Cover photo by Ferdinand Reus
Original cover illustration by Phyllis Rash Hughes

*Still for Steven,
who tended the home fires*

Table of Contents

Mali

Timbuktu

Niger

Gao

MACINA

Ségou

Mopti

Bamako ★

Magnambougou

DOGO *Baoulé* *Bagoé*

Sikasso

1

Return to the Field

The excitement of the chase is properly our quarry; we are not
to be pardoned if we carry it on badly or foolishly. To fail to seize
the prey is a different matter. We are born to search after the
truth; to possess it belongs to a greater power.

—Montaigne

The woman was sitting on a low wooden stool by the side of the
road. Silhouetted by the late afternoon sun, she was cooking fried
potatoes to sell to passersby. The air was full of wood smoke from
thousands of evening cooking fires, and I was heading home at the
end of a long day of research. As I walked by, she accosted me and
asked if I would come take a look at her two-year-old son. She knew
that I was interested in children's health, and thought, like many
others in the town, that I was a medical doctor.

"What's the matter with him?" I asked. She said that her son
refused to eat, and when he did eat, the food would pass through
him and come out as feces, undigested. "Please, come see him,"
she pleaded.

I assumed he was nearby and agreed to take a look at him. We
began walking, and we walked and walked and walked, along
narrow dirt roads, turning one corner after another, until we finally
reached a compound on the outskirts of town. She went inside the
tiny mud brick house and returned carrying the child. With dismay,
I noted his emaciated arms and legs and clearly visible ribs. His
eyes were dull and apathetic. I could tell at first glance that he was
severely malnourished. I looked behind the mother to see who had
been inside with the boy, but no one else was there.

"Who has been taking care of him?" I asked.

"Oh, he just stays here by himself."

1

"Shut in the dark house?"

"Well, he can crawl enough to come outside if he wants."

"How long has he been here by himself today?"

"Since this morning."

"You don't worry about him getting hurt?"

"No, he can't get into anything. He can't walk by himself anymore."

"He used to be able to walk?"

"Yes, and he used to talk, but not now."

"What does he eat?"

"Well, I leave a bowl of rice and sauce for him, but he usually doesn't eat it." She went inside the house and returned with the untouched bowl of food she had left with him that morning.

"Is he still nursing?"

"He was until about three weeks ago, but I weaned him hoping that it would encourage him to eat, but it didn't work."

I sighed and tried to decide what to do.

At the time, I was a graduate student, conducting fieldwork for my Ph.D. in physical anthropology in the town of Magnambougou, across the river from Bamako, the capital of the country of Mali, in West Africa. Since my research involved documenting traditional infant feeding practices and their effects on children's growth, I usually didn't interfere with the infant feeding practices of my informants. In select instances, however, it seemed unethical not to provide whatever help and advice I could. This was one such instance.

I examined the boy, took his weight, height, and other measures, and then spent more than an hour talking to his mother about different strategies she might try to gradually reintroduce him to solid food in a way that his gastrointestinal tract could handle. I knew that children who are chronically malnourished sometimes lose the epithelial lining of their intestines, which renders them unable to digest and absorb nutrients from their food.

The woman listened carefully, clarifying several points about how often, what, and how much to feed him. I also suggested that she keep him with her at all times, talk to him as much as possible, and make a point of putting the food in his mouth for him, making sure that he finished all of it. When I finally got home that night, I entered him in my study log as "Kid #104." Over the next year, I was able to document his recovery, as he steadily gained in weight and height, eventually nearing the standards for his age.

Six years later, on a hot summer day in June of 1989, I found myself once again tracing my way along the dusty back streets of

Magnambougou, on my way to track down #104, now eight years old. I was filled with a mixture of excitement and dread over what I would find. Had I made a lasting impression on his life, or had he slipped back into a downward spiral of malnutrition and disease once I was no longer around to monitor his progress? Or had he perhaps died, falling prey to one of the many diseases or accidents that claim children's lives in Mali?

Whatever the outcome of the morning's search, I was glad to be back in Mali, picking up the strands of my research. I was no longer a naive young graduate student. I had returned as an assistant professor of nutritional anthropology, supported for six months by a Fulbright Scholar Grant to continue and extend my research on child growth and infant feeding practices. During this fairly short time, I had to collect the data that would fuel future professional papers and presentations (critical for tenure at my university).

My happiness at being back "in the field" was not unqualified. My nine-year-old daughter, Miranda, had come with me, as she had the first time, but I had left my husband, Steven, and four-year-old son, Peter, behind in the United States. Moreover, it had taken me several weeks to overcome an unexpected case of culture shock.

Further fieldwork, beyond the dissertation, was absolutely essential for my career development, and I was committed to Mali as a research site. But Steven had a "real job." He had to be at his office from 8 A.M. to 5 P.M., Monday through Friday, fifty weeks a year. He couldn't just pack up and leave for six months. More importantly, it simply wasn't possible for me to take Peter to Mali. Peter has Trisomy 21, also known as Down syndrome, a condition caused by the presence of an extra twenty-first chromosome in the nucleus of every cell. In addition to mild mental retardation and distinctive physical characteristics, Peter has a poor immune system, and he is often on antibiotics for chronic bronchitis. I knew he could not survive the rigors of life in West Africa, and there was never any discussion of all of us going. At four years of age, Peter was just learning to talk and was too young to understand that Mama and "Sissy" were going away for six months; I was afraid he would forget me.

Miranda was along mainly because I needed the company. I also wanted her to experience Mali again, now that she was old enough to understand and remember it more than from her vague early childhood memories. It was important to me that she grow up realizing how different life is in other parts of the world, having firsthand experience of what one might call life-styles of the poor and anonymous. It was her calm and forthright acceptance of our return to Mali that enabled me to overcome my initial feelings of loneliness.

Because I had lived in Mali for two years in the early 1980s, I hadn't expected culture shock on my return, but our first few weeks were difficult and debilitating. Everyone I previously had known in the American community, people who worked for the U.S. State Department or the Agency for International Development, had rotated to other overseas posts. I had no way to contact my Malian friends and informants, as they had neither phones nor mail service. And although Fulbright grants are considered very prestigious in academic circles, I was treated as an "unaffiliated American" by the United States Information Agency (part of the U.S. Embassy) that was supposed to be sponsoring me. I had to negotiate for Embassy check-cashing, mail, and medical privileges, and the U.S.I.A. personnel gave me no help in finding affordable housing.

On my own, it took several weeks to get settled. The problem was to find something larger and nicer than a mud hut, preferably with electricity and an indoor kitchen, and a toilet and shower, but smaller and, more importantly, cheaper than the palatial houses occupied by most Americans, with their five or six bedrooms, generators, tall encircling walls, and large swimming pools. I eventually located and negotiated the rent on a small house next to the American International School, where Miranda would attend fourth grade in the fall.

When we first arrived, we had stayed for a few days in a tiny "guesthouse" on the outskirts of Magnambougou. It was set in a lovely garden, and it had electricity, with lights and an air conditioner. In other circumstances it might have been fine, but the city had only intermittent power. Days passed with no electricity at all, the air conditioner seeming like someone's idea of a cruel joke. Because we were supposed to have electric lights, there were no kerosene lamps, and my flashlight batteries ran out that first night. So we were without light once the sun had set. Most critically, there were no cooking facilities. The owner could provide food for approximately $15 (U.S.) per day—an outrageous sum for Mali, roughly the equivalent of two weeks' salary for an average worker. All the prices at the guest house were calculated to match U.S. government per diem payments.

Our first night in the country, we lay sweating in the dark. My head was pounding from a massive caffeine-deprivation headache, and it was much too hot to sleep. Several times Miranda and I rose and showered together in total blackness, trying to cool off, but the foam mattress radiated our body heat back, and sleep eluded us. I thought to myself "Whose idea was this, anyway?" and replayed in my mind my impressions of our first day.

That afternoon when we deplaned and stepped out onto the tarmac at the airport, I felt the all-encompassing heat of Mali envelop me. Riding into town, I soaked up the sights and sounds of the countryside, looking for evidence of "progress." But Mali looked the same—the road from the airport into town was crowded with cars, mobylettes, donkey carts, bicycles, and people walking. The women all had babies tied to their backs and huge burdens balanced on their heads. Herds of sheep and cows were goaded along with sticks by Fulani boys wearing conical hats. The smells were even the same—dust, wood smoke, car exhaust, rotting food, sewage, ripe mangoes, and more dust. It sounded the same—horns honking, cows mooing, people yelling, the almost forgotten cadences of the Bambara language. It certainly felt the same—hot and sticky, exotic yet familiar.

During the day, hordes of iridescent green flies filled the interior of the guest house, their buzzing a palpable presence, drowning out conversations, preventing coherent thought, and motivating me to find better quarters. As a first step, I sought out Moussa Diarra, my former field assistant, interpreter, and friend, who still lived in Magnambougou. He was working at the American Community Center (my old home) as a gardener. When I hired him to work with me again, the Americans at the Center were amazed to discover that he spoke English fluently and had lived in Houston and New York City as a young man.

My field assistant, Moussa Diarra: the one in the T-shirt.

In addition to Moussa, I hired another old friend, Oumou Drame, to watch Miranda during the day, a night guardian to watch the house at night (a relatively benevolent version of a protection racket), and a young friend of Oumou's to come twice a week to wash clothes in the basin behind the house. Finally, I encouraged another American researcher to share the house with us. Tom Kane was a demographer, in Mali on a two-year Rockefeller Foundation fellowship to study maternal mortality (i.e., why mothers die prematurely). In addition to being friendly and sharing many of my research interests, Tom helped with the rent, and his presence discouraged thieves and provided an aura of respectability for our household in the eyes of our Malian neighbors (it wasn't normal for a woman and child to live by themselves without an adult male). He also had a car.

Besides the troubles of settling in, conditions in Mali contributed to my culture shock. I had expected things to have improved, but instead, Bamako was awash in uncollected garbage, the streets were choked with cars, the sewage drains overflowed, and the government bureaucracy seemed even more convoluted than before. The influx of migrants from the countryside had turned the riverside capital into a noisy, polluted, modern city. Once we had moved into our own house, and I had secured my official research permission papers, I was able to turn my attention to my research in Magnambougou.

I had several projects I hoped to complete. One was to relocate as many of the children from my 1981-83 research as possible. I wanted to measure them again, in order to determine how nutritional status and growth patterns in early childhood affected subsequent growth. Did malnourished children experience periods of catch-up growth, and if so, when—middle or late childhood? Were the ones who were most malnourished in early childhood permanently affected? Had any of them died? Were the ones who were the best nourished in early childhood still taller and heavier than their peers? Had they survived better than other children, or had some of them become relatively more malnourished during late childhood? If malnutrition and poor growth were so prevalent in early childhood, why were so many adult Malians so tall and well built?

I also wanted to gather as much data as I could on children of all ages, to look for evidence of a common growth pattern in malnourished populations, one in which children grow very slowly but continue to grow into their twenties, well past the age when most well-nourished individuals have completed their growth. This extended growth period compensates, to some extent, for their poor growth in early childhood. Did this account for adult Malian size?

Another project was to visit new households, measure all of the members, and conduct extended, semistructured interviews about infant feeding beliefs and practices to supplement my earlier data. The ultimate goal of this part of my research has always been the development of culturally appropriate nutrition education programs, aimed at improving people's understandings of the links between diet and health, and the importance of making sure that young children get enough food, of sufficient quality, to meet their needs for growth and health. The final aspect of my research was to try to determine whether intestinal parasites, thought to be common in most Third World communities, were a major contributor to the poor growth of the children in Mali.

That morning, as I walked along, I pulled out the worn and faded notebook that contained all the information I had gathered about Kid #104, and looked up his real name, as well as his mother's. I began using numbers to refer to the children in my study early during my dissertation research. I thought it would be better to use numbers instead of names so that individuals could not be identified, but the number system turned out to be practical as well.

In Mali, most children are given Muslim names, chosen from the Koran, and there are only a handful of different first names. Every family with many children probably will have boys named Moussa ("Moses"), Amadou, Muhammad (the most common boy's name in the world), and Seydou, and girls named Aminata, Rookia, Oumou, and Fanta. About twenty Bambara lineages comprise most of the family names as well. It would be like doing research in a midwestern city where everyone was named Bob or Mary, Jones or Smith.

Thus, to refer to children by their names didn't identify them very distinctly. In addition to my field assistant, there were three children in the sample named Moussa Diarra. My adopted Bambara name was Mariam Diarra, and I often met other women with the very same name.

The children's numerical designations were unique, and I got so used to thinking of them by their numbers that I often forgot their names completely. "Oh, there goes #89 and his mother," I might remark. Or, "let's go visit #5 and #6 this morning." Another way of remembering which child was which was giving the child or his family some sort of nickname. Thus, we had the Lady from Kangaba (a village in southern Mali, famous as the home of a renowned line of *griots* (praise singers) and the site of a sacred hut), Moussa the Bucket Boy, the Onion Lady, and the Bozos by the river (not an insult, but a reference to the Bozo ethnic group, specifically the family that lived near the river, as opposed to the Bozos near the market). I also had the rich compound, the compound with the VCR, and my other husband's house (referring to a beautiful Fulani boy, with enormous eyes—I often teased his mother that I wanted to take him as a second husband, a notion she found hilarious; even though Malian men often have second wives, *who* would want a second husband?).

As I walked deeper and deeper into the neighborhood, I found my progress punctuated by the necessity of exchanging greetings with everyone I met. At this early hour of the morning, women were heading to the market in a steady stream, on their way to purchase the day's supply of fresh fruits and vegetables, fish or meat. I attracted attention because white people (*toubabs*) are not common on the back roads of any Malian community, but the women were unfailingly polite in offering me the standard morning greetings:

"*I ni sogoma.*" (Good morning.)
"*N'se, i ni sogoma.*" (Good morning to you.)
"*Here sira wa?*" (Did you pass the night in peace?)
"*Toro te.*" (There was no trouble.)
"*I ka kene?*" (Are you healthy?)
"*Toro si te.*" (I'm very fine.)
"*I che ka kene?*" (Is your husband healthy?)
"*Toro si t'a la.*" (He is fine.)
"*I denw ka kene?*" (Are your children healthy?)
"*Toro si t'u la.*" (They are all fine.)

Greetings form an indispensable part of daily life in Mali. Every time you see someone you know, you go through elaborate greetings involving a series of questions about their health, their night or day (did it pass in peace?), their family, and their work. The correct response to each question is a generic "No trouble," or a special word that simply acknowledges the question (men respond with *m'ba*, women with *n'se*). Then, the series of questions will be repeated by the other person. Sometimes each person takes turns asking and answering a question. In rural areas, people always include the query "How are your crops?"

Greetings are very important as a sign of politeness and respect. The higher a person's status, the longer and more elaborate should be the greetings you give them, out of respect. You also stop and make a point of greeting an elder, while two equals approaching each other on the street will begin the greetings as soon as they get in earshot, pass by each other continuing the series but without stopping, and continue the exchange until they are out of earshot going away again.

Men try to outdo each other in terms of who can say m'ba the most, and/or who can say it last at the conclusion of the greetings.

Eight or ten m'bas may be exchanged after all the questions have been asked and answered. The air near a market, or any other place where men gather, will be thick with m'bas flying back and forth. For some reason, women do not engage in the same verbal competition with their word, n'se.

Friends who haven't seen each other for a long time will truly be interested in the information exchanged, but even complete strangers, transacting what most people in the United States would consider an impersonal business exchange, will go through lengthy greetings before getting to the business at hand. You can go a long way in Mali simply by being able to go through the greetings appropriately in Bambara. Because so few French or American residents of Mali make any effort to learn to speak Bambara, my ability to not only greet people, but to actually carry on a conversation, and make jokes (usually at my own expense) gave me a significant advantage.

In his book *We, the Alien*, anthropologist Paul Bohannan writes that "once the people you are studying can understand three out of four of the jokes you make in their language, you can come home," meaning that if you have learned enough of their language and their culture to make them laugh, you have probably collected enough material. I enjoyed making people laugh by extending the greetings to include silly questions such as "How is your bicycle?" or "How are your fish?" or asking a little boy "How is your wife? Did she have a peaceful night?"

During my dissertation research, I learned to speak Bambara fairly well, but I always kept Moussa with me for tricky translations. I found that my Bambara came back very quickly, and I learned a lot of new vocabulary and grammar. Moussa always said I had no accent, but people often didn't understand me the first time I said something to them, because they were expecting French to come out of my mouth and weren't listening properly for Bambara. In Mali, the French language is known as *toubabou-kan*, literally, "the language of white people." For most Malians, the only white people they encounter are French nationals, and their assumption that a white person speaks French is usually justified. People were surprised then, when, in response to a question directed at me in French, I would say in Bambara, "I'm sorry, I don't speak French, but I can speak some Bambara." Once they had gotten over their surprise, they would launch into the greetings, as though to ensure that I really could speak their language.

Language is a source of immense power, and my ability to speak Bambara was one of my greatest assets for carrying out my research, and for surviving on a daily basis. Aside from greetings and cussing, however, my vocabulary was limited to the subjects of my research: pregnancy, breastfeeding, weaning, foods, sicknesses, fever, vomiting, diarrhea, health, kinship, emotions, and economic issues. I could not discuss politics or religion, or lots of other topics. I relied on Moussa to help me out whenever a conversation wandered into an area of my incompetency. It was extremely frustrating, in later months, to come across government agents in remote regions of north-central Mali who spoke French but did not speak Bambara because their native language was Fulani, or Tamasheq, or Bozo. In those instances, my inability to converse in French became a serious handicap, and Moussa's ability to translate between English and French was essential.

I paused on the threshold of #104's compound and peered around the door. Just inside, his mother was bent over, arranging her enamel pots and pans in preparation for heading to the market. She looked up at me and then straightened up, giving no sign of surprise or delight. Instead, adjusting her head cover and balancing her pots on her head, she launched into the morning greetings. When we had completed the standard series of questions, she paused and then said, "I haven't seen you for a long time. Where have you been?" as though I had been away for six weeks, not six years. "I went home," I replied. "Oh," she responded, nodding her head, as though that were the most normal thing in the world for me to do.

She called to her son inside the house. "Look who's come to see you—it's the lady who saved your life." A strapping lad of eight years emerged from the house, wearing a look on his face that was a cross between shyness and embarrassment. He crossed the courtyard and accepted my outstretched hand but kept his eyes cast down, where his foot was scuffing back and forth in the dust. We exchanged greetings. "Do you remember me?" I teased. "Yes," he said. "How could I forget? You used to hang me from the tree [a reference to the suspension scales I had for measuring an infant's weight], and brought me bananas from the market. My mother is always telling people how you saved my life."

In spite of the warm day, I felt goose bumps rise all along my arms and across the back of my neck. Was it really possible that in addition to my own two children, I was really responsible for the existence of this young boy? Was it possible that I had truly made a difference in this one person's life? Pulling myself together, I asked him if I could measure him one more time "for old times' sake," and he flashed me a grin, happy to oblige. Once I was finished, he joined a group of his friends heading to school. After he left, I measured his mother (she giggling and fidgeting the whole time), and then we sat in the shade cast by the house and talked about the day when we had met six years before. She was particularly proud of her son, who had been healthy since his initial illness as a young child; he was doing very well in school and was a cheerful, helpful child.

I left the compound feeling buoyant and confident, eager to search out another child from the original study. Not all of my reunions would turn out to be this heartening.

2

Of Mosquitoes and Men

Sometimes Errol was not a perfect anthropologist, and all this
admirable myth and culture soured into native weirdness.
—Lionel Shriver

The mosquitoes were lined up in a row on the wall above the bed,
like planes on the deck of an aircraft carrier. Seven of them, full
of blood and no longer hungry, they clung to the wall in a stupor.
They didn't move when I turned on the light and sat up, scratching
my leg. Methodically, I smashed them with the heel of my palm,
one by one, leaving a red streak of fresh blood on the wall—my
blood, or Miranda's—to mark each one's passing. It gave me a
certain satisfaction. One last mosquito, swollen with blood, lay
torpidly on the bed sheets. I swatted at it halfheartedly. The weight
of the blood prevented it from becoming airborne, and it hopped
slowly across the bed, followed by my hand, until it reached the
edge, and tumbled off.

Mosquitoes in Mali are both annoying and dangerous. Annoying
because they keep you awake at night, buzzing in your ears, biting
any exposed inch of skin, raising itching, painful welts. Dangerous
because they carry malaria. We faithfully took our prophylactic
antimalarial medicines, two varieties of quinine derivatives,
chloroquine weekly, and paludrine daily, to protect against two
different strains of malaria. We kept the screen doors closed and
sometimes fogged the bedroom with thick, cloying insecticide
before going to sleep, but still they crept in to torment us. Most of
the time the mosquitoes were merely annoying, but I retained my
respect for them, even as I wondered why they existed. Memo to
God: "Why mosquitoes?"

Two events prompted our departure from Mali in the fall of 1983;

both involved death and mosquitoes. The first was the death of Kay, a young Peace Corps volunteer, someone we had come to know through Peace Corps trainings we hosted at the American Community Center and from her visits to the Center for R&R after several months at her remote rural village site. Young, idealistic, in love with her village, Kay exemplified all that was positive about American youth. Out in her village, she had been experiencing severe headaches for several weeks and had doubled, then tripled, her chloroquine dosage, recording all her actions in her diary. Every day the headaches got worse. She finally decided she needed to get to a doctor and rode her mobylette (moped) 50 kilometers on dirt roads through the bush to reach the closest town. There she got into a bush taxi heading for Bamako.

Even though she always took her antimalarial medicine, she succumbed to an apparently resistant strain of cerebral malaria, lapsing into a coma in the bush taxi somewhere on the road to Bamako. The taxi driver dropped her off at the American Embassy. My image has always been one of the taxi slowing down, the door opening, and the driver rolling her unconscious body out into the dusty road in front of the Embassy, without ever coming to a full stop. That's not how it happened; nevertheless, it was too late. She died without regaining consciousness.

The second event was the death from hepatitis of a member of the American expatriate community. Mickey Vakil was actually an Iranian, the son of a diplomat who had grown up in the United States during the reign of the last American-supported Shah. Mickey was in Mali working for an engineering firm. In many ways, he was more American than the Americans themselves, as evidenced by his ardent love of baseball. During the Sunday afternoon baseball games we hosted at the Community Center, he had little tolerance for recreational players. If you weren't serious about the game, or if you weren't very good, you couldn't play on his team.

You don't get hepatitis from mosquitoes, of course, but they nevertheless contributed to Mickey's death. When he went to see the doctor at the Embassy, complaining of not feeling well, the doctor assumed he had malaria and prescribed extra doses of chloroquine, the routine initial treatment. Chloroquine is hard on the liver, and the combination of chloroquine and hepatitis destroyed his. He was Med-evaced to Paris, but the doctors there couldn't save him, and he died, leaving behind a wife and young daughter. I still think of them often, for Mickey's death left scars on us all.

A week after Mickey's death, I was called in to pack up the household belongings (one of the extra jobs I took to support my research). As I followed the wife and daughter into the house, we stopped to pet their dog, who was chained up inside a small mud brick doghouse. A few minutes later I went out to the truck to get more boxes and tape and stretched out my hand to the dog. Instead of a friendly lick, he lunged at me and grabbed the fingers of my right hand, biting deep into the flesh at both joints of my first finger. I got a tetanus shot at the end of the day, and within a week the physical wounds had healed, leaving thick white scars on the inside of my finger. These scars serve as a physical reminder, leading me to think of Mickey often, to wonder at the capriciousness of fate, and to ponder what it would be like to die when you are only 35 years old.

If the deaths of Kay and Mickey prompted us to leave Mali, it was another quirk of fate that had brought us there originally. We went to Mali almost accidentally, the first time, because we had friends from graduate school, Barbara and Gerry Cashion, who were still living there after completing their dissertation research. We had originally planned to conduct research for our Ph.D.s in anthropology in the Nuba Mountains, central Kordofan Province, in the country of Sudan, in East Africa. We spent our first three years of graduate school taking classes, reading books and articles about the Sudan, and studying Arabic. We wrote proposals outlining the well-designed, carefully researched projects we would carry out among the Nuba people. I would study the growth and development of children, and how the cultural focus on wrestling affected children's growth. I had even devoted some time to pilot projects, studying young male wrestlers at a summer wrestling camp (Top of the World) in Indiana and measuring the I.U. wrestling team. Steven would study rain-fed agriculture and how migration from the hills to the plains affected Nuba social organization and adaptation to the environment. With small grants from the university and Sigma Xi, a scientific research society, and a loan from some friends, we set off for Africa, confident that we would return with the data needed to write our dissertations and earn our doctorates. Sudan, "the largest country in Africa," according to every source, the site of "Chinese" Gordon's last stand, and home to the Nuer, a tribe well known to anthropology graduate students because they had been studied by the famous anthropologist E. E. Evans-Pritchard.

Our plans fell apart in Cairo, in July of 1981, during the Muslim holy month of Ramadan. After a delightful six weeks of backpacking and train travel through Europe, we found ourselves stranded in a sweltering, rat- and roach-infested, once grand, colonial-style hotel in downtown Cairo, a city of 12 million people, trying to find transportation south. All the planes to Khartoum were full of holiday travellers, and the ticket agent for the train south across the desert from Aswan refused to sell us tickets, because he didn't think Miranda would survive the journey—24 to 36 hours in open boxcars, if the train didn't break down, without food, water, or toilet facilities. Looking back now, I'm sure he was right, but at the time we were simply upset to be stuck in Cairo.

I had bronchitis, and Miranda refused to nurse because of the heat. Because of Ramadan, food was difficult to obtain during the day. One evening we took the bus out to see the pyramids; I took one look and said, "Big deal, they look just like all the picture postcards I've seen of them—get me out of this place!" After four days, Miranda and I left in the middle of the night, flying "home" to Delaware. Steven followed after a week. We moped about in Delaware, trying to decide what to do with our lives. Had we failed at anthropological research? Were all our years of preparation for naught? I worked days as a key punch operator, and Steven worked nights cleaning a movie theater.

In September, the Cashions came to Washington, D.C., on home leave from Gerry's position with the U.S. Agency for International Development in Bamako. They invited us to return to Mali with them and carry out our fieldwork there. They also had a 15-month-old daughter and assured us their assistance in finding a place to live and jobs to support our research. Grasping at this second chance, we set off once again for the African continent. We knew next to nothing about the country that was our destination (in Bambara, the native language of the largest ethnic group, I could say only "My husband is a very, very fat man," plus a few choice insults and expletives) and knew that we would have to adapt our research plans to a very different context.

When you study people, as anthropologists do, by living with them and becoming participants in, as well as observers of, their lives, you must be prepared for surprises. Sometimes little is known by the outside, academic world about a particular group of people, and what seems like a feasible project turns out to be impossible, or unrealistic, or not as interesting as some other aspect of their lives once you arrive. You can't manipulate the people you study, or conduct experiments, and you must rely on their cooperation in order to collect information. Because of these (quite reasonable) constraints on anthropological research, it isn't unusual for anthropologists to end up studying a different topic, or even a different group of people, than they intended. Personal comfort plays a role as well.

One of our professors from graduate school, Ivan Karp, originally set out to study a group of people who lived on a dusty, arid plain in northern Kenya. Every day he looked longingly at the cool, inviting, green hills in the distance. One day not long after his arrival he asked a friend, "Who lives in those hills over there?" "Oh, those are the Iteso," the man replied. Ivan and his wife packed up their bags, moved to the hills, and became experts on the Iteso. Paul Stoller set out to study the use of language in Niger, but his informants refused to cooperate until he switched to studying what they thought was important, sorcery (*In Sorcery's Shadow*). Daniel Biebuyck went to Zaire (then the Belgian Congo) to study economics, only to discover (as far as Western scholars were concerned) the existence of native African epic oral poetry. Today, he is well-known for his translations of *The Mwindo Epic*, which sparked a new line of inquiry for African scholars. Thus, when we went to Mali, we were following in a long line of illustrious predecessors.

Regardless of our trepidations as we got on the plane with the Cashions, once we arrived, we fell in love with Mali—with its stark beauty, with the bustle of its markets, and with the warm, friendly people who opened their hearts and their lives to our insistent questions, teaching us all we needed to know to survive and flourish and providing the raw data that would allow us to secure our future livelihoods. More than anything else, their wonderful sense of humor, their ability to laugh at the absurdities of life, even in the face of terrible poverty and hardship, meant that our time there made lasting impressions on our lives.

Mali was the reality beyond our book learning of anthropological theories and ethnographic methods. It was where we crossed the line from being students to being anthropologists, from the voyeurism of reading ethnographies to the reality of experiencing a completely different way of life, a completely different mode of thinking, new ways of interpreting the world.

I never did find any wrestlers in Mali, but Steven did find migrant farmers to study. I ended up studying breastfeeding and weaning practices and child growth, combining my academic training with my preoccupation with breastfeeding my first child. Steven studied migrant urban gardeners and changing social organization.

Together, it was our grand adventure, and the fulfillment of a lifelong dream for Steven. We supported each other physically, intellectually, and emotionally, and we delighted in watching our daughter thrive, learning to speak Bambara as she learned to speak English. Our sojourn in Mali was difficult at times, but everything worked out in the end. I sometimes feel as though God reached down his hand, plucked us out of Cairo, and deposited us on the opposite side of the continent, saying "Here, this is Mali; this is where you were meant to go."

Mali is a landlocked country, located in the heart of the great hump that forms the western edge of the African continent. The climate ranges from dense forest in the south, through open savannah-grasslands and river delta in the center, to the northern two-thirds of the country, which is part of the great Sahara Desert. It can be blisteringly hot, up to 140 degrees during the hot season, but with such low humidity that sweat evaporates before it even reaches the surface of your skin. Dehydration can be a real problem, since you don't realize how much moisture you are losing to sweat.

The Niger River bisects the country and affects life all along its route. From its origins in the mountains of Guinea to the south, it runs north past Bamako, a huge "village" of close to a million people, most of whom live in traditional mud huts, squeezed in between the banks of the river and the bluffs to the west. Only a few modern buildings, such as the main mosque, the sports stadium, the Islamic cultural center, and the tourist hotels, tell you that you are in the capital. The river continues north through the Great Inland Delta, created at the end of each rainy season to the south, when the river traditionally overflows its banks, forming a vast delta, the water many miles wide and only a few feet deep.

Along its banks live many of Mali's different ethnic groups: the most populous Bambara, subsistence farmers closely related by language and culture to the Mandinka of other West African countries; the Tamasheq, or Tuareg, matrilineal camel herders and caravaners, often called the Blue Men of the Desert for the indigo from their indigo-dyed clothing, which rubs off on their skin, giving them a dark blue tint; the Fulani, nomadic pastoralists whose herds of cattle roam the inland delta region, migrating wherever pasture is available, and whose women traditionally display their wealth in gold jewelry; the famous Dogon, whose cliff-hugging settlements along the Bandiagara escarpment in northeastern Mali (similar to Mesa Verde) and retention of their traditional religion in the face of Islamic influence have made them the darlings of anthropologists, rock-climbers, and National Geographic photographers; the Bozo fishermen who ply the waters of the Niger in hand-carved and painted *pirogues* (wooden plank canoes). And other groups literally too numerous to mention.

The river surrounds the ancient island city-fortress of Djenné, renowned for its beautiful mosque, and continues on to the bustling port city of Mopti, where huge boats dock to unload cargoes of pottery, dried fish, grass mats, and people, and where the river breaks into many channels. North of Mopti, the river swings east toward Timbuktu, fabled city at the southern end of the caravan routes across the Sahara. The river has shifted its course so that today Timbuktu lies several miles north of the river. It remains a center of Islamic learning and a destination for intrepid Western travellers, who fly in to get their passports stamped, stay in the one tourist hotel, eat gritty food permeated with sand from the Sahara, and fly out again as soon as possible. Past Timbuktu, the river curves south again past Gao and leaves Mali to flow south through Niger and Nigeria before emptying into the Atlantic Ocean. It is impossible to think about Mali without thinking about the river, so great is its influence on the history of the country, as well as daily life today.

Magnambougou, the site of my dissertation research, is one of about 15 squatter settlements located on the eastern bank of the Niger River, directly across the river from Bamako. Like Mali, it was chosen as my research site not because it was particularly suited, but because it was convenient—it was the village at the foot of the hill where we lived.

After staying with Barbara and Gerry for several weeks, we lived briefly in an apartment. Then Steven was hired to run the American Community Center, where the American expatriate community (Embassy and A.I.D. employees, and miscellaneous other Americans) came to enjoy the swimming pool, restaurant, tennis courts, and movies. The Community Center was located just beyond Magnambougou, too far from town for casual visits, so our duties there were limited to Friday evenings and all day Saturday and Sunday. That left weekdays open for research. Best of all, the job came with an air-conditioned, furnished apartment and a car. Hardly the "mud hut in a remote village" one thinks of when considering fieldwork, but the income from the job was essential. Steven commuted daily across the river to his farmers' plots along the railroad tracks on the road to Koulikoro; all I had to do to find my informants was walk down the hill.

When we finished our research and returned to Indiana University to analyze our data and write our dissertations, we were surprised to find that our fellow graduate students treated us with some disdain because we did not "live like the natives." Of course, a prime component of anthropological research methodology, which serves to distinguish it from, say, sociology, is participant observation—one participates in daily life, as well as observes it, and asks questions about it. But when daily life for the women involves hours of manual labor just to supply the basic necessities of life, such as food, water, and firewood, not to mention child care, there is little time left over for research. In addition, I have always felt that moving back and forth between the two worlds of Malian village women and the community of United States expatriates allowed me to develop a conscious awareness of both "emic" and "etic" perspectives. If you "go native," it takes remarkably little time to

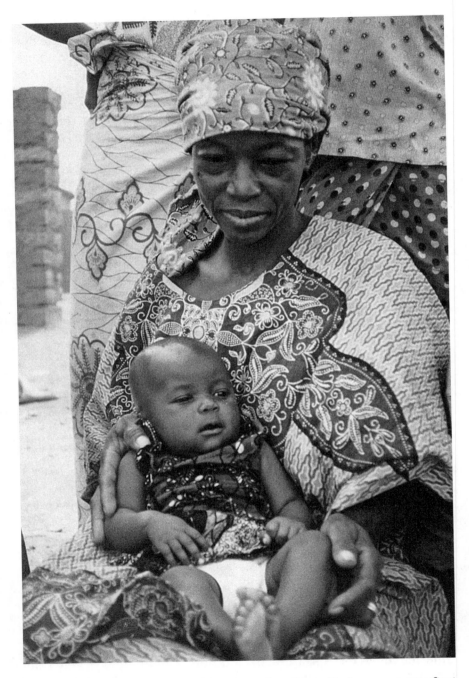

My friend Farima, holding her infant daughter. Farima was my first friend and informant during my dissertation research in Magnambougou. The baby died a few months later from an ear infection.

become enmeshed in the emic perspective and to take things for granted that otherwise would require explanation. I moved in and out of Bambara life and was constantly reminded, by questions from other Americans, of how exotic and unusual village life appeared to them.

Magnambougou is a town of some 15,000 inhabitants who live in "compounds" packed along twisting, narrow dirt paths, with the daily, open-air market forming both the geographic and the social centers of the community. Each compound consists of one or more square or rectangular rooms, made of mud bricks and topped by corrugated iron roofs, which form the perimeter of a large open space. Rooms and courtyard are surrounded by high mud brick walls. If you are walking along back lanes, households can seem forbidding, but admittance to the courtyard is easily gained, once you learn the proper etiquette. Since there are no doors to knock on, nor bells to ring, visitors clap their hands to announce their presence, although my arrival was most often presaged by the chants of children "*toubabou muso be na, toubabou muso be na*" (The white woman is coming! The white woman is coming!).

Magnambougou is occupied by families who have migrated in from rural villages over the past twenty years. People are poor, more so than even the poorest Americans, but Magnambougou isn't a

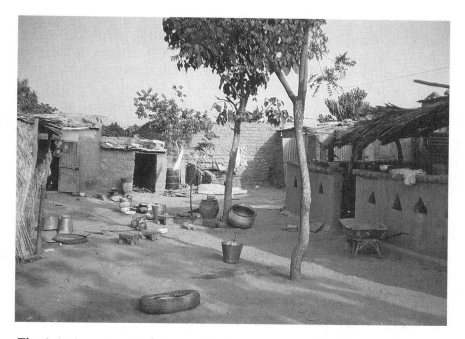

The interior courtyard of a peri-urban compound in Magnambougou.

shantytown of tar paper and cardboard shacks and makeshift tents. The mud brick houses may last for years, and most compounds have spacious courtyards, often shaded by mango trees, where women pound millet, cook, wash clothes, and care for children. "Houses" are really sleeping rooms and places where valuables are kept; most activities—work, play, visiting—take place outdoors. The number of rooms in a compound depends on the number of adult men, sons of one father, who form the backbone of the extended family. If a man has more than one wife, each must have her own room, where she and her young children sleep. Large compounds will have a bachelor hut for those sons too old to still be sleeping with their mother, and some compounds have kitchens, where women can cook when it rains, or when the sun is too intense.

The compounds in Magnambougou have neither running water nor electricity. Water comes from a deep well, laboriously hauled up arm over arm in a rubber bucket. Light at night is provided by kerosene lanterns, or the cooking fires. Cooking is done over an open fire, in black kettles or frying pans balanced on three rocks set into the ground. Each compound has an open-air pit latrine, consisting of a deep hole topped by a mud and concrete cap with a tiny opening in the center, enclosed by a low wall.

Traditionally, the social organization of the Bambara consists of extended families living in large compounds, polygynous marriages (more than one wife allowed), patrilineal descent (last name, ethnic identity, and property inherited from father to children), and patrilocal residence (wives leave their parents to go live with their husband, his parents, and his brothers and their families). This ideal was not always met in Magnambougou, as often only one adult male from a rural family had migrated to the city, and he might have only one wife because of economic constraints.

Except for a few Christian families, the people of Magnambougou follow a blend of traditional and Muslim religious beliefs. Women often do not strictly follow Muslim teachings—they are not secluded, nor do they have to wear veils; they seldom go to the mosque or pray at home, they rarely fast during Ramadan, and they are not familiar with Koranic guidelines concerning infant feeding. Islamic beliefs coexist with traditional religious beliefs and practices. Sickness and death are usually attributed to Allah rather than to organic causes, witchcraft, or sorcery. For many people, Islam can be described as a cloak that one dons when it is socially, politically, or economically convenient. Even very devout Muslims still follow traditional beliefs to some extent.

Most of the women of Magnambougou have had little or no formal education, speak Bambara (and often several other West African languages), but not French, and can neither read nor write in any language. When Americans asked me if I spoke French, I replied truthfully that French would have been of little use in my fieldwork, and I concentrated on learning Bambara instead. Malians, conversely, were always amazed to find a toubab who couldn't speak French but could speak Bambara.

Health services for the residents of Magnambougou are provided primarily by traditional herbalists who sell leaves in the market and by a government-run maternal/child health center (PMI) located in a nearby town. Although the PMI visits are free, the numerous medicines that are usually prescribed are very expensive, and sick children are often taken to a traditional healer first. The nearest hospital is in Bamako, at least 20 minutes away by public transportation. In the early 1980s, few children in Magnambougou had been vaccinated against any childhood diseases.

Miranda, on the other hand, had been vaccinated against all the usual childhood diseases (diphtheria, pertussis, tetanus, polio, measles, mumps, and rubella) plus a number of tropical diseases

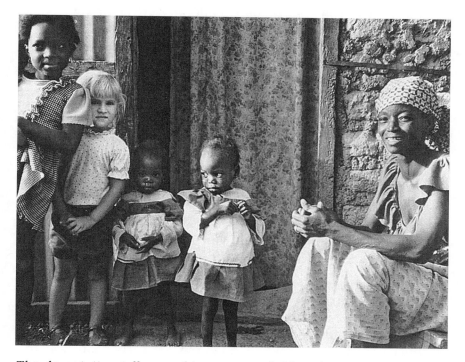

The devastating toll wrought on young children by malnutrition and disease is evident in this photo of Miranda at three years of age. The twin girls were two months older than Miranda. My friend Farima, who often babysat the twins, is pictured at the right. Her healthy five-year-old, Rookia, stands in front of Miranda.

such as yellow fever, cholera, and smallpox. Receiving her smallpox vaccination in 1981, she probably was one of the last children in the world to be vaccinated against the disease, since the World Health Organization (WHO) declared that smallpox had been eradicated in the late 1970s. We didn't want to take any chances, however, and took every precaution we could to ensure her health.

In 1983, on a trip to visit anthropologist friends doing research in the "grassfields" region of Cameroon, we heard of a cholera outbreak in the capital. We visited the Catholic mission hospital in Mbingo to get cholera boosters from "Dr. Rod" and avoided the public water supplies when we passed through the capital on our way back to Mali, even though that meant drinking out of the air conditioner drip bucket in the Catholic mission hostel.

Measles, malaria, upper respiratory infections, and diarrhea are the major illnesses of young children in Magnambougou, and polio is not unknown. A serious outbreak of measles occurred during my initial study in May of 1982; almost every compound lost a child to the epidemic that year. There were only a few cases of measles in 1983, and by 1989 many young children were being vaccinated against measles and other childhood diseases caused by viruses.

There is no vaccine for malaria, which is caused by a protozoan parasite that reproduces in the red blood cells. But if you live through repeated bouts of childhood malaria, you eventually build up a tolerance. As an adult, you might experience several mild cases of malaria during the rainy season, involving a few days of headache, fever, chills, and lethargy, but malaria in an adult is seldom fatal for those who have survived multiple exposures as children. Malaria is a threat to pregnant women because it can cause miscarriages, and of course many young children do not survive malaria. Perversely, it seems that malnourished children are better able to cope with malaria than well-nourished ones, because their red blood cells provide a poor host environment for reproduction of the malarial parasites. In Mali, malaria remains a threat to older children and adults who were not exposed to the disease in childhood.

In the fall of 1983, the combination of Kay's and Mickey's deaths, coming as they did within a week of each other, convinced us that it was time to go home. In the summer of 1989, as though time had diminished, if not entirely erased, the lessons of their deaths, Miranda and I had returned, to a land where early death was too commonplace to be considered a tragedy. With any luck, by tearing my family apart, I was securing its future. But the sobering thought that death, far from home, was once again an entirely real possibility, would never be far from my thoughts.

3

Female Circumcision
Not Just Another Bit of Exotic Ethnographic Trivia

In Africa today, women's voices are being raised for the first time against genital mutilations still practiced on babies, little girls, and women. These voices belong to a few women, who, from Egypt to Mali, from the Sudan and Somalia to Senegal, remain closely attached to their identity and heritage, but are prepared to call it in question when traditional practices endanger their lives and their health. They are beginning the delicate task of helping women free themselves from customs which have no advantage and many risks for their physical and psychological well-being, without at the same time destroying the supportive and beneficial threads of their cultural fabric.

—Scilla McLean and Efua Graham

Moussa and I sat on low stools in the small patch of shade cast by a locust tree in a compound near the market shared by two brothers, Tamasheqs from northern Mali. We had come to remeasure two girls from the original sample. The morning light was already harsh and promised another blistering day, unrelieved by even a breath of wind. I watched the dark opening of the small kitchen hut across the compound, into which the father of one of the girls had disappeared some minutes before. Finally, two spectral figures emerged from the doorway of the hut and shuffled gingerly toward us across the dusty courtyard. Both girls were dressed oddly, with long capes draped over their heads. Their eyes were downcast, their steps uncertain. Their skin was a dusky gray color, not at all the normal rich, vibrant brown of healthy Malian children.

I turned to Moussa in concern and whispered, "What's the matter with them?"

"Nothing," he explained, "but they've just been circumcised."

"When?" I asked, horrified.

Moussa turned to their fathers and asked, then told me: "They did it this morning."

"Please, you can go back and sit down," I called to the girls in a shaky voice. "We can come back another day."

"It's OK, you can go ahead," one of the mothers insisted.

"No. No. I think we need to go," I said hastily, getting up and heading toward the compound gate.

Moussa made apologies to all concerned and hurried after me. He knew me well enough to know that I was very upset. We hurried away down the narrow alleyway toward the morning market. Once we reached the open spaces and the noise and bustle of the market, I stopped to catch my breath.

"Oh Lord, Moussa, do you think they'll be OK?" I asked.

He paused. "I don't know. We usually circumcise girls much younger. It's hard on them when they're this old. They didn't look good."

"What can we do?" I implored.

"Nothing. There's nothing we can do. You know that. Why don't we come back in a few weeks, and if they've survived, we can measure them then."

"All right. Let's go visit someone else this morning."

"How about the Fat Lady from Timbuktu?" Moussa suggested. "She always makes you laugh."

"That's a great idea! We can also check and see how Daouda is doing."

During my dissertation research I had, more or less, gotten used to the fact that the Bambara practice female circumcision, generally what can be called the relatively mild form, involving clitoridectomy (removal of the clitoris). The even milder form, involving removal of the hood of the clitoris, is anatomically analogous to male circumcision in the United States. Clitoridectomy in females would be analogous to cutting off the head of the penis in males. Clitoridectomy is mild only relative to infibulation, the more severe form of genital mutilation.

Infibulation involves clitoridectomy plus cutting off the outer edges of the labia majora, which are then stitched together across the midline to form a permanent layer of scar tissue, preventing sexual intercourse. When a woman is married, the scar tissue is cut open, allowing the husband sexual intercourse. Infibulation is generally understood by anthropologists as a particularly severe, physical means of male control of female sexual behavior, which is accomplished in other societies by practices such as purdah, veils, or social censure for "loose" women. However, circumcision is explained in a variety of ways by the different cultures, mostly African and Asian, that practice it. Often, a religious explanation is offered, such as that found among the Dogon of northern Mali, who believe that all children are born with the potential to be either sex. A boy must have his foreskin removed to make him truly male, and a girl must have her clitoris removed to make her truly female, capable, as an adult, of sexual intercourse with men and safe childbirth.

Among the residents of Magnambougou, female circumcision (clitoridectomy) is usually performed when a girl is about six months old. In this community, girls have clitoridectomies because "It's our tradition. We all do this." No amount of probing revealed any religious justification for the practice, and people seemed to accept it without question. Once, when Moussa wasn't available and I was just spending a lazy afternoon chatting with my good friend Agnes (her European name reveals that she was Christian, not Muslim), we discussed the topic of why the Bambara circumcise their daughters. In response to all of my questions, she just kept saying "tradition." "Well," I told her, "I read in a book about the Bambara [*African Folk Medicine*, by Pascal James Imperato] that the Bambara think that if you don't cut the clitoris off, it will grow to become almost as long as a man's penis." She looked at me as if I were absolutely nuts.

"*Who* told you that?" she asked.

"I read it in a book. Some people here in Mali told that to the author."

"Who?"

"His name is Pascal Imperato. He's a medical doctor. He was here during the smallpox vaccination campaign," I explained.

"No, I mean, who told him that we believe that?"

"I don't know who, specifically, he travelled all over Mali."

"Well, I never heard of that. That's stupid."

"So, what do you think does happen if you don't cut it off?"

"I don't know. Everyone has theirs removed, so I don't know what happens. It's just our tradition."

"Would you like to see what it looks like in an adult woman if you don't remove it? Would you like to see mine?" I asked, half in jest.

"You aren't circumcised?" she blurted out in surprise.

"No, of course not."

"Why 'of course not'?" she mocked me.

"We just don't do it in my culture."

"Why not?"

"Tradition," I admitted, starting to chuckle. "Seriously, let's go in the house, and I'll show you mine if you'll show me yours."

"Oh, sure!" Agnes doubled over with laughter, slapping the ground in front of her with both palms.

"I'm serious," I protested.

"You mean to tell me that American women aren't circumcised, but they still find husbands?"

"Yes."

"Your husband knew you weren't circumcised, and he married you anyway?"

"Yes."

"Well, is your husband circumcised?"

"Yes, most boys in the United States are circumcised as infants."

"Was your daughter circumcised as an infant?"

"No, of course not!"

"But your son was?"

"Well, yes," I admitted. "But it's hardly the same thing! We only remove the foreskin of the penis, not the head of the penis, which would be the equivalent of clitoridectomy for a female. I don't think it takes away from a man's sexual pleasure to be circumcised."

"Strange people, you American toubabs," she chided. "You circumcise the boys but not the girls. How can you do that to your own daughter? Don't you know people will shun her?"

"Not in my culture," I explained.

"You know," she confided, looking around furtively, "the French toubabs don't circumcise boys *or* girls!"

"Come on, don't you want to see what an uncircumcised woman looks like? Let's go in the house, right now. But you have to show me yours as well."

She howled with laughter again. We went around and around; I never convinced her that I was serious, and she never agreed to my suggestion. My interest in female circumcision was a source of much amusement to Agnes, and whenever I saw her after that, she would remind me of our "silly conversation." Usually I didn't have to think about circumcision, and I would put it out of my mind. I told Miranda that if anyone ever asked her if she was circumcised, she was just to tell them "Yes, of course." I knew they wouldn't be so rude as to try and check it out for themselves.

Few Westerners know about female circumcision, and those who do often have difficulty understanding it because they can't fully comprehend the lack of importance that people attach to sex and sexual pleasure (especially female sexual pleasure) in some cultures. When I tried to determine the impact of clitoridectomy on women's sexual pleasure, women didn't understand my questions, telling me "sex is a woman's duty to her husband; it doesn't matter if it feels good for her."

Likewise, the concept of sexual foreplay seemed completely foreign to the Malian women I talked to. They did complain that they couldn't use spermicidal sponges as birth control options, but not because their husbands were particularly opposed to birth control (though many were, the number of children a man has being a direct indication of his wealth and power). Rather, sponges were impractical because their use necessitated that the couple wait for several minutes after the insertion of the sponge before having intercourse. Most husbands couldn't, or wouldn't, wait the required two or three minutes after the insertion of the sponge. "What if it hurts because you aren't ready?" I asked one young woman. "You just turn your face to the wall, and endure," she replied, not really understanding the point of my question.

If I stayed on the subject of clitoridectomy or sexual pleasure too long, women would invariably chastise me, saying, "We Malian women have more important things to worry about than whether or not sex feels good." Whenever the topic of circumcision depressed me, I had only to visit the compound of my friend, the Fat Lady from Timbuktu, whose jolly good spirits never failed to lighten my mood. At the same time, the plight of her house servant and the servant's son, Daouda, epitomized the reality expressed by so many women: they had other problems to worry about; they couldn't concern themselves with the issue of sexual pleasure, or the lack thereof.

Several weeks before the day of these clitoridectomies, as Moussa and I hiked the narrow back streets of Magnambougou looking for my earlier informants, we passed by a compound with a big, red metal door and Moussa asked "Do you remember the Fat Lady from Timbuktu?"

"Of course, now that you mention her!" I replied in delight. "I had forgotten all about her."

"Well, this is where she lives. Shall we see if she is at home?" he asked.

"Yes, let's do."

In 1982, one of the young children in my growth study was a little girl who was visiting her grandmother. The grandmother, a woman of perhaps 50 years, was very much interested in my research. Ethnically, she was a Moor, and she had moved to Bamako from Timbuktu. She was intelligent, articulate, and friendly, and she had a highly developed sense of humor. She was also enormously obese, and came to be known in my field notes as the Fat Lady from

Timbuktu. Whenever I had occasion to be in her part of the community, I would stop by just to chat.

Her daughter and granddaughter went back to their home village after several months, but I continued to visit the grandmother's compound because I enjoyed her company so much. She used to tease me all the time about not having a son yet for my husband (Miranda was almost three years old at the time, and a typical Malian woman would have had another infant by then). She told me that I should wean Miranda so that I could get pregnant again and have a son for Steven. Malian women know that breastfeeding has a contraceptive effect, although they are not aware of the mechanism. When a baby nurses, the mother's pituitary releases the hormone prolactin, which aids in milk production, and also suppresses ovulation, preventing another pregnancy. But this contraceptive effect, known as lactational amenorrhea or lactational anovulation, only works when the baby nurses very often around the clock. At three years of age, Miranda was only nursing a few times a day, not enough to maintain lactational amenorrhea. In fact, my menstrual periods had returned when Miranda was 23 months old. It didn't seem to occur to the Fat Lady that I might want to prevent another pregnancy, or that I would have the means to do so.

Other women in Magnambougou told me I should wean Miranda when she turned two years old, because nursing longer would make her stupid. I knew from my dissertation research that this belief had been reported in several cultures. However, I also knew that most children around the world are nursed until they are two or three years old, and some longer. According to several of my elderly female informants, traditional rural Malians nursed their children until they weaned by themselves, usually between three and four years of age. This was much more in keeping with our species' primate heritage, and what human babies had evolved to expect, and I intended to do the same with all my children.

Of course, the Fat Lady also teased that Steven probably wasn't that interested in me sexually anymore because I was too old and not fat enough. Tongue firmly in cheek, she offered her 12-year-old daughter as Steven's second wife, pointing out that not only was she beautiful (she was), but she was a very hard worker and an obedient child who would do whatever I told her. Every time I saw her, either at her compound, or at the market, she would say, "Bring your husband over to take a look. He won't be able to resist."

When I returned to visit her in 1989, she was overjoyed to see me again. She immediately called over her daughter, now 18 years old and even more beautiful than before, and said, "Look, your co-wife has come to claim you." The girl blushed and ran away. She was glad to hear that I had had a son "for Steven" and chided me for still being "skinny." At 5 feet 8 inches tall, I weighed about 160 pounds when I first arrived in Mali in 1989, hardly skinny by American standards.

The Fat Lady herself was, if anything, even bigger than she had been in 1983. Standing only about 5 feet tall, she weighed close to 300 pounds. The ethnic group to which she belongs, the Moors, like their Saharan neighbors, the Tamasheq, value obesity in their women above all other signs of beauty. To have a fat wife signifies to the world that a man is wealthy, is able to provide plenty of food for his family to eat, and has slaves or servants to do the physical labor so that his wife can relax, lounging around and visiting with her friends and eating sweets. To be fat is to be healthy. Even more importantly, to be fat is to be sexy.

We were sitting on the raised porch of her cement-block house, drinking syrupy-sweet, scalding hot tea and catching up on six years of gossip when I noticed an incredibly malnourished little boy tied on the back of a middle-aged woman who was sweeping up the courtyard of the compound. "Who is that?" I inquired, both my personal pity for the child and my professional interest aroused by the sight of his "overlarge" head and stick-like arms and legs.

"Oh, that's Daouda," she replied, laughing. "He's something, isn't he?" The woman sweeping, Daouda's mother, was employed by the Fat Lady as a general household servant. She came every morning and stayed all day, cleaning, cooking, pounding millet, going to the market—whatever needed to be done. She brought Daouda with her, and he either rode on her back, tied on with a length of cloth, or slept on the ground under a tree. I asked to have a closer look at Daouda, and his mother brought him over, took him off her back, and handed him to me. He took one look at me and started crying. But not the loud, vigorous wail of a healthy child, accompanied by attempts to get away. Rather, his cries consisted of barely audible whimpers as he tried, without success, to turn his head away.

At 18 months, Daouda weighed only 12 pounds and was so weak he couldn't hold his head up or move his arms or legs voluntarily. His head looked huge for his body, the result of his body's incapacity to grow properly after birth because of malnutrition. His arms and legs were mere bones covered by wrinkled, papery skin. His buttocks were pathetic, really just bags of skin hanging in folds from his spine. I could count every rib without difficulty. He felt like a bundle of sharp sticks, and I quickly returned him to his mother, so that he wouldn't be any more unhappy than necessary. I asked his mother what was the matter with him, and she said, "Nothing.

Chapter Three

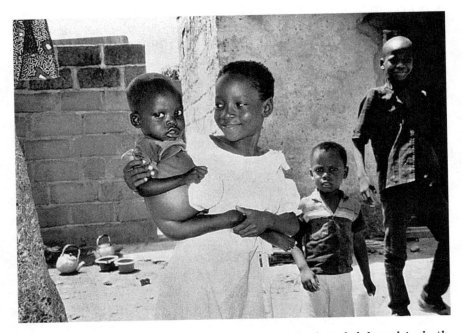

Like Daouda, Bala was extremely malnourished and delayed in both motor and speech development. At three years of age, his anterior fontanelle was still open.

He's OK," and shuffled off to continue her sweeping. Turning to my friend, I asked her what was going on.

She explained that she had taken Daouda's mother on as a servant because the woman's husband was "crazy" and not able to provide for her. The woman was destitute, as neither she nor her husband had any extended family in Bamako. In addition, she had leprosy. When I looked at her closely, I could see that she had one of the characteristic signs of leprosy—her midfacial region was sunken—though she still had all of her fingers and toes. Daouda was her youngest, and only surviving, child.

"What does she feed him?" I asked.

"Well, she nurses him when he cries, and in the morning she gives him *toh* (millet porridge) left over from the night before," the Fat Lady responded.

"That's all?"

"I've tried to get her to give him other food, but she says he refuses to eat."

"Call her over again, and I'll try to talk some sense into her."

That first day, I talked to Daouda's mother for more than an hour, pointing out that all he needed was more food to eat and that he was not growing properly physically and couldn't sit up or walk yet because she was not feeding him enough—not to mention the fact that he was miserable all the time, yet so weak he barely had the strength to cry. I also suggested she take him to the doctor. She listened passively, then looked at me and said, "OK, I'll give him more to eat."

When I returned the next week, my friend the Fat Lady said Daouda's mother hadn't done any of the things I suggested. Daouda looked even worse than before, and this time he didn't even try to cry when I held him on my lap. I again spent a long time talking to his mother about his condition and even offered to give her money for food or to bring food for him. She said that wasn't necessary but didn't seem very interested in anything I had to say. This went on for several weeks, until one day something in me snapped, and I turned to Daouda's mother in frustration and shouted, "Why don't we just kill him? You know, put him out of his misery? We could hold him upside down in a bucket of water! Or we could dash his brains out against the side of the house! Either of those would be kinder than slowly starving him to death! You obviously don't care about him at all, and you know he's going to die, so why don't you just get it over with?"

Moussa looked at me in horror and started to protest. The Fat Lady from Timbuktu started laughing, holding onto her sides to keep from falling out of her chair. Daouda's mother just gazed at me uncomprehendingly and said, "No, I could never do those things. I don't want him to die." "But you do," I said, my disgust with her obvious to everyone in the room except her. "No," she repeated sadly. "Then why won't you give him anything to eat?" "He doesn't like food," she explained. She got up slowly, retrieved Daouda from my arms, and went outside. Soon I heard the steady thump, thump, thump sound as she pounded millet into flour for toh.

I looked at my friend in exasperation. "What is her problem?" I asked.

"Well, you know, she isn't very smart," said the Fat Lady, calmly pouring another glass of tea.

"That's obvious," I retorted.

"No, really, I mean she isn't smart like other people," she responded.

"What do you mean?"

"Well, for example, every day when she comes here to work, she can cook the rice by herself, but I have to show her how to make the sauce for the rice. Every day, it's like she's never done it before."

"You mean she can't remember from one day to the next how to make sauce?" I asked incredulously.

"Right. And lots of other things. If I send her to the market to buy tomatoes and onions, she will get there and then not know what she's supposed to buy, so she'll have to come back. Or she comes back with sweet potato leaves instead and has lost the rest of the money on the way back."

"Has she always been like this, or is it connected to her leprosy?"

"She says she's always been that way, since she was little."

Slowly realization dawned on me—I, the mother of a retarded child, had failed to recognize that Daouda's mother was mentally retarded. It had never occurred to me that anything other than his mother's ignorance and lack of concern stood between Daouda and good health. In retrospect, I realize that I had just assumed, ethnocentrically, that if you were mentally retarded in Mali, you would be unlikely to hold down a job, be married, and have kids. But Malians don't necessarily share American prejudices toward the mentally retarded.

I wondered what I could do to help. If we had been in the United States, I could have referred Daouda and his mother to any number of social service agencies, where she could have gotten treatment for her leprosy, job training, and help with child care skills. Daouda could be enrolled in Women, Infants, and Children (WIC), a federal government program of nutritional education and support and could receive money for food and medical care through Aid to Families with Dependent Children (AFDC). In Mali, no such support networks exist at any level of government. Extended families normally provide help and support of this kind for all family members, but Daouda's mother was alone and without options. The only alternative I could think of was to convince Daouda's mother to relinquish him to the state-run orphanage, but she was not willing to do this. He was all she had. She was convinced that he was just sickly and would soon grow out of his lethargy.

I was convinced that he was destined to die a slow and lingering death from starvation. I had done all I could for Daouda; I had to harden my heart against his circumstances—he was a lost cause. Although I continued to visit my friend every week or two throughout my stay, I ceased talking to Daouda's mother, although I always inquired about his health. Indeed, my first question on entering the compound was always "Is Daouda still alive? He is? Remarkable! Amazing! Unbelievable! Is his mother still feeding him old toh?" We all enjoyed a good laugh about Daouda; there really wasn't anything else to do. If we couldn't laugh, we would have to cry.

Daouda taught me to pick my battles with care. Not only did I have to guard against devoting too much time and energy to lost causes, I also had to set priorities. Perhaps I could, through my research, make a small contribution to the alleviation of malnutrition in Mali. Worrying about Daouda would not help him. Badgering his mother would not help him either, for she had no help herself. The Fat Lady seemed not to care; perhaps she thought she had done enough by giving Daouda's mother a job. Daouda was still alive when I left Mali in December of 1989, but I very much doubt that he survives today. Little boy, you are remembered.

4

Of Worms and Other Parasites

Ordinary is what you are used to. This may not seem ordinary
to you now, but after a time it will. It will become ordinary.
—Margaret Atwood

The rain fell in great sheets, sluicing off the roof, filling the courtyard
with swirling brown water. The water snuck under the front door
and edged across the tile floors of the living room. We chased it back
outside with brooms and buckets, then crossed the courtyard
through ankle-deep water and climbed up on the wall to view the
havoc on the other side. Nothing looked familiar. The broad dirt
road, with its open sewer (usually stagnant) running along the far
side, had been replaced by a raging torrent, sweeping sewage,
garbage, mud, and other debris downhill, toward the river. Children
perched in the lower branches of trees, and we watched as the water
carried a chicken, squawking piteously and flapping its wings, past
our doorway.

"Welcome to Mali!" I shouted to Heather Katz, an undergraduate
from Texas A&M who had arrived the day before to spend the fall
semester working as my unpaid research assistant. Clinging to the
wall, water streaming down her face, she looked over at me and
grinned, then turned her face toward the sky.

The next day we learned that in rural areas of the country, entire
villages of mud huts and herds of sheep and goats were swept away,
never to be heard from again. It was late August, and the
extraordinary storm signaled the end to the three-month-long rainy
season. Following the rains, we would have months of glorious,
practically unvarying weather, cool in the mornings, sunny and hot
by the afternoon.

37

After having taken several anthropology courses, Heather was eager to get started with "the real thing." Early the next morning, following a breakfast of coffee and freshly baked bread (crisp *baguettes*, one of the few positive legacies of French colonialism), we set out to Magnambougou to finish up the final stage of my research project on intestinal parasites. First we walked a mile along the river toward the main road, the "airport road," that connected the capital city of Bamako, across the river to the west, with the airport to the east.

Once we reached the main road, we headed away from the river and walked, looking back over our shoulders for oncoming *baches* (baa-shays) that might be headed to Magnambougou. I exchanged hand signals with several bache drivers, searching for one with spare room headed for Magnambougou. Finally, one pulled over and we clambered up the step and squeezed in among the other passengers, trying to avoid the uncomfortable corner seats, where your legs get cramped.

A bache is a small pickup truck with the tailgate removed. The interior of the truck bed is furnished with hard wooden benches around the periphery, covered by a metal framework that partially encloses the back and keeps out the sun and rain (more or less). Officially, 15 or 16 people can fit in the back of the bache, but often 20 or more are crammed in, not to mention babies in mothers' laps, live chickens and guinea fowl, huge enamel bowls full of cooked food or market vegetables, bundles of firewood, fresh fish, not so fresh fish, anything you can imagine, and then some.

Toubabs are often offered the seats up front next to the driver because these seats are considered more genteel. In reality, it is cooler and more pleasant to ride in the back, where you at least have the benefit of the breeze to offset the smell of sweaty bodies and old fish. Besides, the drivers always turned off their engines at every opportunity—waiting for passengers to load, in traffic jams, going downhill—thinking they were saving gas by doing so, and it annoyed me intensely. No amount of explaining would convince people that it took more gas to start the engine than it took to keep it running for a minute.

People were surprised to see toubabs riding the public transportation system. Most American and French expatriates had cars of their own, and consultants and other short-time visitors usually rode in Embassy or A.I.D. cars or taxis. Only Peace Corps volunteers and anthropologists regularly rode the baches. One problem for the neophyte is that it is very difficult to figure out where a particular bache is headed, how much it should cost, or when and whom you pay. You must be taught all of the intricacies by a friendly (and honest) expert.

We jounced along, trying to keep our balance as the driver swerved around a herd of cows in the road, then careened off onto the dirt shoulder to pick up more people. There are no marked bus stops, though there are some usual, but unmarked, stopping places. You can also get a bache to stop for you anywhere along the road if you know the system of signals, and if the driver has any room.

As always, the seat next to the door was occupied by a young boy who worked for the driver, collecting fares and telling the driver when to stop and let someone off. He swung wildly off the back of the bache, dragging his sandalled feet on the ground and waving to other bache boys going the other direction. He also acted as a watchdog, keeping an eye out for policemen, who like to stop overloaded baches and collect fines.

Toward the end of the line, the boy collected the fares. There are standard fares for certain distances, but no one will tell you what they are if you don't know. You can try to see what other people are paying, but that is difficult because the boy usually has to collect money from a number of people before he can make change for people who don't have the exact fare. I was amazed at the ability of the bache boys to keep track of who had paid what, who needed change, and who hadn't paid yet because they were still fumbling around with their money. Women, especially, always waited until they were asked for the fare to start digging out their money, sometimes a major process.

Women in Mali don't carry purses—they would be too easy for someone to steal. Many an unsuspecting toubab has been relieved of their wallet or coin purse on a bache, and people were always telling me to zip up my bag. Most people carry their money knotted in one corner of their long flowing robes (men) or in the corner of the cloth they use to tie their babies onto their backs (women). Thus, it takes several minutes to locate the money and maneuver it to where it can be reached and several more to untie the knot, search for the fare, and hand it over.

As often happened, the boy tried to cheat me, telling me that the fare was ten times higher than it really was, but since I knew the customary price, I just handed him the correct fare and ignored his rantings. "He thinks we're dumb toubabs!" I said first to Heather in English, then to the crowd in Bambara, earning chuckles and a round of greetings from our fellow passengers, and a lopsided grin from the bache boy, as if to say "You can't blame me for trying!"

My ability to speak Bambara, and the incongruity between that ability and my skin color, was a source of great pleasure to me because I could use it to make people laugh. I sometimes hid my ability to speak Bambara, then made jokes by revealing that I did, in fact, both understand and speak it. I might climb onto the bache and settle in without saying anything, then if the bache was weaving erratically all over the road (not a rare occurrence), I would casually comment, "This driver is a fool!" Or I would listen while several women discussed who I might be and why a toubab was riding the bache, then say, in Bambara, holding out my arm for their inspection "Look, I'm not a toubab, I'm a *fara fin* (black-skinned person), just like you!"

More than anything else, Malians like to laugh—at themselves, at each other, certainly at toubabs ("Only a white man would pay money for a dog! Ha ha ha!"), at the ludicrous world in which they find themselves living—and I liked to make them laugh. I also enjoyed participating in their rituals of respect and kindness, as another way of showing that I was interested in, and sympathetic to, their cultural beliefs and practices.

Giving alms to beggars, blind men, lepers, and mothers of twins are all ways of attaining grace in the eyes of God (Allah). Whenever possible, Malians like to help those in need, as they benefit themselves spiritually as well. However, the sheer numbers of beggars and lepers in the capital city could be overwhelming. As with everything else, there were rules of etiquette for giving alms. To avoid the crush of beggars in downtown Bamako, it is best to pick out one particular person and always give that one some money. "This is *my* leper," I explained to Heather, as I pointed out an old woman with no fingers or toes, sitting on the sidewalk near Dibida, the vegetable market. We exchanged greetings, I dropped some coins into her bowl, and she gave me her blessings in return. "Pick one for yourself, Heather, and the others will leave you alone. You just have to remember to always carry small change, and remember to give something to your leper, but not any of the others, every time you pass by here. The others will respect your choice and not bother you. Likewise, I have my particular mother of twins near the bank. I always give her money and the others know not to ask." "Gee," Heather joked, uncomfortable with the entire situation, "I never had my very own leper before!" "Yes, well, there but for the grace of God . . ." I responded.

Another way of attaining grace was to show respect for old men and women in various ways. Respect for elders is part and parcel of daily life in Mali; all important decisions are made by councils of old men, and a man isn't truly in charge of his own affairs until his father and all of his older brothers have died. When Steven's 84-year-old grandmother visited us in Mali in 1982, wherever she went, people spontaneously dropped to their knees and bowed their heads in respect of her great age (much to her consternation).

One way of attaining grace and showing respect for your elders is by paying their fare on the bache. This is not something the casual tourist is likely to find out about, let alone practice. When we rode the bache with an elderly man or woman, we always paid their fare along with our own, indicating by gestures to the bache boy who else was included in our largesse. This simple action evoked smiles, exclamations of gratitude, prayers to Allah to bless us with many children, and the respect and appreciation of our fellow passengers.

The early morning ride to Magnambougou took about 10 minutes. We jumped off before the end of the line to avoid being crushed by the hordes of people trying to get on for the return trip to Bamako. People pushed onto the bache from the back or climbed in through the side windows (even women with children strapped to their backs!), and you risked your life trying to disembark without getting crushed if you rode to the end of the line. Even my most colorful cussing in Bambara wouldn't stop the pushing and shoving of people eager to get into town for work or school.

"What are we going to do first?" Heather asked as we walked down a side street toward Moussa's house. "First we have to get Moussa. I seldom do any research without him. Then, just for today, we're collecting the final round of urine and stool specimens for my project on intestinal parasites and taking them out to the Vet Lab for analysis," I explained. "Tomorrow we'll go back to measuring and interviewing."

Having Heather along helped me see Magnambougou with fresh eyes. After only a few months, I had already gotten used to the piles of goats' heads on the edge of the market, little kids squatting along the edge of the road to relieve themselves, and the teenager who had polio as an infant, crab-walking his way to a friend's house, waving at us with one sandalled hand.

"Why exactly are you collecting these specimens?" Heather asked. I explained as we continued on our way. This part of my research was designed to figure out whether intestinal parasites, thought to be common in most Third World communities, could be contributing to the poor growth of the children. One of the graduate students at Texas A&M (Karl Reinhard, who went on to the University of Nebraska) was enamored of intestinal parasites as a potential explanation for just about everything. His own research involved looking for signs of parasitic infection in the preserved remains of human feces (known as coprolites) from archeological sites. Imagine Karl at a party, when someone asks, "So, what do you study?" Karl often pestered me to include parasite analyses in my research, so I added it to my list of projects.

Early on, I had contacted the veterinary parasitologists at the Bamako Veterinary Laboratory. I went there (rather than to medical doctors) because the Vet Lab in Bamako is staffed by Malian alumni of Texas A&M's College of Veterinary Medicine. Because of the "Aggie" connection, I knew they were well trained, and I was able to negotiate a good rate for the laboratory analyses of the specimens. The lab provided small plastic bottles for collection, and set up a schedule for me to bring specimens to the lab the same day they were collected. The specimens were analyzed immediately, eliminating the need for chemical preservatives or refrigerated storage.

I expected people in Magnambougou to think I was bizarre, asking for feces and urine in little bottles, but everyone took my requests in stride. Maybe it was because I explained that they would be getting free testing for parasites, as well as medicine to cure any infections that were uncovered. Or maybe it was because Malians are a lot more relaxed and casual about bodily functions that most people in the United States. The first time Moussa said to me, "Excuse me, I have to go shit," I thought I must have misunderstood. Conversely, he didn't understand American reticence or our use of euphemisms: "Everyone does it. And everyone knows exactly what you mean even if you say you're going to the 'little girls' room,' so why don't you just say what you mean?" he wondered.

Only a few people declined to participate in this phase of the research, which I began with 10 families. On one day we distributed the labelled bottles, two per child, and explained what (and how much) was needed. The next morning we collected the specimen bottles. Sometimes the child would not have been able to provide a specimen yet, and we sat around chatting while he or she tried again. It became obvious, early on, that many children had diarrhea and very dark, cloudy urine.

After gathering all 20 bottles for the day, I carefully tucked them in my monogrammed Lands' End attache bag (wouldn't that make a memorable advertisement?) and hopped on the bache for the long trip out to the lab, careful not to let anyone jostle my bag as I pushed and shoved my way aboard, fearing that the bottles would crack or pop open. Odd comments and looks were common; I smelled vaguely offensive. Pretending that I didn't speak Bambara, I was treated to such remarks as "Maybe it's that strange toubab—do you think she's the one who smells?" "No, it can't be her; maybe someone stepped in something rotten." Bouncing along, I looked nonchalantly out the side of the truck, pretending that nothing was going on.

I rode all the way across the river, to the main bache station in Bamako, then transferred to another line that took me about 10 kilometers north of town. From the end of the line it was still a hike of another mile to the Vet Lab, where I dropped off the filled bottles, picked up 20 clean ones, and hiked back to catch the bache back into town.

On the last trip out to the lab to deliver specimens, Heather was along, and the other occupants carried on a lengthy and derogatory discussion about the odor emanating from our corner of the bache. As we neared the end of the line, I blurted out in Bambara, "The smell is because my bag is full of little bottles of shit!"

Everyone laughed and looked around, surprised to discover that I could speak Bambara, chagrined that I had understood their comments, and amazed at my admission. There was a flurry of activity as people squished themselves as far away as possible. One old man was skeptical and, in my defense, suggested that I couldn't speak Bambara very well and had said something I didn't mean to. I carefully opened my bag, reached in, pulled out one of the bottles, and waved it in his direction. "No, it really is shit. Sorry about the smell. We're on our way to the Vet Lab." No one said a word. The old man pulled part of his robe up over his mouth and nose, and turned to gaze out at the roadway, muttering about how weird toubabs could be.

Out of the total of 68 specimens of feces I collected, only 4 showed any signs of the six most common intestinal parasites for which we searched—2 had *Ascaris*, another had hookworm, and the last one had a tapeworm. These children were each treated and their parents told how to avoid reinfection. The girl with the tapeworm, Aminata, had been part of my original research study. In fact, she was the only truly fat child under five years of age that I ever saw in Mali. In my 1989 research, I used photos of well-nourished, and mildly, moderately, and severely malnourished children, to elicit reactions from people as part of a project to understand traditional perceptions of nutritional status. Aminata's photo, taken in 1983 when she was three years old, was my example of a "well-nourished" Malian child.

I returned to Aminata's compound in early August of 1989 to remeasure her and see how she had fared during my six-year absence. After the usual greetings and small talk with her mother and the co-wife, I asked if Aminata was still alive (not a question one would normally ask an acquaintance in the United States—"So, is your daughter still alive?"—but perfectly understandable and acceptable in Mali, where many children die).

Her mother pointed out a short, thin, apathetic looking child, standing shyly behind the group of children who had lined up to stare at me. She looked much younger than the nine years Aminata should have been. At first I didn't believe it was the same child. I rechecked her name in my notes, then pulled out the photo of her when she was three years old and said, "Maybe I have the name wrong; this is who I mean."

Her mother just laughed and said, "Yes, I know she looks different—she was really fat when you knew her before. She's been sick for about four years."

"But she always used to eat so much!" I exclaimed. "You told me that she 'ate like a chicken'—all day long. She even went to the neighbors looking for food. What happened?"

"Oh, she still eats like that, more than anyone else in the family! Every day we give her money to buy meat in the market. Even today she had some."

"Then why is she so skinny?"

"Because she's been sick for so long," her mother replied, speaking slowly and patiently, as though dealing with someone who wasn't too bright. "Everyone knows that you can eat a lot and still be skinny."

Although I hadn't intended to include Aminata in the fecal/urine study, I decided on the spot that intestinal parasites might account for her stomach pains and slow growth in spite of a healthy appetite. "Have you ever seen worms in her feces?" I inquired. "Well, no," her mother replied, "but she uses the pit latrine, not a plastic cup like an infant."

We left the plastic bottles for the specimens and returned the next day to collect them. Results came back from the lab: positive for a tapeworm. Since most Malians are Muslim and don't eat pork, it was probably a beef tapeworm, acquired most likely from eating undercooked beef "kebabs" from the marketplace.

I brought her the appropriate medicine, and watched to make sure she took it. It used to be that tapeworm medicine merely killed the tapeworm, and it would then be excreted, so that one could actually see it, and even measure its length. The new treatment, however, not only kills the tapeworm, but renders it digestible by the intestines, so that nothing obvious comes out in the feces. Thus, we weren't able to confirm that the medicine had definitively killed the tapeworm, but in the weeks that followed, Aminata's symptoms (bad stomach pains, cramps, lack of energy, lethargy) all disappeared. We cautioned her against eating beef from the market. She continued to have a remarkable appetite. She should recoup some, if not all, of the growth she lost during the tapeworm's four-year occupation of her body.

Aminata's experience reminded me that the connection between food intake and health is not at all obvious for people repeatedly subjected to a variety of illnesses and intestinal parasites. Here was the one "fat" child from the community, who always ate prodigious amounts of food. Nevertheless, over the course of several years, she lost her baby fat and stopped growing.

Besides Aminata's tapeworm, only three other children's fecal specimens tested positive for intestinal parasites. However, out of 68 specimens of urine, 34 were positive for eggs of *Schistosoma*, the parasite that causes schistosomiasis (also called "black water fever"). "Schisto" is a disease caused by parasites that burrow through the skin around the ankles and calves when you wade in infected waters, where they have passed part of their life cycle in the bodies of snails. The parasites travel through the body, ending up in the epithelial lining of the walls of the urinary tract. They cause bleeding, which imparts a reddish tinge to the urine. In the long run, schistosomiasis is fatal, but the symptoms may take many years to develop; in the interim, the disease weakens you and causes anemia.

The children in Magnambougou pick up schisto from wading and playing in the Fla-bla-bla ("put them down two by two") Creek, which passes along the northern boundary of the community on its way to the Niger River. Dry for much of the year, the creek contains water during the rainy season and is a favorite place for children to splash and play on hot afternoons.

An unintended consequence of using diapers for infants, then graduating to flush toilets, is that Americans have ample opportunity to see their own and their children's urine and feces. In Mali, children never wear diapers and are trained at an early age to go to the bathroom outside in the bush or to use the deep pit latrine found in the corner of almost every compound. This means that older, more responsible members of the compound, such as parents, do not often see either the urine or the feces of young children. Worms in the feces, or blood in the urine, may go unnoticed and thus untreated (the definitive ethnographic study of beliefs and practices surrounding defecation and urination cross-culturally has yet to be written).

Moussa's nephew, a teenaged boy who accompanied us one day on our rounds to collect specimen bottles, turned out to have the worst case of schisto in the sample. He came with us because he was bored that day and wanted to know what his uncle did when he went "out and about" with the toubab. At one busy and crowded compound, the young child who was supposed to have provided the specimens had been sick and was sleeping when we stopped by. I didn't want to bother him, but neither did I want to "waste" the bottles, so I suggested that Moussa's nephew run into the latrine and provide us with at least a urine specimen.

He was happy to oblige and returned in a few minutes with what appeared to be a bottle full of blood. Moussa and I looked with dismay, first at the bottle, then at him, and his smile of accomplishment turned into a look of consternation and confusion. "What's the matter?" he asked.

"Does your urine always look like this?" I responded.

"Yes, what's the matter? Isn't it supposed to? Doesn't everyone's?"

The lab analysis of his specimen revealed over 500 *Schistosoma* eggs per milliliter, the highest count allowed under the technique used. Upon questioning, the boy said that his urine always looked red; so did that of his friends, he told us, and he had never thought to ask anyone if it was normal or not. He knew that infants had yellow urine but thought the change to red was just part of growing up.

Several months later, I was working in the Macina region of northern Mali with a group of Malian health workers from a CARE project, and we discussed schistosomiasis late one afternoon at the end of a long, hot day. We were being poled across the river in a large pirogue, and I was chastising Mariam, one of the nurses, for dangling her legs over the side of the boat into the water. Mariam was from the Bozo tribe of river fishermen. She told me that in some Bozo communities, the first appearance of red urine in a young boy traditionally was thought to be equivalent to the first menstrual period (menarche) in a young girl. Just as menarche was recognized as a sign that a young girl was sexually mature and could become pregnant, red urine in a young boy was thought to be a sign that he was sexually mature, capable of impregnating a woman.

In Bozo communities, the river is their life, and practically everyone gets infected at an early age. Because schistosomiasis can take a number of years to develop to the stage where blood can be seen in the urine, most boys start showing this symptom during puberty. According to Mariam, many Bozo communities held celebratory rites of passage for boys when they reached this milestone. "Today," she said, as she continued washing her legs in the river, "everyone knows that this is a disease that comes from the river."

Even though the Bozo have been told that going in the river can lead to schistosomiasis, they continue to do it. Partly, it is because the span of time from initial infection to the appearance of early symptoms and eventually death takes so many years. Like the links between food and health, sex and AIDS, smoking and lung cancer, some people find them difficult to believe. Others believe, but still don't change their behavior—the consequences are just too remote. Perhaps even more importantly for the Bozo, to give up the river would be to give up their entire way of life.

At the completion of this part of the research, we delivered the appropriate medicine to each of the children who tested positive for intestinal parasites or *Schistosoma* and warned parents of the dangers of playing in the Fla-bla-bla. Even as I spoke, I knew that it would be almost impossible to keep children out of the water, that reinfection was almost certain, and that parents couldn't afford the medicine. In one sense, the money spent on expensive medicine for schisto was just thrown away, but I felt it was the least I could do in return for the time and effort taken by the parents, and in return for the data necessary to satisfy my own curiosity (and my friend Karl's insistent questions) about the problems of parasites.

The next project on the agenda was to add new children and adults to the study of growth and development and to conduct extended interviews with women and other caretakers about infant feeding, weaning, and child health, as well as intrafamilial distribution of food resources and the decision-making processes involved in food purchases. I was glad the parasite project was finished. I looked forward to meeting new people and spending time sitting under the trees talking, instead of spending hours riding the baches with my bag full of smelly little bottles.

5

The Grande Marché

> Nuer are expert at sabotaging an inquiry and until one has resided with them for some weeks they steadfastly stultify all efforts to elicit the simplest facts and to elucidate the most innocent practices. . . . Questions about customs were blocked by a technique I can commend to natives who are inconvenienced by the curiosity of ethnologists.
> —E. E. Evans-Pritchard (1940)

I tipped my chair back against a mango tree and dozed. At midday the sun was too intense to be out walking around, but I wasn't drenched in sweat—it evaporated before it even reached the surface of my body. A hot breeze swirled through the compound, baking everything in its path. At least it kept the flies away. Around my feet, chickens foraged in the dust for stray grains of rice.

We had spent the morning measuring and interviewing, more of the former than the latter. Measuring all the kids in the family, as well as whichever adults were around, was quick and easy. Interviews required more of a commitment of time from the women of the compound, and they were often too busy in the morning to sit and talk. Mornings were for going to the market and getting started on the midday meal. They had more leisure in the afternoon, if a Malian woman can really be said to have any leisure time at all. Her day usually begins before sunup with at least an hour's worth of millet pounding, followed by lighting the fire and cooking millet porridge for breakfast. The day is filled with heavy manual labor, including hauling water out of the well with a rubber bucket on the end of a rope, chopping firewood, going to the market to buy food for the day, and cooking three meals. At the same time, she is usually either pregnant or lactating (producing milk for breastfeeding), and caring for one or more small children. Only when her first child is old enough to help does her burden become any lighter; women hope to have a daughter first, because girls help more than boys with domestic chores and child care. At least in the afternoons women were at home, instead of at the market, and had a break of several hours before they had to start preparing the evening meal. For many, a visit from a friendly stranger, especially a toubab, was a distraction—they were delighted that I wanted to hear their opinions about topics on which they were the experts.

Few toubabs roamed the back streets of Magnambougou, and I was usually followed by a ragtag band of children chanting "toubabou, toubabou." If they were annoying me, I taunted them back "*fara fin, fara fin.*" This sent any listening adults into gales of laughter, while the children halted in confusion. I felt that my entertainment value somewhat justified my intrusions into people's lives, and it alleviated my guilt over not being able to offer much in the way of tangible goods in return for the cooperation and time of my informants.

We usually visited two or three compounds in the morning and returned to Moussa's house for lunch. Moussa lived with his father, his older brother (and his wife and children), his younger brother (who was unmarried), his wife, his wife's son by a former marriage, and his wife's niece. They had a spacious, well-kept compound at one edge of town near the river, shaded by several tall mango trees. Moussa's wife, Rookia, was a formidable woman, standing over six feet tall and weighing more than 200 pounds. She was fiercely intelligent and had a fine sense of humor. She was also an excellent cook, and early on we agreed that she would provide lunch for "the researchers" each weekday, in exchange for a small sum of money.

Normally, the adult women of a compound take turns, on a daily basis, cooking the food for everyone in the compound. When a man has several co-wives, the one who cooks during the day can lay claim to the husband's attentions during the night. In a large compound with several adult brothers, each of whom has several wives, a woman has to cook only occasionally, maybe one day a week. On the other hand, she may have to cook for 20 or more people at a time, when you count in all the kids. Moussa's compound had two adult women, his wife, Rookia, and his brother's wife, Fatou; so Rookia usually cooked every other day. One taste of Fatou's cooking, however, convinced me that disrupting the usual schedule was worth it. On weekdays, when we were there for lunch, Rookia cooked the midday meal, and Fatou cooked at night.

It's a well-known adage in Mali that toubabs prefer rice to millet, and I was no exception. Every day, lunch consisted of vast

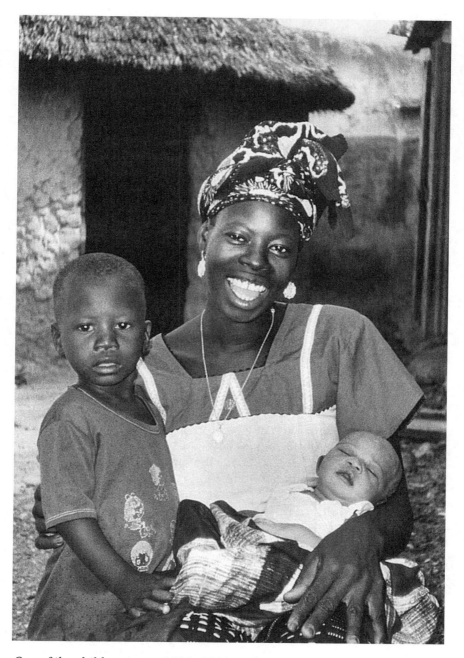

One of the children in my 1981–1983 study, with his mother and newborn sister. The characteristically dark pigmentation in a baby's skin develops over the first four months of life.

quantities of the more expensive rice, served with a different sauce. Rookia's specialties were peanut butter sauce and okra sauce. In deference to my underprivileged upbringing in the United States, Rookia always provided me with a chair to sit on (instead of a stool), my own bowl (instead of sharing from a communal bowl), and a spoon (instead of eating with my fingers). I accepted the individual serving bowl and the chair, but rejected the spoon, much preferring to eat with my fingers.

Eating with the fingers of your right hand is a fine art, one best practiced outside, surrounded by hungry chickens who quickly zoom in to remove all evidence of drips and splatters. Uncoordinated to begin with, and not accustomed to eating with my hand, I always dropped food on the ground. Part of the problem was that I am left-handed—a distinct disadvantage in a culture where the left hand is reserved for cleansing after using the latrine. Food preparation, eating, and handshaking are the province of the right hand. Polite people never eat with their left hand, even if it means spilling a lot of food 'twixt bowl and mouth. The chickens ate well whenever I was around.

Following a brief siesta, I lowered my chair to the ground and announced, "Well, guess we ought to get back out there and collect some more data." In the afternoon, we visited more compounds, measured more people, and conducted more interviews. Part of the semistructured interview had to do with decisions about household budgets. I was interested in how much money each woman was given by her husband each day (in the morning) to spend on sauce ingredients for that day's meals, how many people she had to feed, and how she decided what to buy. I also wanted to know what she would do if she had more money to spend on food.

"Poverty of the parents" is a typical economic explanation for malnutrition in children. In Mali, however, a number of lines of evidence suggested that absolute poverty was not the main constraining factor, in that people with more money basically ate the same foods as the poorest villagers. A number of "development" projects in Mali had been designed to promote income-generating activities, with the ultimate outcome supposedly being better nutrition and health for the children. From my earlier research, I "knew," albeit in an unquantifiable way, that additional household income would seldom be spent on more or different food. This time, in a more systematic way, I would ask questions about income and expenditures, trying to pinpoint the factors that influenced Malian women's spending habits.

It turned out to be very difficult to get straight answers to my questions. Women were often reluctant to tell me how much money their husband gave them, as this partly reflects how wealthy the family is and partly reflects the quality of the relationship between a man and his wife. A favored wife will get more money. A second problem was that women had great difficulty imagining what they would do if they had more money. In response to my query "What would you do if you had more money to spend each day on food?" they would retort, "But where would I get more money?" Another common response was to say that they would buy non-food items such as cloth, shoes, or other items, or else that they would save it. If I said, "No, you have to spend this hypothetical money on food," they would respond, "Why? If it's hypothetical, why can't I spend it any way I like?" I was trying to understand how an increase in income for women might translate into more or better food, and thus into better health for themselves and better growth for their children. But, unaware of my hidden agenda, they didn't want to cooperate.

If I insisted that they had to spend the extra money on food, the most common response was that they would buy bread, potatoes, or macaroni with it. I understood how these quintessentially toubab foods, especially macaroni, held a fascination for people used to eating millet and rice, rice and millet, millet and rice, day in, day out, every meal of every day. But as a nutritional anthropologist, I wanted them to tell me that if they just had more money, they would buy the kinds of healthy, protein- and vitamin-rich foods I thought their kids needed. I wanted them to confirm that it was merely (ha! merely!) the reality of poverty that kept their kids from growing as they should.

Sometimes I would prime them by saying things like "Well, do you think you might buy more meat? How about more fish? And what about fresh fruit? Do you think you might buy milk?" I kept expecting a prosecuting attorney to jump out from behind a tree, pointing his or her finger at me and shouting: "Aha, leading the informant! Invalid data." But no lawyer ever did, and my informants continued to insist that since I wouldn't let them hypothetically spend their hypothetical money on hypothetical clothes, they'd just as soon buy macaroni. Without exception, everyone felt that they were able to purchase food for an adequate diet with the money they currently had.

Several months later, toward the end of our stay, I encountered similar problems trying to ascertain how often people in a rural village ate meat. We were huddled in a small hut, where we had sought shelter from the blowing winds and stinging sand whipping off the Sahara to our north. "So, what do you usually eat for breakfast?" (shake sand off notebook, write answer) and "what do you usually eat at noon?" (shake sand off notebook, write answer, brush sand off face). "Do you eat anything in the afternoon?" (shake sand off notebook, write answer), and "what about for the evening meal?" (shake sand off notebook, write answer, rub eyes with back of hand).

"Now, can you tell me, about how often do you eat meat?" I asked. Perfectly straightforward question, I thought, in my naiveté.

"Whenever someone kills a goat."

"OK. How often does someone kill a goat?"

"Whenever they need money."

"Huh?"

"When someone needs money, they kill a goat and sell the meat to their neighbors. Each family buys a small amount, and when the meat is all sold the person has the money he needs, and the rest of us have meat to eat."

Hmmmm, I thought to myself, not unlike a bank account, just on hooves.

"Why would someone need money?" I inquired.

"Oh, to pay for medicine, or school fees, or a trip to visit a relative, or to go to Bamako to look for work."

"And about how often does someone need money like that, and kill a goat?"

"That's hard to say. It depends."

Aaarrrggghhhh . . . "OK," I sighed. "Would you say that someone kills a goat in this village every day?"

"Of course not."

"Once a week?"

"Not that often."

"Once a month?"

"Sometimes, or sometimes more than that."

"Two or three a month?"

"Probably two."

"So, you usually eat meat twice a month?"

"If you say so."

Whew. I was almost pulling teeth. And how close to any sort of objective reality, I wondered? With dread, I asked the next question: "About how often do you eat fish?"

"Oh, we eat fish every day, sometimes twice a day—at noon and in the evening."

I looked up suspiciously to see if she was teasing me, but she wasn't. "Is it always fresh fish?"

"No. Sometimes fresh, sometimes dried, sometimes smoked."

So far so good. "And how often do you drink milk?"

"Whenever the Fulani come around with their cows, selling it."

Here we go again, I thought. "How often do the Fulani come around with their cows?" I asked brightly. At the same time, I wondered to myself, "How does anyone ever get decent interview data?"

One of the reasons it was difficult to pin down women in Magnambougou on how they would budget their money is that in many parts of the Third World, including Mali, everything is negotiable. Unlike in the retail stores in the United States, where all items have a fixed price, in Mali every price must be negotiated. There are a few rules that govern the bargaining process. First, few goods have an intrinsic value—an object is worth as much as someone is willing to pay for it, no more and no less. There are some general rules for standard prices for particular items, but so much depends on the quality of the item (be it a pyramid of plum tomatoes, a length of tie-dyed cloth, or a young donkey) and the desire of the buyer to own it, that the specific price still must always be negotiated. Second, for the seller, gaining a buyer's regular "custom" is worth taking a loss on some items sold early in the relationship. Vendors vie fiercely for the custom of toubabs who have money to spend on a regular basis, offering deep discounts in exchange for future loyalty. Third, wealthier people are automatically expected to pay more for the same item than poorer people. This goes double or triple for toubabs, the poorest of whom—Peace Corps volunteers, anthropologists, and their ilk— are far wealthier than even well-to-do Malians. Fourth, bargaining over the price of an item is as much a matter of establishing and maintaining social ties as it is getting good value for the franc. A serious bargaining session should be entered into in good faith, with the understanding that each side will make some accommodations to reach an acceptable compromise. The ideal outcome, following a long and satisfying negotiation, is one that leaves both sides feeling they got the better deal.

One of the best places to observe economic activity and vigorous bargaining in Mali is the Grande Marché (French for "Big Market"), centrally located in downtown Bamako. Mere words are inadequate to describe the atmosphere inside the Grand Marché. The Marché is built in an architectural style known as "French Sudanic"—all arches and turrets, faded now to a dirty orange shade. Structurally, it consists of a series of concentric rings of vendors' stalls, with narrow, twisting passageways for aisles. Inside, it is dark and gloomy even on the brightest day, as the only illumination comes from weak light bulbs dangling from bare wires overhead and shafts of sunlight sifting down through gaps in the roof. The very center of the Marché used to be open to the sky, and one stumbled out of the shadowy recesses into the blinding sun, half expecting to find a minotaur at the center of the maze.

When you enter the world of the Marché, all of your senses are besieged—sight, sound and, most profoundly, smell. Your eyes take in vendors selling everything imaginable: incense, myrrh, spices, fluorescent green bras, plastic cups, bicycle chains, cola nuts, ancient trade beads that originated in Venice, gold and silver, monkey heads, and magical powders. Your ears are assaulted by a cacophony of sounds—people speaking in a variety of West African languages, customers and vendors bargaining, greetings flying back and forth, babies crying, and overhead the calls of mourning doves, perched on the highest points of the turrets.

But the most remarkable encounter with the market comes through the nose. The olfactory experience that constitutes the Grande Marché in Bamako is truly amazing. From the tantalizing aromas of unidentifiable foods being cooked, to the sublime smells of incense, myrrh, and bulk spices, heaped in glowing cones, to the odors of sweat, dirt, and stale urine. Permeating all, the mustiness of centuries gone by. The Marché is a concentrated dose of Mali, all the sights, sounds, and material culture of the country extracted and distilled, crowded into one bustling, overwhelming experience. Entering the twisted passageways of the Marché is like stepping through a time-warp into a previous century.

Along one inside wedge of the Marché is the "bead row"—a spacious aisle lined with vendors of beads, bronze figurines, statues, jewelry, purses, and other miscellaneous finery. It takes time and effort to sit down on the small wooden stool provided only to serious customers and sort through the wares elaborately displayed on the floor. But the persistent visitor will be rewarded with an unusual or piquant find.

Among the treasures I discovered were two small bronze figurines, about four inches long. One is a slave. He is bound, with his hands and feet tied to a pole, a look of anguish on his face. The anonymous artist wrought the slave's malnourished state with anatomical accuracy, so that every rib stands out clearly, and his shoulder blades can be seen poking painfully through his skin. The artist even wrought evidence of beating on the slave's back, ranging from fresh wounds to old, healed scars.

The other piece represents a woman in the final stages of pregnancy, kneeling down, perhaps in labor, an avatar of all West African fertility goddesses. As an undergraduate, I once visited the home of a folklore professor who had a fine collection of these small bronze figurines from West Africa, displayed in a glass case with mirrored shelves. Close scrutiny revealed that all of his figurines depicted men and women engaged in various sexual acts, some of them quite intriguing to a naive American undergraduate. Although

I looked diligently in the Bamako Marché, I never found any bronzes quite like his.

At the Marché, I always made a point of visiting my friend Sidi, purveyor of assorted weavings, including Fulani wedding blankets and the beautiful and unique mudcloth (*bogolan-fini*) for which Mali is justly famous. Sidi had a sly face and was a wise entrepreneur; I had made a friend of him by speaking Bambara to him (although Tamasheq was his native tongue), teasing him about his exorbitant prices for toubabs and visiting him whenever I was at the Marché, even when I wasn't interested in buying anything. The color of old mahogany, Sidi had a nervous habit of whipping off his blue turban, rapidly rubbing his hand over his head, which was completely bald, then replacing and adjusting his turban.

One Saturday afternoon, taking a break from data collection, I went to see him to continue our weeks-long bargaining over the price of a beautiful new Fulani wedding blanket. The Fulani are cattle herders who roam West Africa seeking good pasture and water for their animals. They live in tents, and their wedding blankets are actually tent walls, which are used to divide the interior of the tent and provide a modicum of privacy for newly married couples. They are woven on traditional strip looms, using both cotton and wool, and feature geometric designs, stripes, and dots. The colors come from natural dyes and include beige, yellow, white, black, rust, and dark indigo blue. A typical blanket is about 16 feet long and 8 feet wide. Steven and I had purchased a particularly fine traditional wedding blanket in 1983. How many of these do we need, I asked myself? We don't even have a place to hang the one we have! But Sidi had an unusual blanket. It was very finely woven and in good condition, but most striking was the fact that some of the designs were green. I wanted the blanket, but I knew that the first rule of bargaining is "never let the vendor know how much you like the merchandise." So I was maintaining a low profile, visiting Sidi every week or two to bargain the price a little lower. I hoped that by refusing to purchase it until just before I left to go home, I could get the best price possible.

He knew I wanted the blanket. He also knew I wasn't your typical tourist and wouldn't pay his full asking price. Nor did I fall for his ploys that if I didn't buy the blanket soon, someone else would. I countered that I didn't really need another wedding blanket, which was certainly true, and that I couldn't really afford to buy it at all, which was also true. I brought several other toubabs along on different occasions, including Tom, my demographer housemate, to try to find someone to split the cost and the blanket with me.

On this occasion, I had been bargaining and visiting with Sidi for some time when two French tourists approached his stall.

Immediately turning his attention to them, he began unfolding and displaying examples of the different kinds of blankets he carried, extolling their virtues in French. The couple were enamored of a piece of mudcloth, and asked him the price. Without batting an eye he offered a price "for this unique piece" of 25,000 CFA. I knew he had stacks and stacks of similar, if not identical, mudcloth, under the counter. I also knew that the rock-bottom price for mudcloths for toubabs was 3,000 CFA (about $8 U.S.). As the two customers admired the cloth and discussed the price between themselves, he threw me a pleading look, which clearly meant "Keep your mouth shut, please!" The Frenchman countered Sidi's initial offer with an offer of 10,000 CFA. Sidi threw up his hands in disgust, rolled his eyes to the ceiling and said, "Mon Dieu, how do you expect me to stay in business! I am insulted. This is a fine piece of work. You won't find anything like it in the whole Marché. But . . . since you are a special customer, I can maybe come down to 20,000 CFA." Back and forth, offer and counteroffer, Sidi's price inched down as the tourists' inched up. Finally, they agreed on a price of 18,000 CFA, almost exactly halfway between their original starting positions. The money exchanged hands, Sidi folded up their mudcloth and wrapped it in paper, and they departed, very happy with their purchase, and proud of their ability to drive a hard bargain. After all, hadn't they gotten the price down from 25,000 to 18,000 CFA?

With glee, Sidi turned to me and said, "Thank you, my fine friend, for keeping quiet!" "Of course," I replied. "Why should I care if some French tourist is willing to pay 18,000 CFA for one piece of mudcloth, when I would get six for the same price? He's happy, you're happy, and as long as you sell them to me for 3,000 CFA, I'm happy! They're worth whatever someone is willing to pay. You still make a good profit even at my price of 3,000 CFA, don't you?" He chuckled and winked at me. "Now about this wedding blanket . . ."

6

Rural Africa at Last

From a European's point of view Nuerland has no favourable
qualities, unless its severity be counted as such, for its endless
marshes and wide savannah plains have an austere,
monotonous charm. . . . But Nuer think that they live in the
finest country on earth . . .

—E. E. Evans-Pritchard (1940)

About the time measuring kids and interviewing women had started
to pall, an opportunity for research presented itself that would turn
out to have far-reaching (and utterly unforeseen) consequences on
both my professional and personal lives. It began one evening with
a visit from Kathleen Stack and Bakary Traore. Kathleen works for
Freedom from Hunger, a nonprofit organization based in Davis,
California, dedicated to ending world hunger. Bakary was working
for AMIPJ, an acronym for the French version of the lengthy and
barely pronounceable name of a Malian nongovernmental
organization (NGO) created to provide employment to young
professionals in grass-roots development projects. Freedom from
Hunger provided financial and technical assistance to AMIPJ to
carry out a Credit with Education program. At the time, Kathleen
was in Mali on a routine visit. The health officer at the U.S. Agency
for International Development bureau in Bamako had suggested
that Bakary and Kathleen talk to me for help in designing a nutrition
education component for AMIPJ's rural credit, income-generating
project in a region of Mali known as Dogo arrondissement (district).

Kathleen introduced herself, then turned to Bakary. "This is Mr.
Traore, he heads up the Bamako staff that supports the field project
in Dogo. He speaks a little English."

I turned to shake hands with Mr. Traore. As is the case throughout

West Africa, no official business can take place in Mali until everyone has shaken hands with everyone else, even if there are 20 people involved. I was surprised to see that he was very young, of slight build, with a handsome face, finely chiseled features and sparkling eyes; he had a face like an African prince. His demeanor was formal and somewhat reticent, as though he wasn't sure what to think of me.

Without letting go of his hand, I launched into the traditional Bambara greetings. His face lit up as he responded and then took over the series of questions. When we had exhausted the standard greetings, and a few extras, I added nonchalantly, "My Bambara name is Mariam Diarra. It's too bad you are a Traore. I don't think I can work with a Traore. Everyone knows the Traores are worthless and lazy and only like to sit around and eat beans." Bakary cracked up, and proceeded to unleash a string of friendly insults concerning my ancestry and eating habits, of which I understood only the parts about my mother's character and my own fondness for beans. He ended by lamenting the fact that I was a Diarra, consoling me for my misfortune in not having been born a Traore.

"What *are* you two talking about?" Kathleen demanded in English.

"Just trading insults," I answered cryptically. "Bakary is a Traore and I'm a Diarra. That automatically puts us in a joking relationship to one another."

Joking relationships involve official, sanctioned silliness, centered around the trading of insults, which often make reference to otherwise unmentionable body parts or bodily functions. In some cultures, joking relationships are established between certain classes of relatives, by blood or by marriage, such as a boy and his mother's brother in a patrilineal society. You may, and indeed are expected to, treat your joking partner with rudeness and intimacy, but always in a spirit of fun rather than meanness. Joking relationships contrast strongly with the formal distance and respect found in other relationships, such as that between a boy and his own father in a patrilineal society.

In Mali, in addition to joking relationships between specific kinsmen, joking relationships also automatically obtain between people of particular last names. Since my last name was Diarra (by virtue of being Moussa's fictive sister), I was in a joking relationship with anyone who had the last name of Traore. The most common insult, hurled by both sides, was to accuse the other of being inordinately fond of beans. The joke, of course, was that a fondness for beans translated into a predilection for farting, an action Malians find hilariously funny.

Beans and farts aside, Kathleen got down to the serious business of explaining what sort of expertise they needed. "Freedom from Hunger provides the major financial and technical support for AMIPJ's rural credit development program for women in Dogo arrondissement," she explained. "The project is well established, and the women are making money through small-scale projects such as processing and selling rice and millet, trading salt, and selling butter made from *karite* (*shea*) nuts. We asked them what they wanted to do with their profits, and they said their top priority was to improve the health of their children."

"Sounds great," I responded. "How can I help?"

"Well, we think the best approach is through nutrition education, rather than an immunization program or other technology-intensive project. We thought we would start by adding a short nutrition education session to the weekly credit association meetings the women already attend. These meetings are run by the *animatrices* ("animators") who work for AMIPJ. They each live in a rural village and carry out programs in the surrounding villages. They're all young, well-educated Malian women. But we're not sure what kinds of nutrition and health information people need. We're hoping you can help us develop nutrition education messages."

"I____ ___ lot of malnutrition in these villages?" I asked.

"___ there's malnutrition, but there are no data to ___ extent of the problem or the causes. Some staff have ___trition and health, but they have been focused on ___men's associations, managing credit, and providing ___stance for entrepreneurial activities up to now. What ___t?"

"___eed to know how many kids are malnourished, what ___d sex distribution of the malnourished kids, and ___shiorkor or protein-calorie malnutrition is more ___n, you need to know the main causes of malnutrition ___unity. Is this area prone to food shortages?"

"___ sometimes seasonal food shortages, but the area is ___-sufficient in food production. In fact, that's one of the ___PJ chose Dogo for their project. I'm sure some of the kids are severely malnourished, though."

"What do you know about infant feeding practices in the area? Things like when solid foods are started in the diet, when children are weaned from the breast, and what kinds of foods are given to young children."

"We don't know anything about that, really," Bakary chimed in. "But I think some of the mothers don't give their kids anything to eat until they wean them, when they're about two years old. Then they wean them straight onto toh."

"Well, that's a typical perception of outsiders," I explained. "Until children eat the staple foods, mothers often claim they don't eat anything. Fruits, vegetables, peanuts, cow milk, fish, and other foods don't count because they're not millet or rice."

"Can you help us?" Kathleen requested again. "I know you're busy with your own research. Would you have time? And how much would your consulting fee be?"

Visions of data, piles and piles of beautiful data, massive quantities of data, danced in my head. It's not easy to just waltz into a rural village and say, "Can I measure all your children?" Here was a potential opportunity, if I handled it right, of gaining access to hundreds of people from rural African villages, who would willingly cooperate because I was sponsored by AMIPJ. In addition, AMIPJ had four-wheel drive vehicles for transportation, clean huts with foam pads for sleeping, and contacts in every village to arrange for food. They had offered me a potential bonanza.

Bamako had become just a big, dirty city. The "real Africa," the one I'd read about and studied in countless ethnographies, lay out there, beyond the influence of the capital city, beyond the influence of the West. Here it was, being offered on a platter. I tried to control my emotions and sound casual.

"I will need to conduct an anthropometric survey to find out the level and kinds of malnutrition present, as well as the sex and age distribution of malnutrition. I will also need to conduct ethnographic research, perhaps through 'town meetings' to find out if rural beliefs about food, children, and the feeding of children are the same in Dogo arrondissement as they are in Bamako. If your personnel provide transportation and help with the logistics of setting up measuring sessions and interviews in each village and pay for my expenses, and if you agree that I can use the data I collect in my professional research, then I will do it for free. I will provide a report, along with my recommendations for specific nutritional education messages directed at the most malnourished segments of the population."

"Really?" Kathleen exclaimed. "That would be great. How should we go about arranging it?"

Bakary and I discussed details of setting up a reconnaissance trip of three days' duration. Before I could design a proper survey, I needed to have a feel for the region. I also needed to talk to the field personnel, explain what we would be doing, and work out a schedule. Finally, I had to decide if Miranda could accompany me on the longer trip to carry out the actual survey. I wasn't willing to take her out of school for a week, and drag her along, if living conditions were going to be horrible. I was especially worried about what the food would be like. Bakary and I set a date for the initial trip, and we exchanged a few more pleasantries as I walked them out to their car. Returning to the house I carefully closed the screen door behind me, then danced a little jig of happiness.

In the days that followed my spirits soared. I was able to deposit Miranda with an English missionary family in the neighborhood who had two daughters close to her age. The girls were already good friends, and Miranda often spent the night at their house. I had the typical anthropologist's disdain for missionaries, who begin with the premise that their religion is better than the one the people already have, or even that the people in question have no religious beliefs at all. On the other hand, as individuals they were perfectly nice and seemed very responsible. Most importantly, they were willing to take care of Miranda for me. I had some misgivings about leaving her with them for three days, but it seemed the best option. It was easy to convince her that she'd be better off staying with them.

It took more persuasion to convince Moussa that going to the "bush" for a few days was part of his job description.

"Those people live like savages!" he spluttered.

"You sound just like a toubab," I replied.

"Well, they do," he insisted. "They believe in witches and spirits, and the food will probably be terrible. Villagers are very backward. They don't know anything. They never wash."

"You crack me up, Moussa. You've lived in Houston and New York City, and you know what most Americans would think of the way you live; yet you're just as biased against your own countrymen if they live in a rural village."

"I can't help it," he replied. "I grew up in Bamako. I just know it's going to be terrible."

"Well, you can at least try it for three days. It will be an incredible opportunity for me. If it's really awful, neither of us will go back. I'll even bring along extra food and buy you a carton of good cigarettes for the trip."

Moussa finally agreed, and the day of departure for the first trip to Dogo rapidly approached. With some misgiving on my part, and hers, arrangements had been made for Miranda to go home from school with her friends, and Heather and I were packed and waiting for Bakary to come by and pick us up at 10:00 A.M. As the minutes, then the hours, passed, my elation turned to bitter disappointment. Without a phone, I had no way of contacting Bakary to find out what was the matter. Was this just another example of the typical Malian disregard for deadlines and appointments, or was the whole trip called off?

In the late afternoon, Bakary finally arrived. Before I could pick up my equipment, he suggested we postpone our departure for a

day because he needed to go to a meeting the following morning.
"What!" I exploded. "We've had this trip planned for days! I've
made arrangements for Miranda to be taken care of, I've used up
all the food in the house so nothing will spoil, and now you casually
say 'Let's wait another day?' Nothing doing."

It was easy for Bakary to postpone the trip for another day. He
had a wife at home who would take care of his need for food. He
had a wife at home who would take care of his three sons, whether
he was there or not. He didn't understand the imposition it created
for me to pack Miranda off to stay with strangers, because he had
an extended family who would gladly take care of his children on
a moment's notice, whenever the need arose. If you don't have a
refrigerator, and you buy all your food fresh every day, it's hard
to understand why the lack of food in the house is a problem. The
ethnographer in me understood his position—he would get in
trouble with his supervisor if he missed this critical meeting.
Apparently, he had forgotten about it when we scheduled our
departure. At the same time, it really would have been terribly
awkward for me to postpone the trip, even for a day. Was I being
unreasonable?

We argued back and forth. Bakary claimed he really needed to
go to the meeting or his boss would be mad; I countered that we

*Traditional mud-brick houses with circular thatched roofs in Dogo
arrondissement.*

had made a deal that was greatly to his advantage, and he was treating me with disrespect. I also pointed out that his boss knew very well that he was accompanying the toubabs to the field site in Dogo and would not be present for the meeting. "It's either today, or never," I challenged.

Eventually, my insistence, and probably the fact that I was a toubab, prevailed. We loaded our gear into the truck, and set off for Dogo, stopping to collect Moussa along the way. The road to Dogo led south and east of Bamako toward Ivory Coast, away from the river. Once out of Bamako, Bakary relaxed and relations were cordial between us. The further we got from Bamako, the more lush the countryside became. Trees were both bigger and more numerous, and the shrubs and grasses grew thick beneath the trees. Picturesque villages of round, mud-thatched huts were scattered along the road. As we passed each village, dogs ran alongside the truck and children came out to wave, jumping up and down with excitement and shouting "toubabou, toubabou" when they glimpsed our faces. We stopped for late-season mangoes near a tiny roadside mosque, molded of red mud brick and crowned with ostrich egg shells.

Only about 120 kilometers (72 miles) as the crow flies, the trip to Dogo involved two hours of travel on paved roads, followed by two more hours over a twisting, rutted dirt track. After we left the paved road, we bounced along in the heat, holding onto the seat in front of us, but still banging our heads against the windows or ceiling whenever the truck hit a particularly big bump. My head ached. On either side of us were fields, neatly arranged rows of corn, millet, and sorghum, all approaching maturity, as well as low bushes I couldn't identify. "What kind of food is that?" I asked. "Peanuts?"

Bakary turned and looked at me in amusement and disbelief. "That's not food. It's cotton," he explained. "Don't you grow cotton in America?"

"Well, yes, lots of it, but I've never seen it," I explain feebly. "Why do the villagers grow cotton?" I asked.

Again, Bakary raised his eyebrows and looked at me suspiciously, trying to determine if I was kidding. "They have to have clothes to wear."

"Well," I shot back defensively, "I just meant do they grow it for themselves or do they grow it to sell as a cash crop?"

"Sometimes they sell some, if there's any left over," he admitted.

Before I could display any more ignorance of rural country life, Bakary announced, "This is Dogo village, itself, the center of the arrondissement. We must stop and give greetings to the commandant." We pulled up in front of a group of cement buildings.

After the obligatory introductions, explanations, and greetings, we continued on to the AMIPJ compound, situated somewhat apart from the rest of the village. There Bakary introduced us to Falaye Doumbia, the field project director, then went off to see about our dinner in the neighboring village of Belekan.

The only appropriate word to describe Falaye is "beautiful." Over six feet tall, he was the color of rich milk chocolate and possessed a deep, resonant voice. His handshake was strong and confident. In the weeks that followed, I came to admire Falaye's quick, inquisitive mind, his pragmatic approach to the problems of rural development, and his great sense of humor.

Like all AMIPJ compounds, Falaye's household consisted of a large, well-kept compound with two rectangular rooms built of cement block and covered with corrugated iron roofs, in the urban style. In the middle of the compound was a traditional *paillote*—an open-air gazebo surrounded by a low wall, with a thatched roof so low to the ground you had to duck to enter. In one corner of the compound was the pit latrine, surrounded by a five-foot wall. Heather and I were assigned one of the rooms for sleeping, then invited to join Falaye, Macan (the driver), Moussa, and several villagers for a walk through the village, highlighted by coming across a young boy gleefully roasting a fat lizard over a charcoal brazier.

Back at Falaye's, we sat in a circle, chatted amiably, relaxed, and enjoyed the peaceful atmosphere while munching on raw peanuts. Crisp and moist, they taste nothing like the dry-roasted, salted peanuts familiar to airline passengers in the United States. The heat of the day had passed, and darkness fell quickly, as it always does near the equator. From the village drifted sounds of children playing, and dogs barking.

"A little later, we'll go over to Belekan, the next village over. You passed it on your way in," Falaye explained. "They're preparing tonight's meal for us."

Moussa seemed unusually quiet. "What's the matter, Moussa? Still afraid the food will be inedible?" I teased.

"No," he answered. "I don't feel good. My head really hurts. I think I'm getting malaria."

"I have some aspirin, and some chloroquine, in my bag. Would you like some?"

"Sure. That would be great."

I retrieved my Lands' End bag (no longer filled with little plastic bottles) and searched around for the medicines. Someone handed me a flashlight. I fished out three chloroquine tablets for Moussa, the standard initial dose for someone coming down with malaria. As word got out, several of the others requested chloroquine and/or

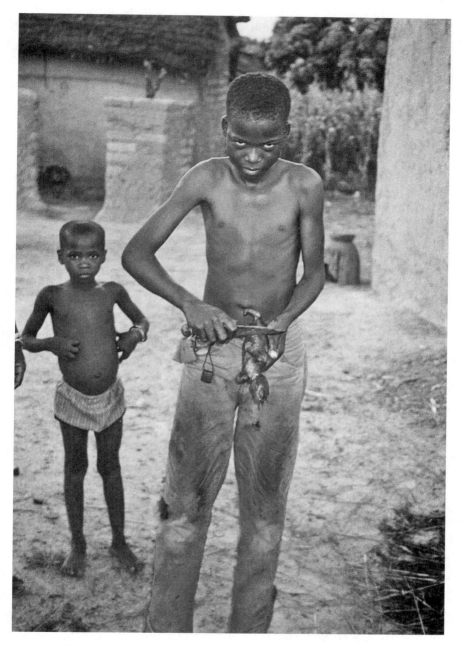

A young boy in Dogo village, scraping the scales from his roasted lizard.

aspirin, and I was happy to oblige. In Mali, it is assumed, usually correctly, that all Westerners carry well-stocked arsenals of medicines and medical supplies, as well as the knowledge of how to use them. If one were to write a book on how to win friends and influence people in Mali, the first rule would be: carry aspirin. In a land of frequent headaches, the mere possession of aspirin was enough to win friends. My well-stocked blue bag, with chloroquine, alcohol swabs, Band-Aids, gauze bandages, tape, and vitamins, came to be known in Dogo as the *pharmacie en brousse* (bush pharmacy). It opened many doors.

The mosquitoes were getting thick, so I fished out my insect repellant, slathered my arms and legs, and handed it to Heather. From her it passed to Moussa, and thence around the circle. "What is this?" Falaye inquired. "It keeps the mosquitoes away," I answered. "Amazing," he said, shaking his head slowly, "you Americans think of everything."

"What do you mean?" I asked.

"You bring along pills in case you get a headache. You bring along other pills in case you get malaria. You even bring along medicine to keep the mosquitoes from biting you." He spoke as though this were silly, as though it mystified him.

"What's wrong with that? There's no point in having a headache when aspirin exists in the world," I responded.

"You Americans just seem soft," he explained. "You can't stand any pain. Like your hands and feet."

"My hands and feet?"

"Yes, your hands are not like the hands of a Malian. Your hands are soft. They don't have any rough spots or hard calluses because you don't do any real work. And your feet are the same way, because you always wear shoes." He directed his next question to the group: "Have any of you ever seen the way toubabs walk without shoes?"

"Yes, yes," they agreed, chuckling. "Like an ostrich!"

"OK, I grant you that," I admitted. "I work with my brain, and my arms for measuring kids, not with my hands. I don't pound millet or grind karite nuts or chop firewood every day. I still don't see the point in suffering unnecessarily."

Before we could continue the discussion, the Land Rover pulled up and Bakary called to us to climb in for the drive to Belekan, and dinner. By this time it was ten o'clock, the sky was completely dark, and I was famished. We stopped after a short drive, then followed Bakary for many minutes along pitch-black, winding pathways. I stumbled several times in the dark. We passed through compounds where children peered at us from hiding places behind their mothers, or from the doorways of small huts, their interiors lit with flickering kerosene lanterns. Eventually we got to the compound of one of the AMIPJ animatrices, where food had been prepared for us.

We were offered seats on small carved three-legged wooden stools, and a number of women bustled about the fire completing arrangements for our meal. The only light was from the embers of the cooking fire and one kerosene lamp hanging from a tree branch. Bakary, Moussa, and Macan joined us, forming a semicircle, and a small bowl of water was passed for hand washing. "Please God, let the food be edible," I prayed to myself. Heather, who had been very quiet all evening, leaned over to me and whispered in my ear "This is *so* weird! I can't believe this is really happening. We're really in a rural African village! It seems totally unreal; it's so exotic compared to Bamako."

One of the women placed a large bowl of steaming corn porridge (*kaba toh* in Bambara, also known as corn *fu-fu* in many parts of West Africa) in front of us. It was arranged in small "pats," formed by plopping gourd ladles full of warm porridge into the bowl just as they are cooling enough to "set." The resulting hand-size portions can be pulled off the pile and dipped in sauce before consuming. A smaller bowl of slimy green sauce, made from okra, onions, and spices, was placed in the center of the corn toh. The food was delicious and plentiful, and I was famished. I ate as much as anyone else, although it took me longer, because I was so inefficient. I could tell that the local villagers were pleased (and surprised) to see a toubab eat with such gusto.

The morning dawned clear and crisp. The smell of wood smoke from a hundred cooking fires permeated the air, a welcome contrast to the noise and pollution of Bamako. Behind Falaye's compound a tall tree was home to hundreds of tiny weaver birds, who chirped and chattered and swooped above our heads. Breakfast consisted of balls of millet dough, spiced with hot peppers and fried in karite butter, washed down with cups of strong dark Nescafe laced with plenty of sweetened condensed milk. After breakfast we set off to visit the villages of N'tenkoni and Merediela.

We passed numerous small villages, tiny clusters of huts set down in the midst of tall fields of corn and millet. Cotton grew in more distant fields, between the villages, as it was less likely to need protection from birds. The road had deteriorated into a narrow dirt path. Men on bicycles, short-handled hoes balanced on their shoulders, pulled over into the weeds to let us pass. They were headed for distant fields, taking advantage of the lull before the corn harvest to prepare next year's fields for planting, fields that had lain fallow for years. Young boys herded small flocks of sheep or goats along the track, jumping up and down and waving. Without warning, Macan veered off to the left, following two barely distinguishable swaths through the waist-high grass. "It's a good thing he knows where he's going," I thought to myself.

After many minutes I glimpsed the conical thatched roofs of a village straight ahead, through the dirty windshield. N'tenkoni was north of Dogo, deeper into the bush, and so small Dogo seemed like a teeming metropolis by comparison. We toured the village, which was practically empty. Most able-bodied children and adults were off in the fields, leaving the village to the elderly and a few mothers with young children. Unlike Magnambougou, the village wasn't laid out in any particular pattern. There were a few lanes between houses, but many compounds could only be reached through other compounds. Most of the compounds were small, with only one room for sleeping and another for cooking and storage.

"Gosh, Moussa," I said, "I have to pee. Can you ask someone to show me to a latrine?"

"Sure," he said. After a short consultation, our guide, son of the village chief, led me to a tiny enclosure, and handed me a gourd full of water.

I passed behind the wall, and stood in puzzlement for some minutes, looking around. Finally, I emerged, and reported sheepishly to Moussa, "There's no hole!"

Moussa went in and looked and quickly returned. "You just pee on the ground, then use the water in the gourd to wash everything out the hole at the base of the wall."

I reentered the latrine and spotted the hole. It passed under the exterior wall. Instead of filling up a pit, waste matter was simply washed out to the periphery of the settlement, where it was quickly disposed of by scavengers of all sizes, including the ubiquitous dung beetles. "Hmmm, an interesting variation on a theme," I thought to myself. This type of system would only work in a small village.

Our tour concluded with a visit to the aging village chief, who held court on a wooden platform under an arbor covered with a luxuriant climbing vine. We returned to the compound of the local animatrice. While everyone else took a siesta after lunch, I wandered out into the surrounding fields, coming across a pit well in the middle of a field. I headed for a huge, leafless tree, which had one large branch that arched out and down to the ground at a steep angle.

I pushed my way through the tall grass and climbed the branch, higher and higher toward the center of the tree. Near the trunk I stood upright and turned to survey the countryside. Fields of corn and millet stretched out in every direction. In the middle distance was the village, N'tenkoni. Copses of trees hid other, more distant villages from view, but I knew they were scattered across the surrounding countryside. I sat down on the limb, dangling my legs, and soaked up the peacefulness, beauty, and utter silence of the rural countryside at midday.

Moussa and Macan had been watching and came out to meet me when I returned. They both thought climbing trees was a pointless and bizarre activity. "Do all toubabs climb trees?" Macan asked. "No," I admitted. Moussa drew me aside and explained that tree climbing is only done by animals.

Following my tree-climbing escapade, we ventured into the village again and came across our first case of kwashiorkor. The little girl presented all of its classic symptoms. Her face was round and puffy, almost as though she had been beaten. Her hands and feet appeared plump, like her face. But the defining characteristic was her enormously swollen abdomen. Bulging against her dress, it strained the fabric, giving her the incongruous appearance of a pregnant woman. Her expression was one of sadness and apathy, her eyes sunken and dull.

Kwashiorkor is a strange disease, with a strange name. Usually found in children two to three years old, it results from a diet that is severely deficient in protein, while at the same time rich in calories. Only this particular combination produces kwashiorkor. Diets deficient in protein *and* calories, ironically, lead to protein-calorie malnutrition (marasmus) but are much less likely to kill you. Typically, kwashiorkor is found in communities where the staple foods are very low in protein. These might include cassava (manioc), yams, or potatoes. At the same time, high-calorie foods such as avocados, bananas, and palm oil are readily available. Kwashiorkor is rare in Mali, where the staples (corn, millet, rice and sorghum) are relatively high in protein, and high-calorie foods are scarce. It is more common in the richer, wetter countries of West Africa, such as Guinea or Cameroon, which rely heavily on cassava.

I exchanged greetings with the little girl's mother, who was seated on a log, holding another, younger child. This child, a boy, was fat and healthy, and chortled with happiness when I chucked him under the chin. Typically, kwashiorkor develops when a toddler ceases to receive her mother's milk because a new sibling has arrived. Even at the age of two or three years, a nursing toddler gets enough protein from mother's milk to stave off kwashiorkor. Once weaned, if she doesn't find another source of high-quality protein to replace mom's milk, kwashiorkor may appear. I knelt down to greet the little girl; even though she had never seen a toubab before, she was too wasted by her disease to either smile or cry in fright. It was difficult to tell what, if anything, she was thinking.

"What's the matter with her?" I asked her mother.

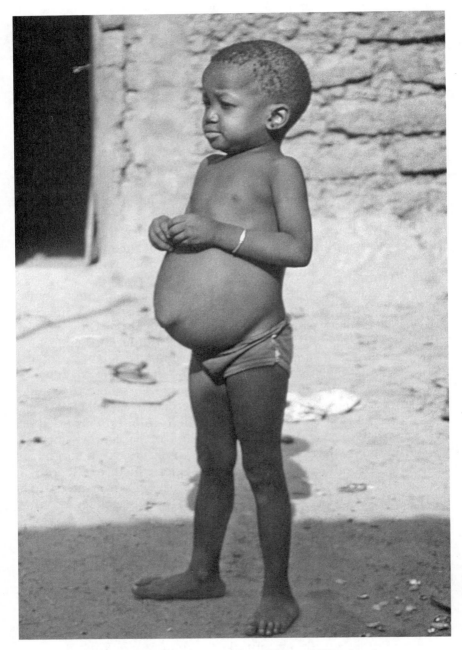

A young girl with kwashiorkor, in the village of N'tenkoni.

"She has *funu bana*," she replied. "She's been sick for about a week. Another child in the village had this disease last week, and he died. Maybe he gave it to her."

Funu bana literally means "swelling sickness" and refers to the transient edema of face, hands, feet, and abdomen typical of kwashiorkor. "Do you have any medicine for this sickness?" she asked, a flicker of hope lighting her eyes.

"Well, the best medicine for this disease is good food," I replied. "You should try giving her a little extra meat or milk with every meal. But not too much all at once!" I warned. One of the difficulties of treating kwashiorkor is that a sudden influx of protein into a protein-starved body can kill the child. I always had to worry that my suggestions would result in harm, rather than cure.

"But she doesn't want to eat anything now. She's too sick. You don't have any medicine for her?" her mother repeated plaintively.

"Food is the only medicine," I repeated, frustrated once again by the problem of ignorance of the basic relationship between food and health in many Malian people. In the food- and health-conscious environment of the modern United States, bombarded as we constantly are by messages about what to eat and what not to eat, it is difficult to comprehend that many of the world's people have never been exposed to the two basic tenets of modern nutrition and medicine: "you are what you eat" and "germs cause disease."

It wasn't so long ago that our own culture was ignorant of these basic principles, as evidenced by diaries or letters written by pioneers of the American West. Why should this woman believe me when I told her the child just needed food to eat? Wasn't this a disease? Weren't diseases treated by medicines? I was an American. Surely I had some magic pill in my bag that I could give her, if I only would.

That night, we travelled on to Merediela, where we ate and slept at another animatrice's compound. Dinner consisted of a pot of succulent beans topped with a zesty onion and tomato sauce, followed by sweet rice pudding. Replete, I sat out in the courtyard, marveling at the stars. We were miles from any electric lights, and the Milky Way looked like a broad swath of cotton stretched across the night sky. It was difficult to pick out familiar constellations that were crowded with stars normally washed out by city glow. I relaxed, contemplating all I had seen and heard, and listened to the heartbeat of the African night. Frogs croaked in the fields nearby, and from far off I could hear someone beating a drum. Incongruously, I could also hear the muted strains of ZZ Top, playing on a tape machine in the animatrice's room, the nightly news from the BBC booming crisply out of Moussa's radio, and the faint strains of the Malian national anthem coming from a television broadcast. Television? Yes. Over at the chief's hut in the center of the village, a crowd of villagers watched television on a set powered by a car battery. The signal from Bamako was drawn in by a tall silver antenna sticking up from the conical thatched roof of the chief's main hut. "I could live here, no problem," I announced to no one in particular. "I guess that means we're coming back with Miranda to measure everyone," Heather answered. "Yeah. I think so."

The next morning, we finalized arrangements with Falaye and the animatrices to come back for a week of intensive measuring, setting up a schedule for which day we would be in each village, making advance announcements to villagers so that they would know when to expect us, discussing who would be available to help with birth certificates, and dealing with potential conflicts with the upcoming corn harvest and karite butter-processing activities.

As we bounced out of Dogo along the rutted path, I leaned out the window and shouted at Falaye, "We'll be back!" I turned my face into the wind. My ears detected a low-pitched murmur. I scanned the countryside and realized I was hearing the voices of anthropologists past, my fictive intellectual ancestors, my mentors. Their ghosts rustled through the millet fields on the outskirts of the villages, curled around the contours of African huts, and pulled chaff and cotton fluff into the air in swirling towers, a palpable presence. The spirit of Evans-Pritchard rode on the wind.

7

Children, Snakes, and Death

Human life, instead of being well regulated and subject to secure human care, is generally more exposed to chance and to the mercies of the natural and the supernatural. . . . As a result, ultimate control and responsibility are neither the privilege nor the burden of humans, who are thereby relieved of guilt.
—Emelie A. Olson

"We have to stop and eat. They've prepared food for us," Bakary explained.

"No. We don't have time. We're already three hours late. The commandant and the animatrices are all waiting for us in Dogo. Soon it will be too dark to hold the training session," I argued.

"I can't possibly work without eating first," whined Bakary.

"Too bad," I snapped. "You should have thought of that this morning."

Our second trip to Dogo had commenced with a car accident. In his haste to be on time, to show me that he could be "responsible," Bakary had an accident with the truck. It cost 90,000 CFA for repairs to both vehicles involved and a bribe to the policeman so that he wouldn't report it. It also set us back several hours, causing us to arrive in Dogo late in the afternoon.

Bakary and I had a rousing argument over whether or not we would stop and eat the "lunch" that had been prepared for us in Belekan before traveling on to Dogo for a training session with the animatrices, who had expected us long before. Bakary insisted on stopping to eat, but I was equally adamant that we had to continue on to Dogo and salvage what we could of the training session. We compromised by picking up the food and taking it with us, but I offended Bakary by refusing to eat with him, once we got to Dogo.

Despite the argument and the late hour, the training session went well, and we all piled back in the truck and drove to Torokoro, the furthest north and most remote of the villages participating in AMIPJ's anthropometric survey. There we were offered a modest meal of rice with peanut butter sauce. I was glad I hadn't just eaten in Dogo, as my appetite for traditional food once again made me friends. It was important to get started on the right foot in Torokoro, our first village. Even Miranda thought the food was good. The rice grains were short and fat, a variety of rice domesticated in West Africa, *Oryza glaberrima*, known locally as *riz locale* (local rice). In many regions of West Africa, this rice has been replaced by another variety of rice, *Oryza sativa*, domesticated in Southeast Asia.

Torokoro was a tiny village of about 80 people. We had the first of our "town meetings" that night, collecting information about infant feeding practices and health problems in the village. Everyone gathered in a large open area in the center of the village. A single kerosene lantern allowed only glimpses of strong dark faces, listening curiously to Moussa translate as I explained the purpose of our measuring sessions.

That night we slept in a traditional mud hut. Its low ceilings were thick with cobwebs; bundles of corn and millet stalks, gourds and amulets, hung from the rafters. We had foam sleeping pads, provided by Bakary, and sheets to protect us from the mosquitoes. In addition, we lit two green Chinese mosquito coils; they would burn slowly for hours, exuding noxious fumes, filling the small room and discouraging mosquitoes. Both the pungent odor and the dull red glow at the tip of the coil were oddly comforting.

The next morning found us methodically measuring almost every member of the village. For each extended family, we began with the oldest male "head of household," who usually had possession of the birth certificates. We took his weight and height, arm and head circumference, and looked at the number of teeth he had (I was interested in third molar eruption patterns). Then we moved on to his first wife, and her children in order of age, oldest first, down to youngest. Next came his second wife, if he had one, and her children in order of age. Etc., etc., etc. After we had finished the wives and children of one man, we moved to his next youngest brother and his wives and children, and so on.

Most men had only one or two wives. Islam officially limits a man to four wives, but wives must be treated equally and well; most men can only afford the bridewealth and upkeep of one or two wives. Not to mention the fact that wives are often good friends and will gang up on a man who is mistreating any one of them. If they aren't friends, a man finds himself mediating among his arguing wives, also an unenviable position.

"Good grief," Heather exclaimed. "This woman has twelve living children! You'd think she'd have figured it out by now."

"Now, now, Heather," I chastised. "Remember that in Mali, the more children you have, the better off everyone in the family is."

"Oh yeah, I remember, the 'pizza' metaphor," Heather said, referring to an example used in lecture. "This family has an extra large, with pepperoni, mushrooms, and double cheese!"

Heather was referring to an analogy I often use in lecture to help students think about the relationship between population and resources. If you are the only one with money, and can only afford a small pizza, but you have lots of friends, then each person gets only a little piece. The more friends, the less each one gets. However, if your friends contribute money to the pizza fund, then you can afford to buy a bigger pizza, especially if some of those friends contribute more than the value of the pizza they eat. The more friends, the more money, the bigger the pizza. It works the same way in many rural subsistence agricultural societies.

Most older women in Mali have six to eight living children, and some have lost nearly that many to disease and malnutrition. It is a common misperception in the West that overpopulation accounts for most of the poverty and malnutrition in Third World countries like Mali. This notion, that simply limiting population growth through birth control methods, would alleviate poverty and malnutrition, comes from two assumptions based on Western economic systems that simply don't apply to much of rural Africa.

First, in the West, wealth tends to flow *down* the generations: parents sow and children reap. Adult men and, increasingly, adult women are the breadwinners in the family, and the adults provide support for the children at least until their late teens, and often long beyond. The more children in a family, the further the family's income must stretch. Or to use the pizza metaphor, it's as though you only have enough money for a small pizza, and it must be divided into smaller and smaller slices as the family grows. It's only logical to conclude that fewer children means larger slices of pizza for each child.

In West Africa, however, as well as many other parts of the Third World, wealth flows *up* the generations. Adults *and* children are breadwinners, and children become net income producers at a very young age, often as young as three or four years. In rural areas, they work in the fields or they herd livestock. In urban areas they peddle wares on the street, or run errands, or work pumping the bellows for blacksmiths. Or they watch the younger children, freeing the mother for income-generating activities. Under such circumstances, the more children in the family, the more workers, and thus the greater the family income. More children means you can afford to buy a larger pizza, and everyone gets a bigger slice than in a family with only a few kids. Especially in the context of rural, subsistence-level agrarian economies, the more children you have, the more fields you can plant, and so more food is available for everyone to eat.

Second, in the West, we tend to measure success and status through the accumulation of material goods—homes, cars, boats, stereos, and so on. As the bumper sticker says: "He who dies with the most stuff, wins."

In Mali, a man's success and status are measured by the number of children he has. A man with no children is pitied or scorned, but a man with several wives and many children is powerful indeed, because he controls the lives and loyalties of many people. A prosperous man's house may be made of mud brick, but it is filled with children and grandchildren who will honor him, work for him, and support him in his old age.

Women pushed and jostled in line, holding children by the hand, babies strapped to their backs with colorful lengths of cloth. About half the population was dressed in traditional garb, wraparound skirts for the women, and loose-fitting short trousers for the men.

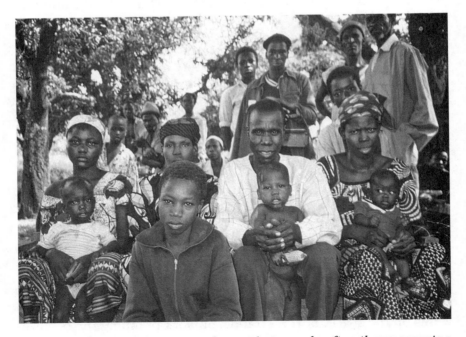

Villagers from Torokoro pose for a photograph after the measuring session.

They were made of the plain off-white material woven from local cotton on narrow strip looms. The rest were attired in a bewildering variety of cast-off Western clothing, several sizes too large or too small, T-shirts advertising American colleges, Michael Jackson, Wendy's, the Phillies, or car-repair shops. Children wore shorts or skirts or nothing at all, and ran about, giggling and shouting. When I glanced up, they ducked behind their older siblings.

I liked measuring babies the best, stuffing their solid, wriggling little bodies into the sling and hanging them from the weighing scales. Young babies, still fully breastfed, are usually fat and healthy and happy; malnutrition and disease have not yet taken their toll. Mother's milk provides all the nutrients and calories they need, as well as living cells that grant immunological protection from disease, and they were too little yet to be crawling around in the dirt. They were full of hope and promise.

Many people in the United States believe that artificial feeding products (infant formulas) are nutritionally equivalent, or even superior, to human breast milk, but it isn't true. The composition of human milk is the result of millions of years of evolution, and it provides all the necessary nutrients, in just the right mixture, to support growth, especially the rapid growth of the brain during the first few years of life. The protein, sugar, and fatty acid content of human milk cannot be mimicked by artificial products based on cows' milk, soy beans, or any other substrate. In addition, human milk contains living cells that provide immunological protection to the infant from a whole host of bacterial and viral infections, and these cannot be duplicated in artificial feeding products. Not to mention that the processes of delivery (breastfeeding versus giving a baby a bottle) are completely different experiences for mother and infant alike. Human babies have evolved to expect breastfeeding for the first several years of their lives.

A great cultural experiment has taken place in the United States and a few other Western countries in this century, including feeding infants artificial feeding products (via hard, cold, plastic nipples on bottles), carrying them around in hard plastic infant carriers, and making them sleep alone at night. Those lucky few who do get to breastfeed are often weaned by six months, or a year at the most. The nutritional and health risks of depriving infants of their mother's milk are well known, yet many physicians continue to promote infant formula as though it were equivalent to breast milk. And women in the U.S. who breastfeed in public or who breastfeed toddlers continue to be the subject of discrimination. As of 1993, only one state (Florida) had legislation guaranteeing a mother's right to breastfeed her baby in public without being subject to arrest for indecent exposure.

Likewise, the health risks of solitary sleeping are beginning to be documented through the work of researchers such as anthropologist James McKenna. His studies of mothers and infants sleeping together and apart have shown that co-sleeping mother-infant pairs have synchronized sleep cycles and similar brain wave patterns. When the baby rouses, the mother rouses. When the baby experiences apnea (a brief episode of not breathing), the mother rouses, and the baby begins to breathe again. Infants sleeping with their mothers spend much less time in the deep stages of sleep. McKenna's research has shown a link between solitary sleeping and sudden infant death syndrome (SIDS). The long term effects of solitary sleeping are still unknown.

Like breastfeeding for several years, human infants have evolved to expect that they will be sleeping in close proximity with other human beings—their mother at first, in order to breastfeed, siblings and other relatives when they get older. The pattern of placing infants alone in a separate room to sleep, and expecting them to sleep through the night at an early age, is another cultural experiment being tried out only recently in the U.S. and a few other Western cultures, with unknown consequences. But I digress.

American babies often smell sweet and clean, redolent with Johnson's Baby Shampoo, Lotion, and Oil. Malian babies mostly smell like wood smoke, with traces of sweat, urine, sour milk, spices, and incense mixed in. It's an acquired taste, but I like the way they smell. As though they live in the real world. They are usually naked except for amulets worn around the neck and waist to ward off evil spirits, especially "Bird," who brings illnesses such as malaria to young infants. Traditionally these amulets contained cowrie shells, herbs, magic stones, or other ingredients imbued with power to protect infants. A more modern amulet might include a scrap of paper inscribed with a Koranic verse. Malian babies also wear jewelry—earrings for the girls and tiny exquisitely beaded wrist and ankle bracelets or decorated bands of iron for both boys and girls.

Name. Birth certificate. Weight. Height. Arm and head circumference. Number of teeth. "Hold still . . . feet together . . . stand up straight . . . look over there . . . give me your left arm." Measuring was uneventful except for the younger kids. Many had never seen a toubab before, and they screamed in fright and confusion. In Magnambougou, little kids often thought I was going to give them an immunization, and their mothers reinforced this view, using me as a bogey man for threats. "If you don't behave, I'll get the toubab to come and give you an injection!" In Torokoro, far from maternal-child health clinics and untouched even by rural health projects, children didn't know what immunizations were, but they were still terrified. To the little ones, I crooned over and over in Bambara, "This won't hurt. Just stand still. Look over there. This won't hurt. You're OK." Having no knowledge of white people, the children didn't find it odd that I could speak Bambara—what other language was there?

Only one potential disaster marred the day. In the midst of measuring a young woman, I heard Miranda crying and screaming, "Mommy! Mommy! Help!" I thrust my measuring tape into Moussa's hands and ran in the direction of her voice. Rounding a corner, I saw her running toward me in terror, pursued by an old Malian man waving a branch threateningly over his head and screeching in Bambara. I folded Miranda into my arms and stood my ground, saying, "*A bla. A bla.*" (Leave her alone.) Just then Moussa caught up with us and demanded that the old man explain what was going on.

It seemed Miranda had gotten bored watching the measuring session and had wandered off to look at some baby pygmy goats, which look like adorable stuffed animal versions of the real thing. Coming back, she found some chickens pecking in the dirt of an empty compound and decided it would be fun to chase them around. She really had them going, squawking and flapping their wings and running every which way, and was having a great time until the old man came out of his hut to see what the racket was all about. He did not take kindly to her chasing his chickens and began berating her, demanding to know what she thought she was doing. Miranda was scared; she couldn't follow his rapid-fire Bambara and didn't know how to explain who she was. When he picked up the branch, she tried to run away but panicked; she didn't know which way to go. She hadn't been physically hurt, but she was hysterical, and the old man was angry.

It took some fancy maneuvering by Moussa to calm the old man down, helped by my offer, which he declined, to pay for any harm done to his chickens. In the meantime, I calmed Miranda down and explained that a serious diplomatic disaster had just been narrowly averted. "I didn't know you aren't supposed to chase chickens," she explained between sobs. "I know, I know. But these people can't imagine kids that don't know better, either. From now on, you stay right with me, OK?" "OK, Mommy," she blubbered. "I promise not to ever chase chickens again."

We worked until noon, then took a break for lunch. The night before, the villagers had presented us with a goat as a gift. I knew that they intended to slaughter it for our meal and begged them not to. In northern Mali, I was inundated with chickens, goats, and sheep in every village I visited, prompting me to quip: "If we do any more nutrition education programs in this area, we'll totally strip the countryside of small livestock, and then the people really won't have anything to eat!"

In Torokoro, we sat in the chief's compound on low wooden stools around two huge bowls of local rice—myself, Miranda, Heather, Moussa, Bakary, Macan, and Abi, the animatrice. The villagers kindly provided the food, then retreated so that we could rest and eat in privacy. Abi acted as server, uncovering the smaller bowl of peanut butter sauce and pouring it evenly over the surface of the rice. A bowl of water was passed around for hand washing. I reminded Miranda and Heather to use their right hands, sitting on my own left hand as insurance. We ate with gusto, enjoying the simple but delicious meal, until Macan reached behind himself and brought forward another bowl. Just as he was about to add its contents to the rice, I rudely thrust my hands out over the rice, palms down, fingers spread, shouting. "No! Stop!" The bowl was filled with a stew made from miscellaneous pieces of the unfortunate goat.

"What's the matter with you?" Macan demanded.

"Please, don't put any of that on our side of the bowl," I begged. "I can't face any unidentifiable 'goat parts' today," I explained.

"But they killed this goat especially for you," Macan said. "They'll be upset if we don't eat it."

"Oh, be my guest," I said. "Just please don't ruin my share of this wonderful rice and sauce by adding goat to it. I have bad teeth," I added lamely. I had often used my bad teeth as an excuse to get out of eating unidentifiable and unchewable pieces of meat. It was an excuse Malians both understood and sympathized with.

"OK, whatever," he said. "But you're missing the best parts."

The Malian men, and Abi, feasted on the tough pieces of goat, occasionally offering me a particularly succulent piece of liver or kidney. "Oh please, no," I responded. Lunch was followed by a brief but refreshing group snooze. I dreamt of prime rib and salad bars.

That afternoon, as we continued working our way through the population of Torokoro, I was startled to find myself faced with a girl who looked remarkably like someone from Magnambougou. For a moment, I thought I really was looking at Kafoune. I shook my head. "This can't be Kafoune!" I exclaimed. "Kafoune? No, her name is Aminata," Heather answered, checking the birth certificate. Then she looked up. "You're right," Heather agreed, "She sure does look like Kafoune from Magnambougou. Something about her eyes, maybe, or the shape of her face?"

During my original research in Magnambougou, one of my

subjects was a young girl named Kafoune. Like Daouda, Kafoune was extremely malnourished. Her twin brother had died at birth, and Kafoune was always small and sickly. Her mother was quite old, or at least worn out by life, with graying hair and a faced lined with wrinkles. At one year of age, Kafoune couldn't hold her head up and didn't make any sounds or respond to any attempts at social interaction. Her head appeared to be too big, the result of her body not keeping up with her head in growth. Her arms and legs were like chicken feet, mere skin-covered bones.

I was surprised to find Kafoune alive, if not well, in 1989. She was very small for her age, and she looked funny. In the United States, professionals who work with developmentally delayed children who have no known diagnosis often refer to them as FLKs—"funny-looking kids." This isn't meant to be cruel, it merely acknowledges that many of these children don't look quite right; their faces are a little askew, probably the result of some genetic abnormality. Kafoune was definitely an FLK. Her forehead bulged, a condition known technically as "frontal bossing." Her eyes seemed too far apart, the bridge of her nose was depressed, and she had a distinct overbite. She wasn't very bright. Her mother had sent her to school when she turned eight, but she hadn't been able to keep up. She spent her days hanging around the compound with her mother.

This girl in Torokoro had the same frontal bossing, wide-set eyes, depressed nasal bridge, and overbite. She also seemed more than a little bewildered by what we were doing. I turned to her mother and gently elicited information about the girl. It turned out that, like Kafoune, this girl had suffered from severe malnutrition as an infant (her mother called it *sere*), but had survived. Like Kafoune, she was not very bright. In the days to come, we would find several more children with "the look." All of them were survivors of severe malnutrition, and all suffered from similar physical and mental manifestations.

The villagers feted us with a small drum performance after the last villager had been measured. Then we were taken to meet the village's oldest inhabitants, a married couple who were confined by old age, arthritis, and blindness to a small hut. Every day, younger villagers brought them their meals and kept them current on all village affairs. Because of their great age, they were treated with the utmost respect. I searched for some appropriate gift and came up with a pineapple brought from Bamako. I gave it to the old woman, and then we left Torokoro to travel the short distance to Merediela.

Before dinner I was treated to the ultimate luxury—a hot shower. A young girl brought me two buckets of water, one cold, the other steaming from the fire. She set them inside the latrine enclosure.

A young girl with the "Kafoune" look in the village of Torokoro. Note her mother's small goiter.

An older girl with the "Kafoune" look in the village of Famabougou.

To bathe I had to hunker down below the low walls of the latrine. I doused myself with cold water using a gourd dipper, lathered, and then rinsed using the warm water. I was so frugal that I ended up with enough to wash my hair. I had to remind myself not to stand up to my full height, which would have exposed much of my body to curious onlookers who had gathered outside the compound wall. To finish, I combined the remaining water in one bucket and sluiced it over my head and body. The water swirled around my feet, then drained out the small hole at the bottom of the wall. On the other side, the grass grew thick and green.

Oh, to be clean after a hot, dusty day of hard work! To have good food to look forward to, to know that my notebook was filling up with data. I was pleased that the first day of measuring had gone so well, Miranda's adventures as a chicken chaser notwithstanding. Life was good.

After dinner, people arrived for our town meeting. They came singly at first, then in small clusters of two or three, and finally in large family groups. Elders, mothers with young children, teenaged boys, almost the entire village. The village chief came up to greet me and thank me again, and the meeting was called to order. I began with the standard questions about health problems in the village, including cases of kwashiorkor. It turned out that two children in the village had funu bana (kwashiorkor), and both were sons of the village chief. I continued with questions about breastfeeding and weaning practices, when solid foods were added to the diet, and what kinds of foods young children usually ate. Who decides how much food a child should eat? What do you do with a child who won't eat? "Do you have any children here with *fasa* or *sere*?" (indigenous terms for what Western medicine calls severe malnutrition). Many people participated in these discussions, arguing with or confirming the responses of their neighbors or offering their own opinions and examples. The village chief was particularly articulate.

"And then there are those children who never grow up," he commented.

"What do you mean?" I asked, shaking my head, not understanding.

"They just never grow. They never reach out for things with their hands, they never sit up or walk, they never talk. Some begin to, but then stop. You keep praying and hoping and looking for medicine for them, but nothing helps."

"What happens to these children?" I asked cautiously, holding my breath.

"Well, if they don't get better after a couple of years, then you know that they are evil spirits, and you give up."

"What do you mean, 'give up'?"

"Well, you take them out into the bush and you just leave them."

"What happens to them?"

"They turn into snakes and slither away."

The words hung in the air for long moments. My heart stopped beating. "They turn into snakes?" I repeated, trying to keep the eagerness and excitement out of my voice, as I asked them to clarify what was, for me, an explosive revelation. I thought to myself, "This is great, this is great. Calm down, and make sure you get it right."

"Yes. You go back the next day, and they aren't there. Then you know for sure that they weren't really children at all, but evil spirits. When you see a snake, you wonder if it used to be your child."

"Are there any children like this in the village now?" I asked. I wanted to see for myself if we were talking about children who were merely severely malnourished, or who perhaps had some recognizable syndrome that would explain why they "never grew up."

"No," someone else replied. "We haven't had any children like that for several years. All our women are careful about walking around at night when they are pregnant."

"Huh?" I blurted.

"That's how evil spirits can take over your child," the village chief explained. "When you are pregnant, you have to be very careful not to go out alone at night, when the bad spirits are looking for someone to take. If that happens, your baby can be born dead, or deformed, or it may look all right at first, but then it becomes a child who never grows up. It's best not even to go to the latrine after dark."

"Yes, I understand now." I told him. Of course, I didn't really understand. How can anyone understand what it feels like to give up on a child who is hopelessly "developmentally delayed"—to take the child of your body, the child of your heart, and abandon him or her to the universe? How can anyone who hasn't experienced it understand the heartache of losing a child? I sat there for a moment reflecting on the choices available for the parents of handicapped children in rural Malian culture. And yet, at the same time, I was elated to be collecting such "exotic" ethnographic data.

Suddenly, I was transported back to another scene (the compound of my friend Ami) and another time (spring of 1982) when I had acutely felt the conflict between being a human being, intimately participating in the lives of my friends, and being an anthropologist, objectively observing and recording the lives of my informants.

Ami first caught my attention when I saw her selling French fries at the market in Magnambougou. At 16 years of age, she was exquisitely beautiful. She was married to a very wealthy Malian man who lived in Paris, leaving her and her infant son to reside with her parents in Magnambougou. We became fast friends, and my visits to her compound were filled with laughter and gaiety, with one exception. Her little brother, two-year-old Yacouba, was frightened of me and fled screaming in terror to hide behind his mother's skirts whenever I came to visit.

Now Yacouba was dead, yet one more victim of the measles epidemic that swept through Magnambougou that spring, and I had come to attend his funeral and pay my respects. The men, gathered in the courtyard for the Muslim funeral ceremony, welcomed me and gestured for me to go inside the house to sit with the other women. As I took my place in the spot indicated along the periphery of the room, I heard the other women keening softly and glimpsed their shapes in the shadowy interior of the room. Sitting inside the house with the other female friends and relatives, I was intensely and consciously aware of the conflict between my personal feelings and my professional curiosity.

I felt real grief over the eminently preventable death of a young child from measles. And Yacouba wasn't just any young child; he was the brother of my good friend, and he had been the source of much pleasure and amusement for us all. At the same time, I distinctly felt the "ethnographic thrill" of being on the inside of a Bambara/Islamic funeral. When I wasn't overcome with tears thinking about Yacouba and empathizing with his mother, I was trying to commit all of the details of the funeral to memory, since it would have been incredibly tacky to whip out my notebook and start taking notes.

I concentrated so hard on committing the scene to memory that even today, more than 10 years later, I have only to close my eyes and I am once again in that room. I can see Yacouba's mother sitting across from me, slumped dejectedly, shoulders bowed, tears silently coursing down her cheeks and dropping onto her outstretched legs, making clean tracks through the dust. It isn't considered appropriate for parents to weep openly when a child dies, I remember thinking to myself, calling on my ethnographic wisdom to help me interpret what was happening. I can still smell the powdered incense that was passed around in a small bowl, each person taking a pinch and passing it on. I can hear the prayers of the men from the compound outside.

Only a few other scenes from my life have that much remembered clarity for me—my children's births, the moment when the doctor told us that Peter had Down syndrome, the audiovisual room at the

My friend Ami, and her son Djibril. I attended the funeral of her younger brother Yacouba, who died during the measles epidemic of 1982.

University of Southern Mississippi where I heard the radio report that the space shuttle *Challenger* had just blown up.

At Yacouba's funeral, I felt that my anthropological interest in the event was inappropriate—I was there under the guise of a concerned friend. I desperately wanted to know what was going on outside, where the men were, but I knew that I couldn't very well get up and go outside. If I had attended as "the anthropologist," the men probably would have let me join them. But I had come as a friend of the mother and sister of the deceased. Conflicting feelings buffeted my heart—feelings of guilt for my professional curiosity, as well as feelings of regret that I had gotten so involved with my research subjects that I would feel real grief at the death of a young child, quickly followed by disgust that I would even want to be so removed, so "objective" that the death of a young child would leave me unmoved. This will never do, I chided myself. One or the other. Anthropologist or friend, which would it be? Participant observation sounds like such an innocuous concept in the classroom. You participate, and you observe. That's fine if you're studying music, or iron working, or even politics. But how can you be a participant observer at the funeral of a friend?

Now, here I was again, listening to the brutally honest admissions of defeat from parents of handicapped children. I was torn between wanting to pursue this fascinating lead ("children who turn into snakes" don't come along every day after all!) and wanting to respect the grief and sorrow of these parents, who had no resources to help them cope. In the long run, giving such children up to the spirits, believing that they turned into snakes, made a certain kind of sense. And maybe that's really what happens, I thought. I had no more questions.

In small groups, the villagers took their leave, weaving out into the night, kerosene lanterns bobbing in the darkness like a string of fireflies. Each person stopped to shake my hand, touched their own heart, and wished me well. After the last one had left, I sat in silence, pondering children, snakes, and death while the stars blazed overhead.

8

Bad Breath, Gangrene, and God's Angels

There is more than one kind of freedom. Freedom to and freedom from. In the days of anarchy, it was freedom to. Now you are being given freedom from. Don't underrate it.—Margaret Atwood

I stood in the doorway, gasping for air, propping my arms against the door frame on either side to hold me up. I sucked in great breaths of cool, clean air and rested my gaze on the distant hills, trying to compose myself. Ominous black thunderclouds were massed on the horizon and moved rapidly toward the schoolhouse. They rolled down the hills like wads of dark cotton, like the fog blankets that regularly obliterate the hills around San Francisco Bay. Thunder growled; the smell of ozone permeated the air. Rain pounded the iron roof overhead, drowning out all thought, while great rivers of water streamed off the corners of the building. Gusts of wind whipped through the trees, blowing the rain into my face. I turned and plunged back inside, back into the fray.

The morning had begun pleasantly enough, with villagers waiting patiently under the huge mango tree in the center of the village. But before long, the approaching storm made it clear that we would have to move inside. The only building large enough to hold the crowd was the one-room schoolhouse, located on the outskirts of the village. Here adults learned to read and write the newly alphabetized written Bambara. General education for children was still a foreign concept.

Inside the schoolhouse, chaos reigned. It was 20 degrees hotter, ten times as noisy, and as dark as gloom. What little light there was from outside entered through the open doorway and two small windows. The entire population of the village crowded onto the rows of benches, or stood three deep around the periphery of the room. Babies cried until their mothers pulled them around front where they could nurse, children chattered, and adults seized the opportunity to converse with friends and neighbors. It was one big party, a day off from working in the fields, with a cooling rain thrown in for good measure. I had to shout the measurements out to Heather, to make myself heard over the cacophony of noise.

The stench in the room was incredible: hundreds of unwashed, sweaty bodies mingled with the ever-present undertones of wood smoke, tobacco, and spices. It was so dark inside the schoolroom that I had to shine a flashlight inside people's mouths, and peer closely, my face right in theirs, in order to count their teeth. Being this up close and personal made people understandably uncomfortable. They guffawed with embarrassment when I looked in their mouths, overwhelming me with the odor of rotting teeth. I had to keep retreating to the door of the schoolroom to compose myself and get some fresh air, to keep from throwing up. Halfway through the morning I gagged once again and turned to Heather in disgust. "I can't stand this anymore. I am absolutely giving up on looking for third molars in adults' mouths."

I was interested in third molar eruption as evidence that rural Malian adults had faces and jaws large enough to comfortably accommodate third molars (wisdom teeth). My hidden agenda was to argue that current understandings of human evolution were skewed, because they took modern Europeans, with their relatively small faces, as the epitome of what "modern humans" looked like. Arguments over interpretations of the fossil record and the date of the first appearance of "modern humans" with "small faces" became irrelevant when the full range of modern humans was appreciated, including particularly West Africans with their large, projecting lower faces and fully operational sets of third molars.

I knew from studies in Magnambougou that most urban adults had beautiful, healthy teeth, including all four third molars, fully erupted and in perfect occlusion. The lack of refined sugar, and the use of traditional tooth-cleaning sticks in many parts of Mali resulted in few cavities. Every morning, adults walked around with the stub of a tooth-brushing stick protruding from one corner of their mouth. Only particular trees provided "tooth brushes"—sticks that were chewed to a frazzle at one end, then used to scrub and polish the teeth. Chemical analysis of these twigs showed that they had antibiotic and anticavity properties.

Apparently, the knowledge of this traditional mode of dental hygiene never made it to Merediela, and I found myself face-to-face with incredible dental wear, multiple cavities, exposed roots, and draining abscesses. I was familiar with all of these dental conditions from working with prehistoric Native American skeletal material, but I had never really pondered what they would be like in the flesh—what it meant for the living people who had to cope with teeth like that. Now I knew firsthand, and it was not a pretty sight, nor a pleasant smell. "It's no wonder kissing isn't big around here," I quipped, trying to find some humor in the situation. "From now on, I'm only looking in little kids' mouths. Next!"

A middle-aged man dressed in a threadbare pair of Levis shoved a crying child forward. I knelt down to encourage the little boy to step up onto the scales and saw that his leg was wrapped in dirty bandages. He hesitated before lifting his foot and whimpered as he put his weight onto it. "How old is this child?" I asked Heather. She consulted his birth certificate. "Four years old," she answered. By that time, he was crying loudly.

"What's the matter with his leg?" I asked his father.

"He hurt it in a bicycle accident," he said.

I rolled my eyes at Heather. "Let me guess. He was riding on the back fender, without wearing long pants, or shoes, and he got his leg tangled in the spokes." Moussa translated this aside into Bambara, and the man acknowledged that that was exactly what had happened.

Bicycle injuries of this kind were frequent, and they would often result in devastating wounds to children's legs and feet. In the country, children wear few or no clothes, and no shoes. They straddle the backs of rickety bicycles, hanging on behind their father or older brother. A moment's inattention, and they get caught. Bicycle spokes can do nasty things to children's limbs.

The father set the little boy up on the table we were using as a desk, gently unwrapping the filthy dressings. The last few layers were crusted over and had to be teased away, exposing the wound. One glance and I had to turn my head away in horror and dismay. The room suddenly seemed hotter, the air thicker than ever.

The festering wound encompassed the boy's ankle and part of his foot, deep enough to see bone at the bottom. His entire lower leg and foot were swollen and putrid; it was obvious that gangrene had a firm hold.

"When did this happen?" I asked the father.

"About five days ago," he replied.

"How did you treat the wound?"

"We just covered it with this cloth."

"Why didn't you take him to a doctor?"

"We thought it would get better by itself," he said, turning to look pleadingly at the boy's mother.

"You have to take him to the hospital in Sikasso immediately," I explained.

"But we can't afford to," he balked.

"You can't afford not to," I cried in exasperation, turning to Moussa. "He doesn't understand," I said to Moussa. "Please explain to him that the boy is certain to die of gangrene poisoning if he doesn't get to a doctor right away. It may be too late already, but I don't think so. He may just lose his leg." Moussa's eyes widened with alarm. Even he hadn't realized how serious the boy's wounds were. As the father took in what Moussa was saying, his face crumpled.

While the boy's father ran to get his cache of carefully horded coins and bills, I dressed the wound with antibiotic cream and a clean gauze bandage. I gave the boy some chewable children's aspirin, as though it would help. I had to do something constructive. The little boy cringed when I touched him, but he no longer cried. Father and son were last seen leaving Merediela, the boy perched precariously on the back of a worn-out donkey hastily borrowed from a neighbor, while the father trotted alongside, shoulders drooping, urging the donkey to greater speed.

Lunch back at the animatrice's compound provided another opportunity for learning about infant feeding beliefs in rural Mali, through criticism of my own child feeding practices. This time it was a chicken that had given its life for our culinary benefit. As we ate, without even thinking, I reached into the center pile of chicken meat and pulled pieces of meat off the bone. Then I placed them over in Miranda's section of the communal food bowl and encouraged her to eat.

"Why are you giving her chicken?" Bakary asked.

"I want to make sure she gets enough to eat," I replied. "She didn't eat very much porridge for breakfast, because she doesn't like millet."

"But she's just a child. She doesn't need good food. You've been working hard all morning, and she's just been lying around. Besides, if she wanted to eat, she would," he argued.

"It's true that I've been working hard," I admitted, "but she's still growing. Growing children need much more food, proportionately, than adults. And if I didn't encourage her to eat, she might not eat until we get back to Bamako."

Bakary shook his head. "In Dogo," he explained, "people believe that good food is wasted on children. They don't appreciate its good taste or the way it makes you feel. Also, they haven't worked hard to produce the food. They have their whole lives to work for good food for themselves, when they get older. Old people deserve the best food, because they're going to die soon."

"Well, I applaud your respect and honor for the elderly, but health-wise, that's completely wrong. How do you expect children to grow up to be functioning adults if they only get millet or rice to eat?" Of course, many children don't grow up at all, on this diet. They die from malnutrition, or from diseases such as measles that wouldn't kill a well-nourished child. Studies of the long-term consequences of childhood malnutrition have shown that adults who have survived are functionally impaired when it comes to sustained work effort. They cannot work as long as adults who were not malnourished as children.

In Magnambougou, the prevailing idea in child nutrition was that children alone should decide when, what, and how much they wanted to eat, but they were usually offered whatever was available, including some of the meat and vegetables in the sauce. In rural southern Mali, "good food" (which included all the high protein/high calorie foods) was reserved for elders and other adults. Children subsisted almost entirely on the carbohydrate staples, flavored with a little sauce. My actions in giving Miranda my share of the chicken were viewed as bizarre and misguided—I was wasting good food on a mere child, and depriving myself.

Villagers' reactions to my behaviors were often very enlightening. This conversation was no exception, and I would have liked it to continue. However, it was interrupted by the arrival of a string of children with miscellaneous cuts and scrapes, coming for first aid. I quickly finished eating and went to attend to them. I did what I could with soap and water, antibiotic ointment and Band-Aids. One little boy sat straddling his mother's hip, his arms draped across her shoulders. She showed me an open sore on the back of one of his buttocks.

"What happened here?" I asked his mother.

"He had malaria, so I gave him an injection of Quinimax. Now the malaria is gone, but his leg is sore," she answered.

"But he can walk on it all right?" I asked, taking the boy's hand and leading him around to see if he could still use the leg.

"Oh yes, he can walk fine."

"Where did you get the needle for the shot?" I pressed, as I held the boy down and administered to the sore.

"From a neighbor," she answered.

In Mali, as in many medically underdeveloped places, injections are thought to be more effective than oral medicines. In many cases, the doctor merely prescribes the medicine to be purchased at the pharmacy; it is up to the patient to find a way to have the medicine injected. This often means tracking down a "neighborhood needle" and paying a small fee to borrow the needle. For a little extra, you can get someone to inject the medicine, or you can do it yourself. The needle may be rinsed in water between uses, but it certainly isn't sterilized. The multiple use of needles leads, not uncommonly, to minor infections at the injection site. As AIDS becomes more common in Mali, it will become even more dangerous. But as unsanitary as this method is, it may be better than having the injection done by the doctor at the clinic, as my friend from Magnambougou, Agnes, can attest.

During the rainy season of 1982, Agnes took her one-year-old daughter to the local maternal-child health clinic because she had a bad case of malaria. The doctor gave the infant an injection of Quinimax, a viscous oil-based chloroquine mixture, one of the strongest means of combatting malaria. Oral chloroquine tablets probably would have done the job, but injections have that special cachet.

Unfortunately, the doctor, a Malian trained in France, had little understanding of anatomy. Instead of giving the shot into the fat and muscle tissue of the buttocks, or the front of the thigh, he administered it in the back of the thigh, directly into her sciatic nerve. This nerve, as thick as a finger, runs the length of the leg and provides communication between the brain and the leg muscles. Damage to the nerve by the needle had left the little girl crippled.

At one year of age, she had just learned how to walk, but she was immediately reduced to crawling again, dragging her useless leg behind her. Agnes fought back, though, taking her to Kati every month for acupuncture treatments and working with her for long hours every day, trying to strengthen her leg. It took more than a year, but eventually she was able to walk again. As horrible as her experience was, it had worse repercussions beyond her own family.

A few months after the Quinimax crippling episode, the little boy next door to Agnes came down with malaria. His mother faced a choice on her little boy's behalf: malaria or paralysis. He had already survived several bouts of malaria. From her perspective, a trip to the doctor carried a more certain risk of being crippled by an inept injection. She gambled, and kept him at home. She gambled, and lost. This time, he died of malaria.

In N'tenkoni the next morning, we were given use of the men's sacred meeting hut for our measuring session. A round hut about twenty feet in diameter, it had a huge center pole made from the trunk of a tree that held up the thatched roof. Because it had two large doorways, it was light and airy and would provide protection in the event of another thunderstorm.

The roof poles were hung with a variety of objects—a bundle of cow bones above one door, a bundle of corncobs above the other. Numerous boys' circumcision toys were wedged into the rafters. Known as *sistrums*, these wooden toys are made from tree branches and strung with serrated discs made from calabashes. Newly circumcised boys wear special clothing and are allowed to parade through the village shaking the toys. The calabash discs make a loud clacking sound, alerting everyone to the impending arrival of the boys, and people come out to give them small presents in honor of their new status as circumcised boys. I had never seen so many in one place.

There was some initial confusion caused by the fact that people outside couldn't really see what we were doing, and everyone tried to crowd in at once. That was straightened out by the chief, however, and measuring proceeded apace, men, women, children, men, women, children. One family at a time filed into the hut through one door, had their measurements taken, and departed through the other door. It was cool and pleasant inside the hut, in contrast to the hot sun and glare outside. Miranda sat off to one side, reading a book, glancing up from time to time, but generally bored by the whole thing.

"Mommy, look!" she exclaimed in mid-morning. "Isn't that an *angel*?" she asked, using our family's code word for a child with Down syndrome. Down syndrome children are often (though not always!) sweet, happy, and affectionate kids, and many families of children with Down syndrome consider them to be special gifts from God, and refer to them as angels. I turned and followed the direction of Miranda's gaze. A little girl had just entered the hut, part of a large family with many children. She had a small round head, and all the facial characteristics of a child with Down syndrome— "Oriental"-shaped eyes with epicanthic folds, a small flat nose, and small ears. There was no mistaking the diagnosis. Her name was Abi, and she was about four years old, the same age as Peter.

I knelt in front of the little girl. "Hi there, sweetie," I said in English. "Can I have a hug?" I held out my arms, and she willingly stepped forward and gave me a big hug.

I looked up at her mother. "Do you know that there's something 'different' about this child?" I asked, choosing my words carefully.

"Well, she doesn't talk," said her mother, hesitantly, looking at her husband for confirmation. "That's right," he said. "She's never said a word."

"But she's been healthy?" I asked.

"Yes," the father replied. "She's like the other kids, except she doesn't talk. She's always happy. She never cries. We know she can hear, because she does what we tell her to. Why are you so interested in her?"

"Because I know what's the matter with her. I have a son like this." Excitedly, I pulled a picture of Peter out of my bag and showed it to them. They couldn't see the resemblance, though. The difference in skin color swamped the similarities in facial features. But then, Malians think all white people look alike. And it's not true that all kids with Down syndrome look the same. They're "different in the same way," but they look most like their parents and siblings.

"Have you ever met any other children like this?" I inquired, bursting with curiosity about how rural Malian culture dealt with a condition as infrequent as Down syndrome. Children with Down syndrome are rare to begin with, occurring about once in every 700 births. In a community where 30 or 40 children are born each year at the most, a child with Down syndrome might be born only once in twenty years. And many of them would not survive long enough for anyone to be able to tell that they were different. Physical defects along the midline of the body (heart, trachea, intestines) are common among kids with Down syndrome; without immediate surgery and neonatal intensive care, many would not survive. Such surgery is routine in American children's hospitals, but nonexistent in rural Mali. For the child without any major physical defects, there are still the perils of rural Malian life to survive: malaria, measles, diarrhea, diphtheria, and polio. Some, like Peter, have poor immune systems, making them even more susceptible to childhood diseases. The odds against finding a child with Down syndrome, surviving and healthy in a rural Malian village, are overwhelming.

Not surprisingly, the parents knew of no other children like Abi. They asked if I knew of any medicine that could cure her. "No," I explained, "this condition can't be cured. But she will learn to talk, just give her time. Talk to her a lot. Try to get her to repeat things you say. And give her lots of love and attention. It may take her longer to learn some things, but keep trying. In my country, some people say these children are special gifts from God." There was no way I could explain cells and chromosomes and nondisjunction to them, even with Moussa's help. And how, I thought to myself, would that have helped them anyway? They just accepted her as she was.

We chatted for a few more minutes, and I measured the whole family, including Abi, who was, of course, short for her age. I gave her one last hug and a balloon and sent her out the door after her siblings. I turned to Moussa and Heather and said, "Guys, I need a break. I'll be right back."

I walked out of the hut, past the long line of villagers waiting patiently for their turn to be measured. They turned to stare as I passed. I went behind the animatrice's compound and sat down on a fallen log. I took several deep breaths, trying to get my emotions under control. Finally I gave in, hugged my knees close to my chest, and sobbed. I cried for Abi—what a courageous heart she must have; just think what she might have achieved given all the modern infant stimulation programs available in the West. I cried for Peter— another courageous heart; just think of what he might achieve given the chance to live in a culture that simply accepted him, rather than stereotyping and pigeonholing him, constraining him because people didn't think he was capable of more. I cried for myself—not very courageous at all; my heart felt as though it would burst with longing for Peter, my own sweet angel.

There was clearly some truth to the old adage that ignorance is bliss. Maybe pregnant women in Mali had to worry about evil spirits lurking in the latrine at night, but they didn't spend their pregnancies worrying about chromosomal abnormalities, the moral implications of amniocentesis, or the heart-wrenching exercise of trying to evaluate handicaps, deciding which ones made life not worth living. Women in the United States might have the freedom to choose not to give birth to children with handicaps, but women in Mali had freedom from worrying about it. Children in the United States had the freedom to attend special programs to help them overcome their handicaps, but children in Mali had freedom from the biggest handicap of all—other people's prejudice.

I had cried myself dry. I splashed my face with cool water from the bucket inside the kitchen and returned to the task at hand.

9

Poulet Bicyclette

Tell me what you eat and I'll tell you what you are. Not only biography and genealogy but the whole field of anthropology could, if one knew the code, be deduced from food.

—Poppy Cannon

The tiny village of Famabougou straddled the road, huts and goat pens spilling down the hills on either side, almost hidden by the fields of millet and corn. Short round ovens heaped with smoking karite nuts were lined up in a row along the periphery of the village. From all directions, people were slowly trickling toward the chief's compound. The shouts and laughter of children filtered through the fields.

Members of the measuring team were all stuffed from lunch in N'tenkoni, and we all wanted nothing more than to take a siesta, but the villagers of Famabougou were waiting. They had gathered in and around the compound of the village chief. A wide covered veranda afforded some relief from the heat of the midday sun.

"Come and eat," the chief gestured. "The women have prepared a special meal for you."

"Oh, no," I groaned. "Moussa, please explain as diplomatically as you can that we just ate in N'tenkoni. They *knew* we were planning to eat in N'tenkoni." Turning to Bakary in exasperation, I said "Didn't you tell the chief he didn't have to feed us? That we were eating lunch in N'tenkoni and dinner in Dogo?"

"Yes, I told him that," Bakary said. "But since they've cooked the food, we really should eat."

"But we're not hungry, and there isn't time," I argued. "Besides, all the women and children are here already. We need to get started.

101

We can't ask them to wait for us to eat again, especially when we've just eaten."

I left Moussa and Bakary to try to smooth things over with the chief and turned to set up the table and measuring equipment. Heather went down the line and gathered all the birth certificates and started putting them in order.

"Hey," she said, "almost everyone in this village is either named Thiero or Keminaani." Neither of these surnames were familiar from Magnambougou, or the other villages.

"*Kemi naani*?" I repeated. "Doesn't that mean '400'? What kind of a name is that?"

"It's an old-fashioned Bambara name," Moussa said.

The village chief, mollified by Moussa and Bakary's promises to eat later, was himself a Thiero. "Sometimes we refer to 'those people' as the *kemi saaba*," he said.

"They call them the '300'?" I asked. "I don't understand."

"It's a joke!" Moussa explained. The villagers laughed and crowded around, poking fun at themselves, and at me. "Look at him," an old woman shouted, pointing at a very short man, "He's only a 250!" The villagers broke up with laughter.

Measuring proceeded apace. Thiero women were married to Keminaani men, and Keminaani women were married to Thiero men. "Clan exogamy!" Heather crowed in delight. "I love it!"

It's one thing to read about a principle of social organization such as clan exogamy in your anthropology textbook, and another thing altogether to see it in operation in a village. In Famabougou, the Thieros all traced themselves back to a common ancestor, the first Thiero in the region. Not everyone knew exactly how they were related to this founding father, but if your name was Thiero, you were part of that clan. Ditto for Keminaani. But your clan membership didn't just tell you who your ancestors were or which living members of the village you were related to. It also affected who you could marry, as the rule of clan exogamy meant you had to marry outside your clan. If you were a Thiero, you couldn't marry anyone named Thiero. You didn't have to marry a Keminaani— anyone who wasn't a Thiero was a potential marriage partner. However, most of the non-Thiero people in the village were Keminaanis, so chances were good that you would end up with a Keminaani. Under the system of patrilineality, a child ends up with the last name of his or her father. Thus, each child's clan membership was unambiguous, even though, genetically speaking, most people in the village were a combination of Thiero and Keminaani.

On and on we worked. By now, we had the routine down. Heather organized each family's birth certificates in order and announced the name. When the person stepped forward, I guided them onto the scales, then bent over to read the weight and called it out to Heather, who wrote it down on the data sheet. Next, Moussa led the person over to the height measuring device, and helped position them, feet together, head up, eyes looking straight ahead. I lowered the cross-bar down on the top of their head and again called out the reading to Heather. Then head circumference, which required that women remove their head scarves, and men remove their hats. Braids sometimes got in the way, making an accurate measurement impossible. Arm circumference, simplest of all. For the children (never again the adults) I looked in their mouths and counted the number of deciduous and permanent teeth.

Not for Malians the childhood pleasures of wiggling and worrying loose teeth until they give way at last, placing them reverently under the pillow at night to await an exchange from the Tooth Fairy (and we think their traditions are odd!). Some of the older children still had three or four deciduous teeth, pushed out of the tooth row by emerging permanent teeth, but still hanging on, bent at odd angles. Moussa taught them how to rock the teeth back and forth, explaining that the permanent ones would move into correct position once the deciduous ones were out of the way.

Next in line was a teenaged boy with only one leg. The other had been amputated high on the thigh. He maneuvered gracefully with a pair of homemade crutches, even though it was clear he had outgrown them long ago. "What happened to your leg?" I asked.

"I was bitten by a snake, year before last," he answered, smiling and pivoting on one crutch. "I can still beat most of the other boys in races!"

He handed his crutches to a friend and jumped up on the scale, arms outspread for balance. I called out the weight to Heather, then added, "Make a note that he has only one leg, so I'll know not to include his weight in the statistical analyses."

No matter how prepared you are for fieldwork—no matter how well trained in the philosophy of research, sampling strategies, research methodologies, survey techniques, interviewing, naturalistic inquiry, participant observation, anthropometric measurements, and others—you are never prepared for what actually happens to you in the field. No one ever mentioned one-legged children in my Research Methods class.

Much of the time I worked without thinking, and the high levels of malnutrition that would emerge in analysis weren't always noticeable during the data collection stage, as only Heather knew the chronological ages of the kids from the birth certificates. From time to time I would be jolted out of my complacency when I looked in a child's mouth: the boy I had just measured, who looked to be a sturdy three-year-old, had permanent central incisors, both top and bottom, indicating an age closer to six or seven; the girl who seemed to be an oddly proportioned eight-year-old had fully erupted second molars, making her at least twelve. There were, of course, children who were obviously malnourished—every rib visible, their elbows and knees the largest part of their arms and legs, respectively. Children with kwashiorkor were rare, only one or two per village, although every adult was familiar with the disease known as funu bana. And every village seemed to have its Kafoune, an FLK with "the look."

One problem plaguing nutrition education programs in communities with widespread malnutrition is that people simply get used to the way children look. If the typical child is mildly to moderately malnourished, then that becomes the standard. That's just "how children look," not a problem to be fixed. Even I was affected by the constant stream of underweight children. After months in the field, they began to look normal, and only severely malnourished children caught my immediate, conscious attention. *Normal* is what you're used to. When I returned to the United States, I would be disgusted by all the fat little kids I saw at the mall, mindlessly stuffing their faces with French fries and hamburgers from their Happy Meals.

Malnutrition among the adults was even more subtle in some ways. They didn't exhibit the painfully thin arms and legs of the children. In fact, they looked pretty good, if you didn't notice how short they were. At 5 feet 8 inches tall, I was used to being taller than most women back home, and as tall as the average man. Many of the women in Magnambougou, and Bamako generally, however, were taller than me, and well built. Malian men in the capital were often well over six feet tall, some over seven feet. A common question from students or colleagues following presentations of my research, has always been: "How do all those short little kids grow up to be such tall adults?" The answer, of course: "They don't. The short little kids don't grow up. They die."

In rural Dogo arrondissement, the adults were relatively short, compared either to American standards, or to their more urban counterparts. Average height for the men would turn out to be just over 5 feet 7 inches; for the women, a shade over 5 feet 3 inches. If Malians could grow up well nourished, in an environment free of parasites and disease, they would probably be heavier and taller than Americans. It won't happen in my lifetime.

During the afternoon of measuring in Famabougou we did occasionally come across someone with a surname other than Thiero or Keminaani. One was Bilo Bissan, a noble hunter. He was dressed in traditional, homespun cotton clothing, including an elaborate "hunter's shirt." The shirt was encrusted with dried blood, and adorned with numerous hunter's fetishes sewn in seemingly random patterns. Multiple amulets hung from his neck, and he wore a special hunter's cap on his grizzled head. He refused to remove his hat when it came time to measure his head circumference. Another bit of missing data. I was struck by the gold hoop earring dangling from his right earlobe.

"I am a mighty Bambara hunter," he intoned in a deep bass voice, grinning as I involuntarily took a step backward. "Don't worry, I won't shoot you." Bilo set his gun against the wall of the chief's house. It was ancient, a handmade ball and powder affair, made of spare car parts and intricately carved wood and decorated with fetishes, like the hunter's shirt. A fine patina on the wood showed where the gun was customarily held.

I knew we were safe from the gun, but there was still something slightly creepy about Bilo Bissan. In contrast to many of the rural villagers, who had kept their heads bowed throughout their encounter with me, Bilo's eyes drilled directly into mine. It felt as though he could tell what I was thinking, and strong waves of power emanated from him, disturbing the air whenever he moved. He frightened me. It was the same reaction I'd had when once confronted with a Komo mask, wooden avatar of the staggeringly powerful Komo spirit that enforces social conformation and assists in divination and problem solving in traditional Bambara societies. My intellect told me this was just an old man, as the Komo mask had been just a hunk of carved wood covered in chicken blood, millet beer, and other sacrificial offerings. From each, though, some other sense had picked up vibrations of extraordinary power and danger. Moussa felt them too, and moved away, raising his eyebrows in chagrin when he saw that I had noticed.

"What's with the earring?" I murmured in an aside to Moussa, trying to lighten the mood, as the hunter stepped up to the height measuring board. Moussa was careful not to touch the hunter, giving only verbal instructions on how to stand, where to look.

"I don't know," Moussa replied, "it must be part of the special hunter's code. I don't know much about hunters, myself."

Traditionally, hunters held a special, magical, almost mystical place in Bambara society. They wore special clothing and were the keepers of secret, sacred knowledge about the bush and about the spirits of the animals they killed. It was intimated that some hunters could even turn themselves into animals. Griots sang their praises in special hunters' songs and memorialized great hunters, who were remembered down the generations. Environmental change, population growth, the introduction of Islam, the expansion of agriculture, and new government laws prohibiting the hunting of most wild animals had all but robbed hunters of their exalted role. No new young men would be inducted into the secret hunting societies, no new songs would be written in their honor. Bilo was among the last of a dying breed.

As the sun sank rapidly toward the horizon, the last chubby brown baby was handed back to his mother, and we packed up our equipment and headed back to the truck. I was looking forward to a cold shower from a bucket, and a late dinner of kaba toh that was being readied for us in Dogo. Bakary, who had disappeared for the afternoon, caught up with us on the path and announced grandly, "The chief wants us to come and eat the food they prepared for us."

"You've got to be kidding," I said wearily. "I thought we'd been through that already. Surely they don't expect us to come eat it after it's been sitting around all day in this heat. It was at least 100 degrees today."

Bakary just stared at me, puzzled. "What's that got to do with anything? It will be a grave insult if you refuse to eat with them. After all, it is the host's responsibility to feed his guests, and he did arrange for all of his villagers to stay in from the fields today so you could gather the data you need."

"First of all, Bakary," I said, trying to contain my anger, "the chief was told that we would be coming *after* lunch, *after* we had eaten in N'tenkoni. He was told not to fix any food. Second, the villagers could have worked all morning, since they knew we weren't coming until *after lunch!*" I could hear my voice getting higher and louder, my language deteriorating into a mix of Bambara, broken French, and English. "Third, and most relevant, that food has been sitting around all day in this heat. By now, it will be full of bacteria. It will make us all very sick if we eat it."

"But the chief will be angry," Bakary repeated, ignoring my arguments. "We have to go eat."

"Fine, Bakary, you go eat! Miranda and Heather and I will wait by the truck." I stalked off in protest. When we reached the truck, which had been parked on the main road in the shade of a tree, I threw the equipment in the back and flopped down on the grass, exhausted. A small circle of children gathered around to giggle and stare.

"Why is it so hard to be a good anthropologist?" I asked the children rhetorically, in English. They snickered and hid behind their hands.

"Do you really think it will make us sick?" asked Miranda.

"Definitely," I said. "They probably don't make bacterial

contamination scores that go up that high. We can't afford to get sick."

"How can they eat it, then?" Miranda wondered.

"They're used to it," I explained. "From the time they begin to crawl, and eat solid foods, they get bombarded with bacteria. If it doesn't kill them, they eventually get used to it. Of course, diarrhea does kill lots of them, when they're little."

"Yuck," said Miranda.

After a short time, Moussa appeared. "It was pretty bad," he said. "It's probably just as well you didn't try it. Bakary and the others are still eating." He reached in the truck and pulled out a Frisbee and proceeded to teach the group of youngsters gathered around the fine art of floating a Frisbee.

Sometime after midnight, I awoke, wrapped in absolute darkness. Even the glow of the mosquito coil had been extinguished. The door was marked by faint lines discernible only when viewed from the corner of the eye. I extricated myself from between Heather and Miranda, opened the door slowly, and stepped out into a world of magic. The light from thousands of stars illuminated the courtyard of Falaye's compound. Star shine. Turned sideways from its familiar orientation, Orion hung low on the eastern horizon, his body crowded with stars.

Drums beat in the distance, the throbbing heartbeat of the village. Who else was awake at this hour? Why were they drumming? Was it a meeting of the highly secret, no-women-allowed, members-only Komo society? Was Komo dancing? I longed to go in search of the drummers but was held back by fear, and respect. Fear that I would lose my way, stumble and fall, be attacked by wild animals, be possessed by spirits. Respect for the drummers' privacy, fear of being caught. Komo isn't impressed by toubabs. Life goes on, with or without anthropologists, observers, tourists—exotic and romantic as it seemed to me, for the villagers it was simply business as usual. Midnight drummers, celebrating, mourning, perhaps divining, not for my intruding eyes.

The eager crowd pushed and shoved its way onto the porch of the Health Center, yelling and shouting. The men waved fistfuls of birth certificates, the women talked all at once, calling "me first, me first," the children grinned and danced on nimble legs, then jumped off the porch over the heads of those massed below. The sun was barely over the horizon, and I had had only one cup of coffee, but already we were starting the measuring session. As the center of the arrondissement, Dogo had a population of more than 500 people, and they all wanted to be measured first.

I couldn't blame them. Everyone had work waiting at home or in the fields, and there was little shade in the yard of the Health Center. The women had their daily round of domestic and agricultural chores. There was water to be hauled up out of wells, firewood to be gathered and chopped, millet or corn to be pounded, fruits and leaves to be harvested from the kitchen garden, or from the bush, meals to be cooked, compounds to be swept, and clothes to be washed. Always there were children to be nursed, nurtured, watched, comforted. In addition to the daily chores, there were huge mounds of karite nuts to be sorted and roasted, and the roasting fires to be attended. Men were busy as well, for the first ears of corn were ready to be harvested. Children had been kept in the village, when otherwise they would be out and about with the herds of goats and sheep, or using their slingshots on birds, lizards, and bush rats.

With Falaye's help, the crowd was pushed off the porch and organized, and measuring began in earnest. We had to work fast if we were to finish everyone before tempers wore thin from waiting in the hot sun. After a few false starts, we caught our rhythm and funneled people up the steps onto the porch, through the measuring routine, and down the steps again. Falaye was a model of industry and organization and made the work more efficient.

It soon became apparent that iodine deficiency was a major problem in Dogo village; as the day wore on we took to joking about the size and magnificence of individual goiters. Iodine is an essential nutrient needed by the body for proper brain growth and development and hormonal functioning. The main symptom of iodine deficiency is enlargement of the thyroid gland located in the front of the neck. In many cultures, a slight swelling of the thyroid is considered sexy, a sign of beauty. But untreated iodine deficiency leads to the development of a goiter, a very large, lumpy overgrowth of the thyroid gland. If a pregnant woman doesn't receive enough iodine in her diet, she can give birth to a child with a condition known as "cretinism," marked by permanent mental retardation. Usually, iodine deficiency takes many years to manifest itself in a visible goiter, so it is most often found in adults. Goiters are more common in women, who have higher iodine requirements because of the hormones associated with menstruation and pregnancy. Iodine deficiency is rare in the modern United States because salt, the one food everybody eats, is supplemented with iodine. In other parts of the world, the iodine content of food depends primarily on the iodine content of the soil where the crops are grown. If the soil is deficient, it may be difficult to get enough iodine.

Prior to Dogo, I had simply been noting presence or absence of goiters, and they were few and far between. Iodine deficiency was such a problem in Dogo, however, that goiters were detectable even

Falaye Doumbia and Heather Katz organize the birth certificates for the measuring session in Dogo village.

The author and Moussa Diarra weigh an infant in a suspension scale, while waiting villagers look on with amusement.

in young boys. Almost all of the adults had goiters, and some were quite large. I began calling out "small," "medium," or "large" to Heather to give some indication of the degree of goiter development.

One woman had a goiter the size of a basketball distending her neck and weighing heavily on her chest. It was lumpy and discolored. "This one takes an 'extra-large'," I quipped to Heather. She looked up from writing numbers. "Criminy! It's huge! That one must weigh at least 10 pounds!"

Moussa and Heather both laughed until tears ran down their faces. "Come on, you guys. Be serious!" I admonished, giving Moussa a stern look. "It's a good thing this woman doesn't know why we're laughing."

Later that night I asked the government health agent who ran the Health Center in Dogo what he was doing for the goiter problem in the village. His reply: "What goiter problem?"

Following the huge goiter, we had several more 10 pounders and 5 pounders, as well as a woman with polio who walked on her knees. She had no trouble getting up on the scales, and we recorded her weight, but height was trickier. She couldn't stand on her feet, even with help. From her rough and calloused knees down, her legs were worthless. "Well, it would be rude to tell her she can't participate," I said to Moussa. "She's come all this way, and waited in the heat, to be a part of the project. We'll just have to measure her height from the knees up."

She shuffled onto the height measuring board, and I lowered the cross-bar onto her head, thinking again of my class on anthropometric measuring techniques. There is no standard for "kneeling height."

"Be sure to make a note about this, so I don't include her height in the average," I reminded Heather. "So noted: kneeling height only," Heather announced. We were all getting punchy. Too many hours of working in the hot sun without a break, too many injuries, too many diseases, too much hardship. Joking was our only release.

We didn't even break for lunch, because that would have meant leaving a dwindling, but still substantial crowd of people waiting in the sun while we relaxed in the shade. On and on we worked, until the last villager had been added to the growing pile of data sheets. More than 300 people were measured that day, between sunrise and late afternoon.

We dragged ourselves across the road to Falaye's compound and collapsed. Miranda had spent the day inside the room where we slept, but she hadn't just been lounging around. She had been busy. Using her imagination, she had created an entire community of people, filling page after page with descriptions of each family, their occupations, appearance, likes and dislikes, religious affiliation, yearly income, number, names, ages, and sexes of adults and children. Some were wealthy, lived in mansions, owned yachts, belonged to the country club. Others were poor, lived in urban housing projects, lost children to drive-by shootings. There were bakers and fashion models, race car drivers and investment bankers, janitors and amusement park barkers, children and babies. A whole society, operating by cultural rules contained inside her head—lives undreamt of by the scores of rural African villagers who surrounded her.

Refreshed by an hour's rest, we mustered up enough energy to bathe and put on clean clothes. Heather and I turned our hand to making tea over a small charcoal brazier. Tea brewing in West Africa, as in many parts of the world, is a fine art, but in West Africa it is practiced exclusively by men. Amid much joking and merriment, we managed to boil water in a small bright blue teapot but had to have help adding the tea and sugar in proper proportions. Finally, Macan, as the youngest, and therefore lowest-status male in the group, took over the ritual of tea making, filling glass after glass of sweet hot tea, reviving both body and spirit.

Dinner was delivered in the midst of another thunderstorm, but we huddled close together in the darkness under the paillote, eating by flashlight. Millet toh with a sauce made of chicken and spices. "Hmmmm," I murmured, "*poulet bicyclette.*" I had met my match, a piece of meat beyond my powers of mastication. Surreptitiously I removed it from my mouth and lobbed it out into the darkness.

"What?" said Bakary. "Poulet bicyclette?"

"Yes," I repeated. "Poulet bicyclette—bicycle chicken."

"What exactly is bicycle chicken?" Bakary asked, sounding offended. Moussa snorted in the darkness.

"You know, a chicken who has spent its life riding a bicycle—what little meat it has on its bones is all tough and stringy. Poulet bicyclette. Besides, this wasn't cooked long enough, contributing to its toughness."

"What can you expect?" said Moussa. "Falaye has to have food cooked for him by others. All week we've been feasting on food cooked by the animatrices themselves."

It was true. In Mali, women cook and serve, men eat. In the villages, we had mostly eaten food cooked for us by the animatrices, all of whom were women, and excellent cooks. Falaye didn't cook his own food; he couldn't, because he was a man. He paid village women to cook for him, and the quality was uneven, to say the least. Malian men have been known to go without food for several days if they can't find a woman (mother, sister, wife, daughter) to cook for them. Men cooking, men carrying babies on their backs, and women wearing pants and bikinis were toubab activities that amazed and puzzled Malians. A toubab in a bikini was the ultimate in perversity. Why bother to cover up your breasts, which are for feeding babies, but let everyone gawk at your thighs, the sexiest part of a woman's anatomy?

Every society has activities that are normally considered to be the province of only one sex. Officially termed "the sexual division of labor," it is more often expressed as "everyone knows that only women do _____." In Mali, only women cook, unless it's for wages, in which case men can be "chefs" (not unlike the French and United States distinction). In Mali, only men weave cloth on the narrow strip looms, sitting in rows of five or six for companionship, weaving from dawn to dusk, surrounded by huge, brightly colored balls of thread. Only men sew clothes. In Cameroon, on the other hand, only women sew clothes. We are all taught from our first moments of life that certain activities are appropriate for someone of our gender, and others are inappropriate. By the time children in the United States reach preschool, they have learned their lessons well—most of the girls don't want to play with trucks; most of the boys don't want to play with dolls. But these are cultural attitudes, drummed into us in a multitude of ways by parents, siblings, peers, schoolteachers, television, and even strangers. Other ways of organizing the world come to seem unnatural and bizarre, rather than merely alternatives to our particular way. Poor Falaye, doomed by his gender and his culture to eat whatever was fixed for him by the women.

It was fractionally cooler in the shade of the baobab tree, and we leaned back against the trunk, annoyed but resigned. Heather and Miranda occupied themselves counting and scratching their mosquito bites. Heather had more than 200 bites on one leg. Miranda had only a few, though hers would turn out to be more dangerous, by far. We watched as Macan pedalled past on a bicycle commandeered from some unsuspecting stranger on the road. A hundred yards away, the AMIPJ truck sat with an empty gasoline tank. Bakary had siphoned gas from the truck to fill up the tanks of the mopeds belonging to the field personnel, gambling that we could make it to the gas station at Oulessabougou before running out of gas ourselves. Almost, but not quite. Despite Macan's best efforts, zooming up hills full throttle and coasting down with the clutch pushed in, the truck spluttered to a stop some two miles short.

No problem. Cadge a bicycle from the next man riding by. Talk him into loaning you his bike for an hour for 1,000 CFA (about $3 U.S., a vast sum). Unload the bike, lash the spare gas can to the back, hop on, and pedal hell-bent for leather to the gas station. Buy one liter of gas in the can, ride back, and return the bicycle to its owner, who has spent the interim chatting, resting, and bumming cigarettes from Moussa. Siphon the gas from the can into the truck, pick up the toubabs, who have walked up the road to take advantage of a patch of shade, and head into town to fill up. No problem. Homeward bound.

10

I Give You Rural Africa

As the traveler who has once been from home is wiser than he who has never left his own doorstep, so a knowledge of one other culture should sharpen our ability to scrutinize more steadily, to appreciate more lovingly, our own.

—Margaret Mead

Standing on tiptoe, I scanned the passengers climbing down the stairs from the jet onto the tarmac. I saw Steven immediately—I'd recognize his gait anywhere (toes out, just like the Australopithecine footprints at Laetoli). I tried to keep him in sight as I was jostled and shoved to and fro by the crowd. The babble of excited voices, French, Bambara, some German, some English, made it impossible to hear his shouted greetings. Without an expediter from the Embassy (he was just a tourist, after all), it took some time to clear customs and get his luggage, but finally he emerged from the chaos and gave Miranda a giant hug. We all climbed into the taxi I had brought along and headed to the house. I had a million questions—how was Peter? How was my mother (who had gone to Texas to stay with Peter during Steven's visit)? How was he, Steven? Had it been terribly hard, being alone with Peter for four months? What did he think of Mali, this time around? Amidst hugs and kisses, smiles and laughter, all the questions were answered.

"Will we be able to go to Dogo?" he asked, once we were settled around the dining room table at the house.

"Yes," I replied. "This weekend, Bakary and Macan will take all of us down for a three-day trip. I'll be giving a preliminary presentation of the results of my research to the animatrices, but once that's done it's just a pleasure jaunt. We'll pay for gas and food, but they'll make all the arrangements and do the driving. Tom may

115

come along, too, but Heather says she wants to stay here."

"Is it really as wonderful as you described in your letters?" Steven asked.

"Even better," I said. "This is the Africa we studied about in our graduate classes, Steven. This is the Africa of the classic ethnographies we read, Evans-Pritchard and Victor Turner, Meyer Fortes and Paul Bohannan, Hilda Kuper, Elizabeth Colson, and Elizabeth Marshall Thomas. Not Bamako, with its car horns honking, radios blaring, piles of rotten food and trash, streets full of potholes. The best part is that Bakary says the villagers of Dogo have agreed to dance for us."

"What do you mean?" he asked.

"I wrote you about hearing the drums and music far into the night during my earlier trips. So I asked Bakary if the villagers would have a dance while we were there. He asked them and they not only said yes, they said they would put on a special dance in my honor!"

A few days later, we were there, watching the villagers assemble for the dance.

We sat high above the dance ground, on raised platforms built of thick logs, held up by notched corner poles. I dangled my legs over the front edge of the platform, swinging them back and forth. Before me, on the ground, Miranda slept in a low-slung metal chair, exhausted by the excitement of having her daddy come visit, and by the long, hot, dusty trip down by bouncing truck. Steven sat on my left, my housemate Tom on my right.

In the dusk of early evening, the dance ground spread out before us. We had an excellent view and would be spared the worst of the dust clouds raised by the dancers. Every large rural village in Mali has a dance ground. This one consisted of an oval area some 60 feet long, devoid of vegetation, and swept clean of debris, the dirt hard-packed by generations of pounding feet. Five high wooden platforms were spaced around the periphery, providing positions of honor for old men and other important guests.

The whole village had turned out to honor us. Only a few would be dancing. The rest were gathered around the edge of the dance ground, adults standing in back, children standing in front or sitting on the ground. A few children frolicked by themselves in the center of the ring but gave way to the drummers, who lit small fires of brush and twigs and used torches of burning reeds to heat the drum heads and tune them by adjusting the tightness of the laces. As the drummers continued their heating and tuning, a line of women entered the dance ground and began to form a circle.

The center ring was made up of the older women, women my age (in Mali, by the time you reach your thirties, you're getting old), who sang and danced, slowly and rhythmically, shuffling around in a continuous circle. Some held large hemispheres made of calabashes, decorated with a net covering laced with cowrie shells. These were tossed into the air with a spiral motion, making a wonderful clickety-clacking noise as they fell back into reaching hands. Back and forth, twist and turn, shuffle forward, respond to the call sung by one of the younger women.

Outside the ring of older women, the young, nubile girls danced in a larger circle, more quickly, more energetically. The outermost circle was composed of young boys, just kids, who raced around and around the women and girls, running rather than dancing, stirring up dust. The drummers provided the rhythm for the dancers, an intricately woven beat that accommodated both circles of women. Some women dropped out to rest for a while; others joined from the sidelines; all nodded and bowed when they passed our viewing stand on their way around the circle.

At one point, many of the spectators joined in on the chorus of a call-and-response song. Point, counterpoint. Clear soprano soaring up and out, above the crowd, responses in a hundred deeper voices. I asked Falaye what the song was about. "They've been singing songs about your work. About how you came here and they all gathered together, staying in from the fields for the whole day so you could measure everyone. They were singing about how wonderful you are and how much good your work will bring to the villages of Dogo."

"Gosh," I responded, inarticulately. "And what about this song?"

"This is an old standard. It's about the necessity of having many children to take care of you in your old age, to help you, to make you happy. They've added some new verses about the importance of keeping the children healthy so they can grow up to keep you company when you are old and give you many grandchildren."

Beside me on the wooden platform, Steven sat mesmerized, trying to take in every detail and commit it to memory. Tom, conversely, was fascinated by the goiters. Night had fallen, and the full moon wouldn't rise for hours. The only light came from the fires that still burned in the center of the dance ground. As the women passed between us and the fires, their faces and necks were silhouetted in the firelight. Every second or third woman had a goiter. "Wow, look at that one!" Tom exclaimed. "Whoa! That must be the 'goiter from hell' that Heather told me about!"

"Hush, Tom," I admonished. "Enjoy the dancing, and try to stop worrying about the goiters."

The next few hours had a mystical, time-out-of-time, otherworldly quality. The dancing and singing continued, but one by one the women dropped out and joined the watching crowds. The fires in the center burned low and went out. The stars hung low over the dance ground. A group of men brought out buckets of water and used their hands to spray it in great arcs in every direction, dampening down the dust and clearing the air. "Whew! Why didn't they do that earlier?" I wondered. We could barely see in the darkness.

Gradually the idle chatter of the crowd ceased. Everyone grew quiet, then murmurs could be heard among the crowd furthest from our position, where the main trail from the village approached the dance ground. The drums began again, a faster, more strident rhythm. "Look," said Steven, pointing. "Can you see the two dancers?"

I couldn't see them until they were right in front of us—two young men, dressed in simple costumes and tasselled caps. One had a whistle, the other a gourd rattle. My initial disappointment that they weren't dancing with masks gave way to amazement at their artistry. They began slowly, dancing with careful, precise movements. But soon they were leaping and twirling in a frenzy of barely controlled energy and power. They posed, they postured, they strutted, they danced in imitation of different animals— antelopes, lions, elephants, monkeys. They danced toward us and then away, taking turns showing off their prowess, competing for our attention. The pungent odors of wood smoke and sweat filled the air.

The dancers were disconcerted by Miranda, who continued to sleep even when they danced right in front of her. They stomped and cavorted so hard the ground shook, and one blew his whistle in her face. The taller, better dancer, the star of the production, danced furiously in front of Miranda, the rattles on his legs clattering loudly. He flung his head from side to side and shook his arms over his head, raining sweat. Miranda slept on, oblivious to the spectacle.

On and on, around and around, the dancers whirled and turned, feet pounding, rattles shaking. Finally, the band of drummers corralled and chased one dancer out of the ring. The other was harder to get rid of. They chased him around and around, but he kept breaking loose and coming back to dance in front of us. Finally, they pushed him out of the ring, and he fled along the path into the village. All was quiet for a moment. We climbed down from our perch, stiff and sore from the hours of immobility. Steven gathered Miranda up in his arms, and we followed Falaye back to his compound, and sleep.

The next morning we feasted on millet *fru-fru* (fried millet balls) and coffee. One of the men from the village had agreed to guide

Steven and Tom on a trek to the top of the hill behind the village. While they were gone, I stayed in the village and held class for the animatrices, Falaye, and Bakary, under a mango tree. I used a blackboard to illustrate my preliminary findings, describing the incredibly high levels of malnutrition among the young children, and the dangers of goiters, and offering suggestions for first steps the animatrices could take to tackle the monumental task of overcoming malnutrition in the kids. They asked lots of questions, and we brainstormed for several hours, thinking up different approaches and debating their merits. Was immunization more important than starting solid foods at an earlier age? How much did contamination of the food—from sitting around in the heat, from dirty hands—contribute to illness? What could be done about the iodine deficiency that led to goiters? How could nutrition education messages be incorporated into the regular meetings of the credit societies?

The sun moved up in the sky until it stood overhead. I returned to Falaye's compound and went inside the sleeping room to check on Miranda, who had spent the morning reading a book. I was just beginning to worry about Steven and Tom when they showed up at the door, sweaty and out of breath, their faces red with sunburn and exertion.

"Water," Steven croaked. I pointed to the covered pot sitting on a raised platform of sand near the doorway. It was covered with a metal plate, and a cup was turned upside down on top. Every Malian hut has one of these large pottery jars. The water seeps slowly through the sides and evaporates, keeping the water inside cool and refreshing. Steven downed five cups of water before relinquishing the cup to Tom and collapsing on the floor.

"Did you have a good time?" I asked.

"It was great," he said. "The view from the top of the hill is amazing. You'd think you were looking at New England if it weren't for the thatched roofs. I've never seen Mali look so green. We came through the millet fields on the way back. That was spooky. And we saw some incredible tunnels."

"Whoa, whoa," I exclaimed. "One thing at a time!"

Steven got up to drink some more water, then related his morning's adventure in greater detail. Their guide was an old man, who zipped up the hill barefooted, without apparent effort, and arrived at the top unwinded. Steven and Tom, on the other hand, even with the advantages of relative youth and hiking boots, were hard pressed to keep up with him. The path, if such existed, was hidden under thick brush, and the stony hillside meant one slip down for every two steps up.

"I kept worrying that I would step on a snake," Steven said. "The

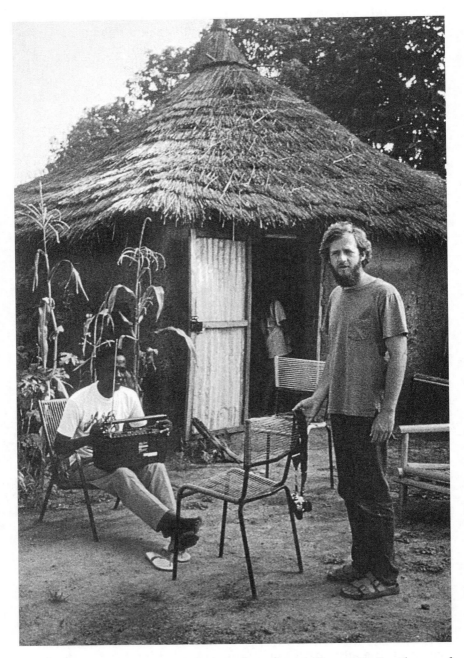

The author's husband, cultural anthropologist Steven Dettwyler, and field assistant, Moussa Diarra, relax after a long day of helping with the research in N'tenkoni.

view was incredible, but the best part was going through the millet fields on the way back here. The millet is almost ready to be harvested. It must be 18 feet tall! Inside the fields it's like being inside a forest. It's dark and cool. Whenever Tom got more than a few paces in front of me, I couldn't see him anymore. The millet just swallowed him up. If you got lost in there, you'd never find your way out."

"What did you mean about seeing tunnels?" I asked.

"Oh, that part was great. There are all these tunnels inside the millet fields, that lead down into the ground. The old man said that in the past, people hid in the tunnels, during intervillage skirmishes."

"That must have been a long time ago," I said.

"At least a hundred years, I would think," Steven answered. "Before the time of the French occupation. We saw nine or ten tunnels, and the guide said there were lots more. They look just like shallow wells, about the size of a manhole cover. They go down about three feet and then turn horizontally and disappear under the millet. He said they're all interconnected under the ground, and people could stay in the tunnels for a long time, until it was safe to return to their village."

We waited for lunch outside, under the deep shade of a huge locust tree. As we sat there, just relaxing, a young man walked up and quietly introduced himself to Falaye, shook our hands, and took a seat. He kept his eyes on the ground.

"This is the main dancer from last night," Falaye said, introducing us all around.

"Oh my," I exclaimed. "He seems so quiet and shy today! He must be exhausted, too."

Falaye translated my words into Bambara and the young man raised his head and smiled, revealing a huge gap between his two upper front teeth. He *was* shy, and exhausted, and a little embarrassed. He told how he had spent six years learning to dance, as an apprentice to the village's master dancer, who was too old to dance any more. He was only 25 years old, but already he was known throughout the region for the grace and power of his dancing.

After a delicious lunch of local rice and peanut butter sauce (no detachable goat parts!) and a short siesta, we packed up and drove on to N'tenkoni, where we would spend the second night. I showed Steven the tree I had climbed and the walk-through hut where we had conducted the measuring session. The animatrice, Tiedo Ba, saw us settled in her compound, then took us to meet the traditional midwife at what served as the village's maternity clinic, a three-room mud hut with a corrugated iron roof, where all the women of N'tenkoni and nearby villages came to give birth.

The midwife was middle-aged and her shoulders drooped, but she was exceptionally articulate and gave us a thorough tour of the rooms. On the right was the birthing room, a six by ten foot rectangular space with a sloping floor that allowed for easier cleaning. Following a birth, water was sluiced onto the floor from a bucket, and ran downhill, emptying through a small opening where the floor met the wall. The midwife had no equipment or supplies, only a stool to sit on, a reed mat for laboring women to lie on, and a "birthing kit" provided by the government, which she could not replenish. It contained empty bottles of alcohol and iodine, razor blades for cutting the baby's umbilical cord, rubber gloves, and a broken pair of clamping scissors.

The middle room was the reception area, where patients and visitors could wait, while the room on the left was equipped with a bed for recuperating mothers and infants. It was occupied by a shy young mother, who was excited to be able to show off her new baby to the visiting toubabs. Appalled by the lack of facilities, Tom ventured to ask the midwife if she had ever lost a woman in childbirth.

"Only one," she responded with a mixture of pride and regret. "Only one, in more than 30 years. I've delivered many babies, and only lost one mother." She gazed pensively out the open doorway toward the millet fields.

"What happened?" I gently prompted her.

"She was from a neighboring village, about four kilometers distant, and walked here after two days in labor. She was exhausted. When the baby started to come out, I could tell that it was lying the wrong way, because one of the arms came out first. The baby couldn't be born in that position. As soon as we saw the arm, we decided to send her to the hospital in Sikasso, to the south."

"How did she get there?" I asked.

"On the back of a donkey cart," she continued. "It took all night just to get to the main road and flag down a truck to take her to the hospital. Then the doctors in Sikasso said they couldn't help her and sent her in a taxi to Bamako instead."

"But that's several hours back this direction," I protested.

"Yes, I know. But we thought the hospital in Sikasso could help her, and it was closer, so she went there first."

"Did she make it to Bamako?" Tom asked.

"No. She died while they were crossing the bridge into the city. She had lost too much blood and was just too worn out. The baby died too."

We all stood in silence for a moment, imagining the scene in our minds. On the one hand, I was discouraged that a woman should lose her life in childbirth because of the lack of medical facilities. On the other hand, I was truly amazed that more than thirty years of midwifery without equipment or supplies, without the option of Caesarian sections and intravenous drips and blood transfusions and fetal monitors, without even electricity for lights at night, should result in only one maternal death.

"Did you ever consider sacrificing the baby to save the mother's life?" I inquired.

"What do you mean?" the midwife responded.

"I mean, maybe you could have cut off the baby's arm. That might have made it possible to reach inside and rotate the baby so it could come out head first, and the baby probably would have bled to death, but the mother might have survived."

The midwife shuddered and closed her eyes. "I could never do something like that," she said. "I could never purposefully hurt the baby like that, and I don't know how to turn the baby."

"It was just a thought. You have a remarkable record here," I reassured her. "Quite remarkable."

That night Steven and Tom went off to palaver with the village men; Miranda and I went to sleep early. I awoke to the sounds of women pounding millet in the predawn stillness of the African morning. Husbands and children slept on, but women's work for the day was well underway. Thunka . . . thunka . . . thunka . . . thunka. I dressed and stepped outside, where hundreds of yellow weaver birds twittered around a tall tree, festooned with tiny woven nests like Christmas tree ornaments. The air was crisp and cool, giving no hint of the heat to come. Gradually the sky lightened and the darkness retreated. I made a quick trip to the latrine, washed my hands in the bucket left outside the cooking hut for that purpose, then ducked inside to watch breakfast preparations.

The interior of the cooking hut was warm and cozy, and I huddled near the glowing fire on a three-legged wooden stool. Balanced neatly on three rocks half-embedded in the ground, a large pot of thick millet porridge was bubbling. Tiedo greeted me absentmindedly as she stirred the porridge and adjusted the heat of the fire by pulling a few pieces of firewood out from under the pot. From the shadows behind me came the contented snufflings of a baby nursing. One of the village women was sitting there. Because her infant was only a few weeks old, her co-wife was cooking breakfast for their compound, leaving her free to visit friends in the early morning hours.

After breakfast we went on a trek around the village. On our earlier trips, I really hadn't had a chance to see the village of

N'tenkoni itself. We wanted to observe the villagewide karite-processing activities, and we hoped to find a traditional carved wooden door lock to add to our collection. I also wanted Steven to meet Abi, the little girl with Down syndrome, but it turned out that she had gone with her mother to visit relatives in another village.

Most of the men of the village had gone off to work in the fields. Normally the women would have gone to the fields also, but it was karite time, and all able-bodied women and girls were recruited for the incredibly labor-intensive activities involved in extracting vegetable oil from the nuts of the karite, or shea, tree (*Butryospermum parkii*). In the fall, when the karite nuts are ripe, parties of young girls and women spend several weeks collecting huge mounds of the nuts. The nuts are slow roasted in giant earth ovens lined up in rows of five or six on the periphery of the village. These ovens are round, stand about four feet tall, and are partitioned into top and bottom halves. Below the partition a fire is kept burning day and night. Above the partition, the oven is filled with nuts. After several days of roasting, the hulls are easy to remove.

The nutmeats are then pounded in huge wooden mortars, similar to the standard millet-pounding mortars, but at least three times as large. Groups of women and young girls make parties out of karite pounding by singing songs, clapping their hands, and dancing to the rhythm of the pounding sticks. Once the nutmeats are thoroughly pounded, the residue looks like thick mud. This residue is then transferred, little by little, to a flat stone mortar, similar to those used by the Hopi to grind blue corn. This special mortar, used only for karite, is set on a slant, with the lower edge emptying into a calabash that has been sunk into the ground. Instead of taking the usual standing position, women kneel and further grind the karite sludge with a small wooden grinding implement. The resulting liquid, which has the appearance of Hershey's chocolate syrup, runs down the mortar, gradually filling up the submerged calabash.

When the calabash is full, water is added to the syrup, and the whole mixture is beaten, using only hands and forearms. Whomp, whomp, whomp, slurp, slurp. As the young girls beat the sludge, it turns a frothy cocoa color and increases in volume. The final stages of karite processing involve several rounds of boiling the pale brown sludge and skimming off the dark impurities that rise to the surface. With each boiling and skimming, the color lightens, until the final product is ready—karite butter, a solid, pure white vegetable oil. Karite butter is highly saturated, so that it remains solid even at very high ambient temperatures. It looks just like Crisco. The karite butter is rolled into balls of varying sizes and stored for use during the coming year or exported for sale to regions

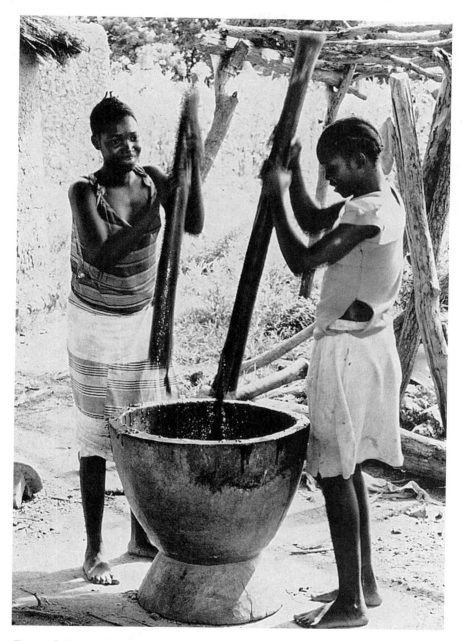

Two adolescent girls use wooden pestles to pound karite nuts in a huge wooden mortar.

without karite. In much of the country, karite butter is the main
source of cooking oil and is added to sauce for millet or rice. It is
also rubbed into the skin as a lotion and put on burns or other minor
injuries as an aid in healing.

In every quarter of the village, different stages of karite processing
were underway, from cracking nuts to communal pounding fests
to whipping the syrup with water. The boiling down had even begun
in some compounds. "Now I understand why the teenage girls have
larger mid-upper arm circumferences than the teenage boys," I
remarked to Steven. "Just look at those arm muscles!"

"No kidding," he replied. "This gives a whole new meaning to
the term labor-intensive."

"Mommy," Miranda said, gesturing to a group of old women
cracking nuts in the shade of a grove of mangoes. "Why do the old
women here have such flabby breasts?"

"Miranda!" I chided. "What a thing to say!"

"Well, look at the woman over there. Her breasts sag down clear
to her waist," she persisted.

"All old women's breasts sag," I said. "You just never see any
old white women sitting around outside under a tree, naked above
the waist, that's all."

It is not uncommon for authors of travel books about Africa to
state with authority that African women's breasts sag more than
those of modern, Western women because they go through so many
cycles of pregnancy and nurse so many children. Of course, travel
writers usually spend only a few days in any one place and seldom
take the time to understand the lives of the people they describe,
preferring to use their own explanations for other people's actions.
That is why, for example, one can read in travel books about the
"antique" sewing machines still in use throughout West Africa.
These treadle sewing machines are operated by foot power and are
identical in every respect to the one my grandmother used on the
Kansas prairie, but they are *not* antiques. They are newly
manufactured, probably in China or the former Soviet Union, for
export to Third World countries where electrical power is either
nonexistent or unreliable. A treadle sewing machine makes perfect
sense in Mali. An electric sewing machine is an improvement over
a treadle only if you have electricity. It's not unlike the
computerized systems that have replaced the card catalogues at
modern university libraries, which have the unfortunate effect of
rendering the library holdings inaccessible whenever the power is
out or the computer is down.

I suppose it's understandable for the casual observer to conclude
that the typical African pattern of nursing many children for two
or three years apiece accounts for their lack of mammary pertness

Two young girls continue the process of extracting karite butter from the nuts. The girl on the left grinds the nuts to a fine liquid state, while the one on the right whips this "syrup" with water, using her hands and forearms.

The interior courtyard of a rural compound in Dogo Arrondissement. Several millet-pounding mortars can be seen in the foreground, and a karite nut oven is visible in the background.

in later years. Because of Western prudishness, plus our bizarre insistence that breasts are primarily sexual objects (rather than amazingly functional body parts designed for feeding infants), one seldom sees American women breastfeeding in public, and many Western observers are fascinated by the casual manner in which rural African women feed their children as they go about their daily chores. It forms a striking contrast with their own society, where even some breastfeeding promotion literature depicts breastfeeding as an activity best done in a white negligee in the privacy of one's bedroom.

The more likely explanations for sagging breasts in African women are more mundane—years of pounding millet and chopping firewood without the benefit of a support bra, exacerbated by the practice of tying children onto their backs with a cloth that encircles the mother's chest very tightly. It has to be tight, or the baby risks falling off. The pressure of the baby wrap pushing down on the breasts causes them to migrate southward, as it were.

Fortunately for Malian women, Malian men (and more importantly, Malian babies) don't care whether the women's breasts sag. The ability to produce breast milk is not related either to the size of a woman's breasts, or to their pertness, and the men are much more interested in women's *thighs* . . .

After watching the karite processing for some time, we continued our tour of the village and hesitantly and politely inquired whether there might be any door locks in the village. Traditional door locks are ingenious contraptions, carved out of wood, that function to protect huts from burglary. They are often carved in the shape of bodies with huge ears (to listen for petty thieves), and each tribe and part of the country has its own style. Where Islam has infiltrated, with its prohibition against representational carvings, the door locks are carved in intricate geometric shapes. Where the modern world has impinged, the beautiful carved wooden door locks have been replaced by the equally functional, but less aesthetically pleasing, metal padlocks. We hoped to add to our collection of fine old door locks, all of which had been purchased from an art dealer in Bamako.

Door locks are a relatively cheap art form to collect, as they usually have little religious significance and are replaced when they wear out. People willingly part with them for a reasonable price, and since the old ones end up on the garbage pile or, more likely, are added to the cooking fire, we felt little guilt about offering to buy one right off the door. Even as remote and traditional a village as N'tenkoni has few remaining wooden door locks, but we finally found one. It wasn't particularly old, or particularly well carved,

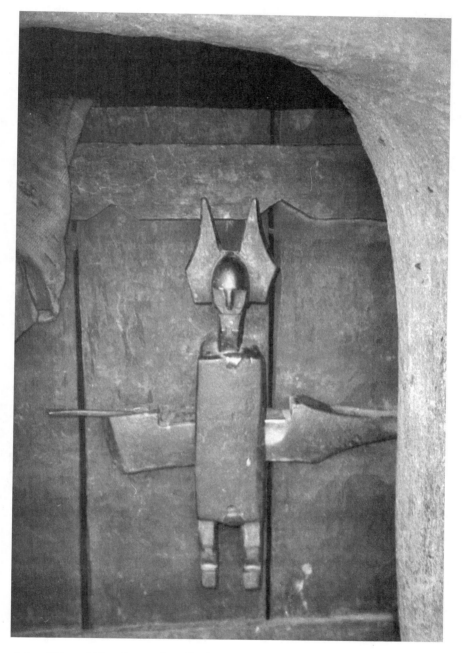

A traditional Bambara door lock.

but we bought it anyway, as a memento of our visit. The man whose storage hut it adorned gladly accepted our first offer, an indication that we had offered way too much.

An old woman, who had been watching our transaction with puzzlement, remarked that if we were willing to pay good money for old junk, she knew of another door lock nearby. Tom said he was interested, so we all followed the old woman to her compound. It was a spacious, immaculately clean compound, with a large central area surrounded by numerous round huts used for sleeping and cooking. The old woman put down the bowl she was carrying and hobbled over to the main kitchen hut. Stepping over the threshold, she reached inside the dark hut and pulled the door shut, revealing an exquisitely carved, ancient door lock.

"Oh no!" I said to Steven, stopping in my tracks. He gripped my arm tightly.

"What's the matter?" said Tom. "It looks pretty nice to me."

"Nothing's the matter, Tom," I explained. "Just that that's the most beautiful door lock we've ever seen. It's much nicer than any of the ones we have in our collection. Look at that carving. Look at the patina on the sides—the shiny areas polished smooth by the touch of thousands of hands. See, you grab it here, and here, to operate the key," I demonstrated the locking and unlocking of the door with the bent metal key.

"Well, I guess I'll buy it, then," Tom said, looking around for Moussa to help with the negotiations.

Steven and I retreated to the other side of the compound to commiserate on our misfortune at having lost the opportunity to acquire this door lock to someone who, we felt, wouldn't properly appreciate its beauty and significance. There was nothing we could do, and there were no other door locks of comparable quality in the entire village. We asked.

11

Turtles All the Way Down

There is an Indian story—at least I heard it as an Indian story—about an Englishman who, having been told that the world rested on a platform which rested on the back of an elephant which rested in turn on the back of a turtle, asked (perhaps he was an ethnographer; it is the way they behave), what did the turtle rest on? Another turtle. And that turtle? "Ah, Sahib, after that it is turtles all the way down."

—Clifford Geertz

Our brief time in Dogo was over all too quickly. Back in Bamako, we had a surprise visit from Gerry Cashion, who had first introduced us to Mali years before. He was working for the United States Agency for International Development in Lagos, Nigeria, but had come to Bamako for a few days on business and heard that we were there. Mary Jo Arnoldi, another anthropologist we had known from graduate school, was also in town. Mary Jo, who works for the Smithsonian Institution, is an expert on Bambara and Bozo puppet theater. We all spent a night on the town, eating couscous and stewed lamb in grand fashion at one of the restaurants. Afterward, even though it was near midnight, Gerry insisted we sit for a photograph at one of the studios (who knows why they were still open?). We posed as Malians usually do, looking straight at the camera, very formal and serious.

Too soon, it was time for Steven to leave, and time for me to get back to my research. Throughout November, I continued my growth and development work in Magnambougou. In order to increase the sample size of children in later childhood and the early teen years, I undertook to measure as many of the children at the Magnambougou school as I could. Moussa had made arrangements

131

with the principal to allow us access to the names and birth dates of the children in each class. We began with the first graders, a class of some 90 or more eight-year-olds crowded into a long, hot, narrow room. Every child has to have a uniform, made by a local tailor. They must bring their own desks or share with others, and they also have to bring their own food for lunch, or buy from street vendors, as the school has no cafeteria. The road across from the entrance to the school is lined with women selling fried dough balls, some filled with meat or vegetables, fried bean balls spiced with red pepper, fried potatoes, and macaroni. At the lunch break, crowds of noisy children jostle for position, trying to be the first to get something to eat. Others run home for a quick meal, and of course, many simply don't eat during the long day.

In the early grades, children sit two or three to a desk, and the rooms are so crowded that the students have to clamber across the tops of other desks to reach their own. They all stood up in unison and sang out, "*Bon jour, madame! Bon jour, monsieur! Bon jour, mademoiselle!*" when Moussa, Heather, and I entered the room. In those early grades, there are approximately equal numbers of boys and girls. As we progressed up the grades, the ratio became more and more skewed in favor of boys. School fees are expensive, and few parents can afford to send daughters, who will "just" end up as wives and mothers, or even more than one son. In addition to the expense, girls are needed at home, to help with domestic labor and child care. In both rural and urban parts of Mali, boys lead relatively leisurely lives until their teens, while girls are expected to start helping with domestic chores and market selling almost as soon as they can walk. In some rural areas, boys help by herding livestock, and work in the fields as well, but in urban Magnambougou there really wasn't much that boys could do to help at home. If they didn't go to school, they just hung out with their friends, playing games and hunting small animals and birds with their sling shots.

We worked out an efficient routine for measuring the kids quickly. When we were really cooking, it took less than two minutes per child. Call out their name, get them up to the front of the room, shoes off, onto the scale. Onto the height measuring board, arm circumference, head circumference, wrist breadth, head length and breadth, number of deciduous and permanent teeth, calling all the information out to Heather for recording. Finally, out the door to the open schoolyard, where they frolicked and giggled and talked about us, peering back in through the windows and doors. In just a few weeks, we measured hundreds of children. Hard data! Row upon row of numbers, marching across the page. No slippery interpretations to be made here, no guesses, no language barriers.

Just an incredible range of variation in each class. Officially, you can't start school until you are eight years old, but some parents want their children to start sooner. If you are a particularly tall six- or seven-year-old, you might get away with a doctored birth certificate, or perhaps a small bribe to the admissions officer would be sufficient. If you did an anthropometric survey limited to six- and seven-year-olds in all the first grades in Malian public schools, you would conclude that Malians had perfectly adequate nutrition and growth, since only the very tallest six- and seven-year-olds can pass for being eight.

At the same time, there are other children who, for one reason or another, didn't start school when they were eight but who have an opportunity to attend later on. Since they haven't been in school before, they begin with the first grade. They might be able to muddle through starting at a higher grade if school were taught in Bambara, but it's taught in French. Since French is the official language of education and government, schools in Mali will probably always be taught in French. However, some people are working to get Malian history and literature taught in addition to the French subjects. For now, the children begin in first grade, even if they're 10 or 11 years old.

Thus, in one classroom you get a core group of children who are the appropriate age for that grade, plus some several years younger, and a larger group several years older. Children in the first grade ranged in age from a particularly tall five year old to several children aged ten. The resulting variation in body size and shape was even more apparent in the upper grades, as some children began their adolescent growth spurts early, while others were delayed, either because of normal genetic variation or chronic malnutrition. In the sixth grade (supposedly the 14-year-olds), we measured 16-year-old girls who were fully developed, alongside skinny 12-year-olds who looked as if they were only 10. It was, for the most part, boring work, not nearly as frustrating as interviewing, but not nearly as interesting either.

In the evenings, I worked on my report on the Dogo surveys for Freedom from Hunger, and prepared interview forms for some research in northern Mali that I would be conducting as part of a nutrition communication project for the Academy for Educational Development, in conjunction with CARE. Developing the interview forms was easy enough, with Moussa's help, and we conducted a pretest in Magnambougou, then revised and finalized the forms. Getting photocopies copies made of the forms was more difficult and required several trips to Bamako, including one particularly memorable occasion.

The Bambara are known for their proverbs—little sayings that fit any occasion and often carry a moral or message. Like everything else, Bambara proverbs only make sense in the context of Malian culture. One day, Moussa and I were sitting in a taxicab in downtown Bamako, stuck in a traffic jam. We were still trying to get the interview forms copied, and we also wanted to buy supplies for my trip north and groceries for Tom, Heather, and Miranda, who would be staying in Bamako.

My usual cabbie, Siddiqi, was playing a scratchy tape of an old Simon and Garfunkel album I had given him, and leaned out his window to gesture wildly and scream at the cars in front of him blocking the way. It was Friday, just before noon, and the streets were packed with cars, mobylettes, bicycles, and pedestrians, all on their way to the Grand Mosque for prayers. As we inched our way forward, a powder blue Mercedes squeezed alongside, then wedged its way up onto the sidewalk. The door opened, and a middle-aged man emerged. He was elegantly garbed in a beautiful embroidered *boubou*, the traditional long flowing robe of Malian men. He opened the trunk of the Mercedes and extracted a securely trussed, very large, very angry sheep. The sheep was sent off, on the shoulders of a younger man, undoubtedly to be slaughtered.

The crowds of pedestrians separated and re-formed, moving faster than the traffic. On one side, a man calmly sauntered down the street, weaving in and out of the line of stalled cars, carrying a toilet upside down on his head. On the other side, a teenage boy walked toward us wearing a T-shirt proclaiming in English "I'm po', but I'm stupid."

"What a colorful place," I remarked to Moussa. But Moussa was in no mood to be amused by our circumstances. It was hot and stifling in the car, and we were going nowhere fast. He spoke sharply to the driver.

"Well, I should have gone the other way," Siddiqi said. "This is going to take forever."

"Just when it's time to go to bed isn't the time to say you're hungry," Moussa retorted in Bambara, using an angry tone.

"What did you say?" I asked Moussa, not understanding the Bambara phrases. He translated, but it still made no sense to me. "What is that supposed to mean?" I asked.

"It's a typical Bambara proverb. It means that he should have planned ahead. He knows it's Friday, and almost noon. He should have turned left just after we came across the bridge, to avoid this mess," Moussa explained.

"But I still don't understand. What's that got to do with being hungry right before bedtime?" I asked.

"You have to plan ahead if you want to eat right before bedtime, since it takes a long time to cook millet or rice. You can't wait until the last minute and then say you're hungry. It's too late then, so you might as well keep quiet," he answered.

"Oh yeah. I see what you mean now," I said. "That proverb wouldn't make any sense in the United States, though."

"No? Why not?"

"Well, the part about planning ahead is good advice, as is the admonition not to complain if you get stuck in a bad situation because of your own poor planning. We might say "Don't be penny-wise but pound-foolish," or "You made your bed, now lie in it." But the part about the food doesn't work."

"Why not?" Moussa asked again.

"Because in the U.S., if I want to eat something right before bedtime, I just raid the refrigerator. I eat a dish of Blue Bell ice cream, or a bowl of cereal and milk. Or I heat up some leftovers in the microwave. I might even call out for a pepperoni and mushroom pizza. We have lots of yummy things to eat that can be ready at a moment's notice. We don't have to plan ahead."

"Ah yes . . . pizza," Moussa said, a dreamy look coming over his face. "I remember pizza. And all the restaurants in New York City that were open late at night."

"America, the Land of the Midnight Snack," I quipped, reaching through the window to open the door from the outside and climbing out. "Let's get out of here, Moussa. We can walk quicker than this." I paid Siddiqi for his trouble, and we left him sweltering in his cab.

We found a small video rental establishment near the Embassy with a functioning, state-of-the-art photocopy machine, and negotiated a good rate with the proprietor, behind closed doors. Normally, only the boss operated the photocopy machine, so it took more discussion before he was convinced that I could be trusted with his rare, expensive, almost mystical machine. The other employees watched in amazement as I rapidly copied and collated my forms. They were impressed with my obvious expertise. I even knew how to add paper!

We completed our shopping, and I sent Moussa off in a taxi with the groceries. I stayed behind in Bamako, because I wanted to pay a visit to a friend. Sue Hammerton, a nurse from Rochester, New York, was in Bamako temporarily as part of the Sister Cities Program, conducting training sessions for health clinic workers in Bamako. We had become good friends, and for several weeks we met on Friday afternoons to make cookies at the Protestant Mission, where she was staying (cheap rates, clean rooms, "No Card Playing Allowed"). The kitchen at the mission guesthouse had an oven, an amenity I had sorely missed. We made peanut butter cookies and sat in the common room talking about our work, commiserating about the difficulties of accomplishing anything through the official bureaucratic maze of the Malian Ministry of Health. Sue was a kindred spirit, and our therapy sessions of cookie baking and complaining did much to make the time after Steven's departure bearable.

Before leaving to go north, I made a special trip to Magnambougou to visit Ami, a little six-year-old imp of a child whose bright spirit had captured my heart the first time I laid eyes on her. Ami belonged to a double compound of Dogon people who lived near Moussa's house. Her mother and oldest sister had been part of my research years before. I had always felt sorry for Ami's mother, a young woman who had had more than her fair share of heartache, even for a woman of Mali. Her best efforts to make sure that her children got enough food to eat and stayed healthy were to no avail. Her first child, a tall, sober girl, had been part of my dissertation study, and one of the better-growing children. Her second child had serious birth defects, including "deformed genitals" (according to clinic records), and no arms. She was deeply ashamed of him, assuming that she had done something wrong to cause his problems. He was seldom brought out of the house, but he was loved and cared for. When I revisited the compound in 1989, I was told that the girl had died of malaria, and the boy of measles, some years before.

The third child was Ami, and the fourth was a girl about one year of age who had hydrocephaly. Hydrocephaly is caused by a failure of the spinal fluid to drain properly from the brain, causing increased cranial pressure and abnormal growth of the bones of the head. Untreated, it leads to mental retardation and early death. I gasped the first time Ami's mother turned around, and I saw the child she had strapped there. The girl's head was three or four times normal size, and she couldn't hold it up by herself. In the United States, surgery can often successfully relieve the intracranial pressure, harmlessly draining the excess spinal fluid through a shunt into the abdominal cavity. In Mali, there was no treatment.

In some ways, Ami made up for her mother's other sorrows. Ami was carefree and energetic, sassy and bold. She wasn't afraid of the toubab. When she heard my voice, she would come running to the door of the compound and sashay out, extending her hand to shake mine, inquiring "*ça va? ça va, toubabou?*" I can still hear her mocking voice and see the tilt of her head as she asked me what I had brought her that day, her hands darting into my pockets, checking out my bag. She once told me I should give her money to buy macaroni in the market. I was happy to oblige and got into the habit of carrying small change so I could give her "macaroni money" whenever I saw her. She would respond with extravagant graciousness: "*Merci! Oui, merci beaucoup, toubabou.*"

I often made a point of passing by her house after visiting Daouda at the Fat Lady's compound, to lift my spirits. Ami was my antidote to depression. I teased her that I would take her away from her mother, to live with me, and she replied that she just needed a few minutes to pack her bag. I suggested that when it came time to go to sleep at night, she would cry, but she assured me that she wouldn't. "You wait and see. I'll sleep for you, all night long. I won't cry. Not me! You can take me home for good!"

Ami was so full of life. Her exuberant charm was an affirmation that the human spirit can survive and triumph even in the most difficult of circumstances. My last image of Ami, the one I will always carry in my heart, is of a small child, all smiling face and waving arms, bursting with affection and goodwill, undaunted.

12

Dancing Skeletons

For a moment of night we have a glimpse of ourselves and of our world islanded in its stream of stars—pilgrims of mortality, voyaging between horizons across the eternal seas of space and time.—Henry Beston

We clattered down the rickety stairs and turned the corner of the building. Once we were well out of earshot, we turned to each other and blurted out simultaneously, "Did you see his arms?"

"His upper arms were much too short! His short sleeve shirt hung down below his elbows!" Claudia said.

"When he crossed his arms, they were right below his chin!" I added. "What could cause that?"

"I don't know," she replied. "Some obscure genetic syndrome, perhaps? The rest of him looked fine."

I was in the river-port town of Segou, with Claudia Parvanta, a nutritional anthropologist who worked for the Academy for Educational Development (AED). We were on our way to Macina, in northern Mali, as ethnographic consultants for a vitamin A deficiency project funded by AED. The project was being logistically supported by CARE, which has an extensive health project in the rural villages across the river from the administrative center of Macina. We had stopped in Segou to stock up on fresh fruits and vegetables, coffee, powdered milk, meat, and toilet paper and had just finished a quick visit to the headquarters of a UNICEF nutrition project.

"You realize that only a physical anthropologist would even notice something like that," Claudia pointed out.

"Yes. We see the world through a glass strangely," I commented. Claudia just laughed.

Physical anthropologists, at least those of us who study variation in living human populations, see the world from a distinctly different perspective than normal folks, even other anthropologists. Without conscious intent, we always note a person's physical appearance—not just the apparent characteristics that our society teaches us are important, like skin color, facial shape, and weight-for-height, but a myriad of other, more subtle variations that nonphysical anthropologists probably never notice: this man's legs are too long for his body; that woman has a perfectly symmetrical face; this person has a sloping forehead just like a *Homo erectus*, that one has brow ridges that would fit a Neanderthal; this student's tiny round ears proclaim his West African ancestry as much as (if not more than) the shade of his skin, that one has a face like an Aztec.

This way of seeing is both a blessing and a curse. In my line of work, it means that I can look at a child and make a quick assessment of his or her nutritional status on the spot. In northern Mali, I could sweep my eyes across a line of children who had run out from a village to crowd around the CARE truck and immediately get a feel for the level of malnutrition in the village. Without recourse to measuring tape or anthropometer, I could spot the children with marasmus, kwashiorkor, or goiters. The flip side, though, is that there's no way to turn off this ability, to just see what other people see, to not be struck by the physical condition of the people who surround you. A most dramatic example of this came near the end of my research in Macina.

A haze of dust hung in the air, whipped up by the hot dry winds blowing off the Sahara. The sun was a golden orb, faintly visible, climbing up from the eastern horizon. Huge tents had been erected on the outskirts of the village, forming three sides of a large rectangle. Under one tent sat the dignitaries—CARE administrative personnel, the regional medical director, a number of health clinic workers, the CARE animatrices, as well as village elders, and two anthropologists. Pennants fluttered in the breeze. Several hundred villagers were massed under the other tents, women and children in their finery spilling out around the edges, forming bright splotches of color against the monochrome sandy brown of country-side, village walls, and sky. To the east, people lined the road heading out of the village. Far away, across the flat, tawny plain, a plume of dust announced the arrival of another CARE vehicle, bringing people from other villages in the region. A cry rose up from the crowd and hovered in the air. Women danced in place, and men waved as another Land Rover approached, stopping briefly to disgorge its passengers before heading out to pick up more.

The occasion was the graduation of several of the CARE villages into "self-sufficient" status. In the villages surrounding Macina, the CARE projects focused on sanitation and illness prevention. They began in each village with wells to provide sanitary drinking water. With the cooperation, economic contributions, and physical help of the local people, CARE personnel built concrete-lined and capped wells, surrounded by concrete block fences to keep out the goats. According to CARE philosophy, safe, clean, drinking water was a prerequisite for health improvements. Once a village had a well, it could also start dry-season gardens to raise vegetables to supplement the meager diet of millet and dried baobab leaf sauce. Water was the cornerstone of the CARE project in the region, but the group also provided tetanus immunizations for pregnant women (if you immunize the woman against tetanus, it also protects the newborn) and immunizations against all the usual childhood diseases for children. Other projects included village sanitation (to keep the streets and common areas clean of goat manure, food debris, and other refuse that attracted flies), household sanitation (to keep each family compound clean), birth hygiene (giving birth on a mat instead of the ground; using a new razor blade to cut the umbilical cord, instead of whatever sharp object was handy; putting alcohol on the umbilical stump, instead of the traditional practice of daubing it with cow manure), and the use of homemade oral rehydration solution (ORS) as a treatment for childhood diarrhea.

Each village, with the help of the CARE animatrice assigned to it, had formed a Village Health Committee, a group of influential men and women who would continue the education and community action programs after CARE was gone. Over the course of a year, the village would be weaned from the technical advice and motivating presence of the animatrice. She would visit once every two weeks, then once a month, then once every three months. Finally, the village would be declared independent, and the animatrice would be assigned a "virgin village" and begin the process anew.

A number of villages had just been declared independent, and CARE was hosting a celebration at one of them. There would be formal speeches by the dignitaries, music, stand-up comedians, masked dancers, feasting, and visiting. The mood was festive, self-congratulatory, and very optimistic.

Claudia and I had taken the day off from our research project on vitamin A deficiency to join the party. We sat in the front row with the CARE animatrices. A young girl climbed up onto my lap. She gazed at my face, her wise eyes rounded in amazement, and entwined her fingers in my straight brown hair. A group of some 20 children had gathered in front of the place where the notables

Anthropologist Claudia Parvanta and CARE health workers watch the festivities at the CARE independence celebrations at Kene.

were sitting. They were dressed in their holiday best, faces scrubbed, the girls' hair plaited into neat rows. They stood expectantly, waiting. On one side of the open area, three drummers appeared. They lined up in a row and began to play, hands flying, heads tilted back, eyes closed. Each seemed oblivious of the others. At first the rhythm was choppy, but then it settled into a complex and lively beat, and the children began to dance.

As I watched the children dance, the oddest feeling came over me. Goose bumps rose along my arms, and the hair stood up on the back of my neck. "What's wrong with this picture?" Suddenly, it dawned on me. The children—dancing with abandon, smiles on their faces—looked like dancing skeletons. They were the living embodiment of Camille Saint-Saëns's "Dance Macabre." They were the warrior skeletons from Ray Harryhausen's film Jason and the Argonauts—dancing, instead of fighting. They flung their arms and legs about like kindling, knees and elbows jutting out of painfully thin arms and legs like knots in the wood. On the boys, naked from the waist up, I could count every rib, see the outline of clavicle and sternum in front, scapulae and vertebrae in back. Even their faces were haunting—a thin veneer of skin stretched tight over zygomatic arches, the outline of skulls and jaws visible for all to see. Yet bright eyes blazed, and there seemed to be no end to their energy as they danced.

I watched as long as I could (only a few minutes), then disentangled the little girl's fingers from my hair and set her down on the ground. I stood up, transfixed by the sight in front of me. Dancing skeletons.

I fled, in anger and horror, pushing my way past the dignified government men in their immaculate blue boubous, past the CARE personnel, whose faces registered puzzlement and annoyance. I left chairs overturned in my wake. Hot tears coursed down my cheeks, and I refused to acknowledge Claudia's shouted questions. Once free of the tent, I strode off around the edge of the village to the west, following the outer walls as they curved in upon themselves until I was out of sight of the tents. I walked and walked, past groups of startled women who were bathing and washing clothes by a well, past a knot of young boys herding goats. I mumbled a few words of greetings in Bambara and stalked on.

Eventually, I reached the far side of the village. My anger subsided, and I took a few moments to breathe deeply and compose myself before sitting down under a tree. I must have sat there for twenty minutes or so, trying to purge the image of those children from my mind. I focused on a grove of mangoes in the middle distance. Before long, my natural curiosity overcame me. I wanted to talk to the people who lived here. I rose and entered the back side of the village through a narrow passage in the high wall.

At first, I was disappointed, because almost no one was at home. Most people were taking part in the celebrations. However, wandering around the nearly deserted village gave me an unprecedented opportunity to examine and reflect on the villagers' "stuff," the material aspects of their culture. I studied the design of the village, the seemingly random layout of the narrow twisting alleyways, the walls surrounding most compounds. I noted the arrangement of sleeping and cooking rooms within each compound, the way the living spaces were demarcated and divided, decorated and defined.

I tried to imagine what would be left for an archeologist to find several hundred years after the village had been deserted. Not much. The mud bricks of huts and surrounding walls would dissolve, melting away under the forces of rain and wind. Thatched roofs would collapse and rot, along with baskets and leather goods. Wooden stools, dolls, and masks would disappear, gourds would decay. Perhaps some of the massive millet-pounding mortars, hewn from thick logs, would survive. Maybe a wooden pounding stick or two. A few imported iron utensils, spoons and such, some Chinese enamel basins, potsherds from the large vessels used to hold drinking water, ashes from cooking fires, occasional fish and goat bones, pollen grains. Not a lot from which to reconstruct the vibrant and complicated life people led here—no masks danced in honor of *chi wara*, the antelope-man who taught the Bambara how to till the land, no puppets, no lion costumes, no woven mats to keep out the sun, no amulets to protect babies. Little that would tell of the laughter, the hopes and dreams, the friendships, the disappointments, the keening sorrows, the rhythms of the days and the seasons.

For over an hour I wandered aimlessly, stopping to talk to those few villagers, all women with young infants, who had remained at home. Some were rendered speechless, at first, by the site of a lone white woman appearing unannounced at their doorway, but all welcomed me warmly, and let me sit and hold their babies. I told them about my children. They fed me lunch, millet toh with dried baobab leaf sauce, of course, and cool clear water to drink.

When the sun, still just a bright spot in the sky, had passed far to the west, I returned to where the CARE Land Rovers were parked in a grove of trees and waited. As we zigzagged across the countryside, dropping off chiefs from surrounding villages, Claudia broke the long and uncomfortable silence.

"Did somebody say something that upset you?" she asked.

"No," I replied. "It was the kids. I couldn't stand watching them dance."

"What do you mean? What was the matter with the kids dancing?" she wondered.

"Did you look at them? I mean *really* look at them? Their little arms and legs were like sticks! I wanted to rush out and tell them all to sit down, to conserve their energy, to save it for growth or fighting off disease. How can they dance, when they're so malnourished?" I wondered.

One of the CARE administrators broke in, indignantly. "Are you saying that we haven't accomplished a lot in these villages?" he demanded. "The CARE villages are much cleaner than they used to be, and cleaner than those that haven't been part of the program. The infant mortality rate is one of the lowest in the country, and we have the country's highest coverage rate for immunizations also."

"No, I'm not saying that. The work you've done so far is excellent, as far as it goes. But without a major push in terms of improving nutritional status, what difference will it make—for the kids and for the village—in the long run?" I asked.

"What do you mean?" he asked, warily.

"OK. Look at it this way," I explained. "Kids used to die here of neonatal tetanus, right? When they were only a few weeks old. Some of them survived the neonatal period only to die of measles or diarrhea when they were one or two years old. Many children died of diarrhea from drinking contaminated water and because no one knew about oral rehydration solution. Now the kids don't die of tetanus or measles, because of the immunization program. They don't die of diarrhea because of the wells and the ORS program. Instead, they die of lingering malnutrition when they're three or four, or five or six years old. Is this really an improvement? Where is the benefit? You have more kids surviving, but the nutritional status of the kids in that village was among the worst I've ever seen! They'll eventually die from their malnutrition. If they manage to survive, they'll be permanently affected, both physically and mentally. They looked like dancing skeletons. It made me sick to my stomach. I'm sorry, but it did."

"They didn't look that bad to me," he protested, turning to Claudia for confirmation. "I didn't notice anything unusual about them."

"You aren't looking through the eyes of a physical anthropologist," I pointed out.

"They did look pretty bad," Claudia conceded. "Worse than many we've seen. That's why you need our nutrition education program!" she added brightly.

"Are you saying we should have been concentrating on improving nutritional status instead of, say, immunizations? Then we could have our well-nourished children die of measles?" he inquired archly.

"Aye, there's the rub!" I exclaimed, triumphantly. "Well-nourished children don't die of the measles! They still get it, but they're only mildly sick, for a few days instead of months, and they don't die. Just as children who have sufficient vitamin A in their diets don't die so much from respiratory infections, or from diarrhea either."

"Don't get me wrong," I continued. "I'm not saying you should stop what you're doing already, I'm just saying it's not enough. If you pour all these resources into keeping kids alive, without following up on their long-term health through more extensive gardening projects and nutrition education programs, then you're just wasting everyone's time, money, and energy."

"Well, we're cooperating with this vitamin A project, aren't we?" he demanded.

"Yes, but vitamin A deficiency isn't the only problem here," I said. "These people have very little to eat. Millet and dried baobab leaf sauce, day after day. They have almost no variety, and not much to give the little kids. Even where they grow carrots in the

CARE gardens, only the adults eat them. They think little kids can't eat them because they have no teeth. You've built wells, convinced people to grow gardens, and introduced carrots as a good source of vitamin A. The people have gone along with all your changes. They like carrots! But no one ever thought to tell the people that carrots can be added to the sauce, or cooked by themselves and mashed up for little kids. We only discovered that through our interviewing. And no matter what subject we tried to explore, within five minutes people were talking about the droughts and the dam, and how there used to be so many more trees, and so much more food to eat. In the Bozo villages they only wanted to talk about how their lakes had dried up and there were no more fish. One woman said her four-year-old son saw a fresh fish in the big weekly market in Macina and asked her if it was a mouse. She cried, because her son didn't know what a fish looked like. How could he be a true Bozo without any fish? And the Bozo detest being millet farmers. They're not very good at it, and they consider it beneath them. This part of the country is a mess."

"What do you suggest?" he asked.

"Oh, I don't know," I sighed, turning my face to the window. "How about a massive airlift to Oklahoma?"

In the distance, villages appeared at irregular intervals, perched atop their accumulated mounds of dirt and debris, rising out of the plain like islands. Each village had its own mosque, a humble yet somehow noble creation of mud brick, with crenelated ramparts reminiscent of a medieval castle. We were driving through desolate country. Once a relatively lush open-forest savannah, the trees had died from lack of water, though most were still standing. The droughts of 1974–75 and 1984–85 had hit the area hard, and the river no longer flooded its banks, thanks in part to a hydroelectric dam built far upstream to provide electricity to the capital city. Without the annual flood of the river to sustain them, most of the trees had died. A bizarre landscape, a forest of dead trees, the life sucked out of them. It looked as though someone had invented a kind of neutron bomb that only killed plants. Blasted. Scorched earth. We passed a huge tree that had been split asunder by lighting, its hollow heart exposed. Thousands of termite mounds sprouted from the sand like a miniature forest of toadstools, like little hobbit villages. Termites flourish on dead wood.

Only the majestic baobabs survived, silent sentinels standing watch, protecting the villagers and the land. Traditional Bambara religious beliefs can be described as animistic—believing that spirits inhabit natural objects such as trees and animals, as well as places such as springs, rivers, and mountaintops. It was easy for me to believe, as they did, that giant old baobabs are inhabited by

Tall grass and verdant trees reflect the comparatively lush environment of villages in Dogo Arrondissement, in southern Mali.

The hot sun beats down on a village in comparatively arid northern Mali. The young trees in the center are protected with brush cages from the ever-present goats.

powerful spirits. I nodded to them, in greeting, as we passed.

My brief research in the villages around Macina only served to confirm what I already knew. Mali, like almost every other country in Africa, was a hodgepodge of environments and ethnic groups, artificially thrown together into one nation by European colonizers at the end of the nineteenth century. An amalgam of people speaking hundreds of distinct languages, with diverse cultural adaptations, facing vastly different problems in different regions of the country. How could a coherent nutrition plan for the whole country be devised? Did it even make sense? And how could one hope to understand the problems facing people without living among them for years, experiencing their lives, learning to see through their eyes?

Would our whirlwind survey of vitamin A deficiency in Macina mean anything? We had found out that the main problem with night blindness (the first outward manifestation of vitamin A deficiency) was among pregnant women, not young children, as expected. It was so prevalent among pregnant women, in fact, that they regarded it as a normal part of pregnancy. When we explained that it was a nutritional problem that could be prevented and cured by eating more of specific foods, they were very interested and said they would try our suggestions, when possible. But then, invariably, they asked, "And what foods do you suggest we eat to avoid morning sickness?" To this eminently logical question, we had no answer.

Also, we had found out that the traditional cure for night blindness was eating a piece of roasted goat liver. Animal liver is, of course, an excellent source of vitamin A, but the villagers had no way of knowing this, at least not by Western, scientific standards. How had this efficacious traditional cure been developed? And what were we to make of the beliefs surrounding the consumption of liver as a cure for night blindness? Before the patient could consume the liver, it was first thrown into a dark room, and the patient had to crawl around on hands and knees searching for it. If she didn't find it, then she couldn't eat it.

Finally, we had discovered that vitamin A capsules were available in the local markets (if you knew how to ask for them) and that many people knew that they were a cure for night blindness. Did it make any sense to promote the cultivation and consumption of vitamin A-rich foods in this desolate and forbidding landscape, when capsules were available?

We had accomplished a lot in a very short time. At the same time, I realized that I could never know Macina the way I knew Magnambougou, where I had spent more than two and a half years of my life. Chances are that I will never return to Macina, but in my mind's eye, the skeletons dance on.

13

Mother Love and Child Death

> The 72 women reported a staggering 686 pregnancies and 251 childhood deaths (birth to 5 years). The average woman (speaking statistically) experienced 9.5 pregnancies, 1.4 miscarriages, abortions, or stillbirths, and 3.5 deaths of children. She has 4.5 living children. [When a baby dies] Alto children form the funeral procession. In this way they are socialized to accept as natural and commonplace the burial of siblings and playmates; as later, perhaps they will have to bury their own children and grandchildren.
>
> —Nancy Scheper-Hughes (1987)

I sat on a hard wooden chair next to the narrow hospital bed, holding my daughter's hand, watching the slow rise and fall of her chest. The IV tube snaked down from above and entered at the crook of her arm. Its steady drip, of saline solution and Quinimax, provided little comfort. Miranda lay, unmoving, beneath a crisp white sheet. Beads of sweat appeared on her forehead, coalesced into large drops, and sluiced down into her hair. I leaned my head on the edge of the bed and moaned. "Please God, don't let her die." I repeated the phrase over and over. "Please God, don't let her die."

Even as I pleaded, bargained, for my child's life, I was acutely aware of the irony of my request. Here we were, in Mali, where nearly every adult woman had lost several children to early deaths, and I was asking God to exempt me from the loss of even one of my children. "Make an exception for me, God. Remember that I'm an American. We're not used to losing our children." How could I ask God for this special favor, when pain and death surrounded me, just outside the whitewashed walls of the American Embassy compound? Why should God listen to my plea, in the midst of all that suffering? How did I dare to ask more from God for myself than for the women I studied? "I know it's not fair of me to ask, but I ask anyway. Please God, don't let Miranda die."

It all began on a Sunday afternoon in November, when Linda, from the Embassy, had brought Miranda home after a pool party. Linda often entertained the American children whose parents worked for the Embassy or A.I.D. She told me that Miranda had spent the afternoon lying down inside the house, while the other kids went swimming and ate cake and ice cream. Linda was so worried about Miranda's lethargy and high fever that she took her by the Embassy on the way home, called the doctor to come in, and had a blood sample drawn to test for malaria. He sent her home with some erythromycin and Tylenol, saying it was probably just a virus.

Miranda slept through the night, and the next day she seemed better. She ate an egg for breakfast and asked for macaroni and cheese for lunch. Tuesday morning the guard from the adjacent American School came over to tell me that a radio message had come from the doctor—Miranda had malaria. We had been faithfully taking both our chloroquine and our paludrine antimalarial pills. Between the two of them, they were supposed to take care of "garden-variety" malarial protozoans, as well as the chloroquine-resistant strains that had evolved in areas of high chloroquine use.

Tom gave us a lift to the Embassy, and the doctor took another blood sample for testing and gave Miranda three large orange tablets of Fancidar to swallow. Fancidar can itself be fatal to people who are allergic to sulfa drugs, but it was the treatment of choice. Miranda wasn't able to keep the Fancidar down, so the doctor told me to put her on an intensive schedule of the same chloroquine tablets we had been taking for prophylaxis. I took Miranda home in a taxi and spent the day watching her fever climb—102, 103, 104, 105. She slept fitfully, her body racked with the cyclical fever and chills of malaria, as well as the less well known but entirely typical symptoms of headache, vomiting, and diarrhea.

I immersed her in the bathtub, but she radiated so much heat that she made the tepid water hotter, rather than its bringing her temperature down. I added ice cubes to the bath water but quickly exhausted the meager capacity of our tiny Polish refrigerator. I steadied her head while dry heaves shook her body. She lost weight, literally before my eyes, as the fever burned up her body, melting away the pounds. Her forearms took on a sharp, angular appearance, and her eyes appeared ever larger in her face.

I made her take three chloroquine tablets, then three more a few

While we measured people in the village of Siramana, Miranda amused herself by playing with a baby pygmy goat.

hours later. I tried to get liquids into her, but they came right back up. We waited for the chloroquine to work. Tuesday night she slept on the floor in Tom's air-conditioned room, while I sat beside her, sponging her face with wet cloths. Wednesday morning I had trouble rousing her from sleep, and it was obvious that the chloroquine tablets weren't working. Tom took us back to the Embassy.

The previous day's sample showed no change in the malaria count. The doctor took yet another vial. Then he gave her a shot of chloroquine in the buttocks. "Let's try this," he suggested. "Take her home and keep her cool."

Thursday morning she was no better, and she was becoming seriously dehydrated. We had to get back to the doctor, but Tom was away on a trip, so we had to walk from our house to the main road. Miranda stumbled often and wanted to sit down, but I made her keep going. We were able to catch a bache across the bridge, but I carried her from the bache park to the Embassy, a distance of several miles through the noisy, crowded, garbage-strewn streets of downtown Bamako.

As I walked toward the Embassy, awkwardly trying not to drop her, people would call out, teasing, "You shouldn't be carrying that child! She's a big girl. Make her walk!"

"*A man kene. Sumaiya b'a la,*" I explained. "She's sick. She has malaria." The teasing stopped, replaced by litanies of Islamic blessings.

"Her blood is still swimming with malarial parasites," the doctor reported. "I've never seen anything like it. The only other thing I know to try is Quinimax. We need to set up an intravenous line anyway, to get her rehydrated. We can administer the Quinimax in the IV, directly into her veins. If that doesn't knock the little buggers out, then nothing will. It's her only chance."

My confidence in the doctor was shaky, to say the least. He was new in country, a gynecologist by training, and Miranda's was the first case of malaria he had treated. But I had no other options, except to have her medically evacuated to France. I hoped it wouldn't come to that.

During the long, hot afternoon, the ghosts of Kay and Mickey flitted around the edges of the room. I thought about all those women I had talked with in rural villages in the region of Macina. As part of the vitamin A research, I had conducted interviews with older mothers about their reproductive histories, asking them to tell me how many children they had given birth to, how many had died, how old they were when they died, and what they died of.

Again and again, I was staggered by the extent of loss and suffering these women had experienced.

In the village of Touara, I spoke with Safiatou Dombele, who had lost three of ten children.

"I'd like to ask you some questions about your children," I explained to the middle-aged woman.

"OK," she replied.

We were sitting off to one side of a spacious room in which six mortars were arranged haphazardly. All morning long, women had filtered in to pound their day's ration of millet into flour, to share the work, and to enjoy the social interaction of talking with their neighbors. At each mortar, several women clustered around, pounding in complicated rhythms. When the wooden pestles hit the mound of grain, the tiny millet seeds flew up to the edges of the mortar, but very few spilled over. Every so often, a woman would throw her pestle up into the air and clap her hands before catching it in midflight, without missing a beat. Laughter and excited voices filled the room, echoing off the high ceiling. The thatched roof was supported at intervals by forked tree trunks set atop large rocks.

Young children clung to their mothers' legs, peering out at me with impish grins on their faces. Many women had babies tied onto their backs with lengths of brightly colored cloth, their heads lolling back and forth. The babies were rocked to sleep by the powerful and familiar rhythms of the millet pounding. The room had two open doorways, set in opposite walls, and the room itself formed part of the network of trails through the village. Many people passed through on their way from one part of the village to another. Thousands and thousands of feet had ground the dirt floor between the doorways into a powder-filled trench some eight inches lower than the floor on either side. I adjusted my seat on the low wooden stool and proceeded with my questions about this woman's reproductive history.

"How many pregnancies have you had?" I asked the woman. She looked down at the wiggling toddler sprawled across her lap. "This is my tenth child," she responded quietly, patting the child gently on its naked bottom and fingering the amulets that hung from a string around his neck. "His name is Oumarou."

"Let's start with your very first child. I want to know the sex and age of each child, and if the child has died, I would like you to tell me how old the child was when he or she died and what you think the cause of death was. If you don't want to answer these questions, or if you want to stop at any time, just let me know."

She nodded her head, looked off into the distance, and began to speak in a low voice. Three of her children had died. The first, a daughter, died when she was two years old.

"What did she die of?" I prompted.

"I don't know," she replied.

"Well, I mean, did she die from an accident? Did she fall and hit her head? Or was she sick before she died? What kind of symptoms did she have? Diarrhea? Fever?" I probed for a response.

"I don't know," she repeated. "She wasn't here when she died. They just told me she died, they didn't say from what."

"Who told you she died? Where was she?" I asked, somewhat confused.

"When I became pregnant the second time, my husband sent her to live with her grandparents in Djenné. Her grandmother wanted her to live with them, to keep them company. She was only two years old," she explained. "The next year, they sent word that she had died. My second child was a boy. He died after only four days."

"OK," I sighed. "Do you know what he died of?"

"Well, he had a high fever, and convulsions. His back would arch and his fists would close up. When that happens, you know the child is going to die."

"Sounds like neonatal tetanus," I murmured to Moussa. The traditional treatment of the newly cut umbilical cord was to smear it with cow manure. The CARE health project's birth hygiene unit had had remarkable success eradicating that particular practice.

"So your first and second children died. You have had another child die?" I continued.

"Yes, my third and fourth children are still alive, but the fifth child died, when she was three years old," she answered.

"And what did this child die of, do you know?" I asked.

"Well, she had white stuff on her tongue and in her mouth, and a sore in her throat. We call it *kungolo chi*," she said.

I was writing fast and furiously, but stopped and looked up. "Moussa," I said, turning to him for translation help for the first time in an hour. "What is she saying? I've heard kungolo chi [literally, "cut head"] used to refer to the sunken fontanelle caused by severe dehydration, but a three-year-old shouldn't still have an open fontanelle. What does she mean 'a sore in her throat'?"

Moussa asked her to explain, listened for some time to a rapid flow of Bambara, then turned to me and translated.

"They have a disease here they call 'a sore in the throat.' Some people say it is the same as kungolo chi. When a baby has this disease it is almost always fatal. The sore in the throat pulls on the fontanel and causes it to sink down. The baby won't eat or drink and has diarrhea. Then it dies," Moussa explained.

"Is there any cure for this disease?" I asked.

The woman looked at me with an air of resignation. "You can

search for a traditional healer. She goes to the river and gets clam shells, then she pounds them up in a little mortar until they are like millet flour. Then she licks her finger, dips it in the shell dust, and reaches down into the baby's throat and rubs the sore with the clam shell dust. That can make it better sometimes, especially if the baby throws up, but it didn't work for my child. She got worse and worse and then she couldn't breathe anymore and she died on the fourth day. You can search and search for medicine, but if Allah decides it is time for the child to die, there isn't anything you can do. Many children used to die of this." Her voice cracked and she covered her face momentarily with her hands.

I hesitated. "They don't die of this anymore?"

"No, it seems to have gone away," she answered.

I turned and spoke to Moussa, thinking out loud. "I think I know what this is. She must be talking about diphtheria. It's caused by a virus, and it causes a membrane to grow across the back of the throat, choking the baby's air supply. The traditional cure probably worked at least some of the time, by rupturing the membrane before it could grow completely across. It's a horrid disease."

"I've heard of that. It's the D in the DPT vaccines," Moussa said.

"Exactly. That's why it's not so common anymore. The prevention part of the CARE health project includes vaccination against it. What about your other children?" I asked the woman.

Her son had grown quiet. She flipped him over and nestled him in her arms. He latched on to nurse, and soon fell asleep, his face buried in her breast. "My third child is still alive," she said. "She lives in Konkonkourou [a nearby village] and has two children of her own now."

"My fourth child is my son Mamadou. He is about sixteen years old now. Number six is Sibiri, he's twelve. Number seven is a daughter, Aminata. Number eight is my daughter Oumou. I had two miscarriages after her, then another daughter, Sali, and now Oumarou."

"So you've had ten children, seven of whom are still alive, plus two miscarriages?" I asked in confirmation.

"Oh, I've had more than those two miscarriages," she said, idly scratching designs in the dirt with a stick.

"How many?" I asked.

"I don't really know. I didn't count," she answered.

I had only a few more questions. She dislodged Oumarou from her breast and tied him, still sleeping, to her back. Then she hoisted her calabash full of millet flour onto her head and disappeared out the door, bending low to clear the lintel. Another woman came to take her place on the stool in front of me, handing her pestle to a young girl, who entered the rotation of pounding like a schoolgirl joining a jump rope game.

She had the look of a Fulani, with relatively light skin, a long straight nose, and beautiful large dark eyes. She sat staring at the ground, twisting her head-tie in her hands before retying it around her plaited hair. She had given birth to seven children, of whom the first four had died.

"Tell me about your first child," I prompted, after giving my usual spiel about the purpose of my questions.

"My first child was a girl," she started. "She died when she was two months old."

"What did she die of?" I asked.

"Malaria," she replied.

"What about your second child?"

"She died when she was one week old, of fever and convulsions," she said, trying to hold back tears.

"Neonatal tetanus again," I thought to myself. "And the third?" I asked.

"He died when he was about five. He had malaria and fever," she answered.

"What kind of symptoms did he have?" I inquired.

"He had malaria for a long time. Then he got funu bana."

"Would you describe funu bana to me?" I requested.

"He would swell up. His hands and feet would get big. And his stomach. It used to get huge. Then it would go down again. He didn't want to play anymore, and he stopped talking. Finally, he died. That was about a year ago," she added.

"Kwashiorkor," I wrote down on the interview form. "And the fourth?"

"She died when she was six days old, of fever and convulsions." Abruptly, she stood up and ran out the door, flip-flops flapping wildly, tears streaming down her face.

I felt like crying myself. The constantly repeated litany of children born and children died. It upset me just to listen to it. How could these women bear to live through it? I wrote down "neonatal tetanus" next to the fourth name.

The next day, in the village of Zambala, the story was much the same. One young woman had given birth to four children, all of whom had died before the age of six months, "of fever." Another, whose first child died during birth, saw the second die at two weeks; the seventh, eighth, ninth, tenth, and twelfth died like the first, during birth. She still had five children surviving, but seven had died. Yet another woman, whose first six children had died during their first year of life. She had only two surviving children, both now grown and moved away. Malaria, fever, cough, diarrhea, stomachache, headache, sore in the throat, kungolo chi, convulsions, funu bana, measles. Every woman had a story to tell, of heartache and sorrow, of children lost. And yet some women spoke of their profound losses with little expression of emotion.

"How can they stand it?" I asked Moussa later, as we headed back to Macina in the CARE Land Rover at the end of the day.

"Well," Moussa began, searching for a way to explain. "You have to realize that death is a fact of life here in Mali."

I smiled at his choice of words.

"I'm serious," he continued. "We all grow up knowing many people who die. Most of them are either very young or very old. Every person has experienced the death of numerous relatives, friends, and neighbors. We've all had siblings, especially younger siblings, as well as half-siblings, nieces and nephews, and cousins who have died. No one escapes. You never really get used to it, exactly, but you come to accept it, and even expect it. A woman expects that some of her children will die. Why should she be any different than her grandmother, her mother, her aunts, her sisters, her friends? You can't let the death of a child destroy your life."

"I never really thought of it that way, Moussa," I replied. "Although I've been told that among some tribes in Kenya, people say you can't really count a child until it has survived the measles."

"People say that here, too," Moussa said. "And people don't think about what will happen when their kids grow up. We can't plan ahead, or try to imagine what the child will be like, because we never know how long the child will live."

"You know, many of my students experience the death of a grandparent during their college years," I said. "As professors, we joke about the relationship between exams and convenient grandparental death. But often, it's not just an excuse to postpone an exam—the student's grandparent really has died. It's a matter of generation length; the grandparents are getting old, and some die. For most of these students, it is their first experience of death, and it devastates them."

"No one in Mali could grow to adulthood without having lost many friends and relatives," Moussa said.

"In the United States, the death of a child is considered just about the worst thing that can happen to a parent. There are even support groups you can join to help you deal with the loss," I explained.

"Here, everyone would belong," Moussa quipped, laughing.

"How can you laugh?" I admonished him.

"You have to laugh," he responded. "Otherwise you'd have to cry."

"Some of the women do cry. In some cases, it's been twenty or thirty years since these children have died, and the mothers have other grown children, even grandchildren, but they still choke up when they talk about the ones who died."

"That's true," Moussa agreed.

"I was puzzled by some of the women, though. For every one who was really upset, there was another who didn't seem to care much one way or the other. Or was I just misinterpreting them?" I asked.

"Well, in some places, it's not considered proper to express too much public grief over the death of a child, especially a very young infant," Moussa explained. "It's considered inappropriate to cry in public, for instance, even though everyone knows you are crying inside."

"Inside your heart, or inside your house?" I asked.

"Both," he replied. "Partly it's considered offensive to Allah, because people say he has made the choice to take the child back to Heaven, and you shouldn't mourn such a fate, because the child is with God," he said.

"Yeah, people say that in the U.S., too, but it always seemed of little comfort to me," I said.

"Do you think some mothers really don't care if their kids live or die?" he asked, skepticism apparent in his voice.

"Well," I hesitated. "You have to wonder. Most women here don't have any choice—about whether or not they marry, about whom they marry, when they have kids, or how many kids they have. More than a few women have told me they don't get along with their husbands and didn't want the kids they had. Do you remember the woman in Magnambougou with nine kids, who left her husband back in 1983?"

"Yes, I remember her," Moussa admitted. "She was secretly taking birth control pills so she wouldn't get pregnant again. Her brother posed as her husband so that she could get the pills. And when the youngest child was weaned, she left. But all her children had survived, and she certainly didn't neglect them. Except at the end, by leaving," he added weakly.

"The point is that she didn't want any more kids, she thought nine was plenty, but her husband wasn't satisfied. He wanted more. He even took a second, much younger wife, because he thought the first wife had gone through menopause, and that's why she didn't get pregnant again. That's also why he didn't try very hard to track her down. She wasn't of any use to him anymore. She had a choice, but only because her brother helped her. Most women don't have that option. They have to marry the man their parents pick out. Then they have to stay, even if they don't like their husband, and they have to keep on having children, even if they don't want to. It's hard for me to imagine being married to someone I didn't love, let alone going through pregnancy and childbirth, and then being expected to take care of a child I hadn't wanted in the first place.

But if I found myself in that situation, and then the child died, I don't think I'd be all that upset. It certainly couldn't compare to how I would feel if something happened to Miranda or Peter."

"So what's your point?" Moussa asked.

"All these malnourished children we see, or the dead ones we hear about during the life history interviews—they aren't all necessarily the cherished offspring of women who married for love and were able to choose when and how many children to have. Some of them, at least, must have been unwanted to begin with."

"Well, lots of women don't like their husbands, but don't all mothers just love their children, naturally?" Moussa asked.

"Some people think so," I replied. "And it's certainly an ideal image of motherhood in many cultures. But there's lots of cross-cultural evidence to refute the idea, including plenty of child neglect and abuse in the United States. Probably most of the apparent apathy we've seen toward child death comes from the combination of a woman's understandable expectations that some of her children will die, based on her own childhood experiences, and cultural sanctions against grieving in public. But not having any control over her reproductive life must contribute in some cases."

"Nobody talks about it, in the child survival literature," I pointed out. "One group argues that the main causes of child malnutrition and mortality in the Third World are either the absolute nonavailability of food, or poverty, the lack of money to purchase sufficient food. If food production is the problem, then genetically improved, higher-yielding strains of millet, rice, sorghum, or corn are the solution, or more pesticides, or herbicides, or fertilizers. If poverty is the problem, then income-generating programs and economic reforms are the solution.

"Another group argues that the main causes are ignorance and inappropriate cultural beliefs and practices. Ignorance in the sense of simple lack of knowledge, such as not understanding the relationship between food and health, or not understanding the critical importance of good nutrition during the first few years of a child's life. Thinking that quantity of food is more important than quality. It's certainly part of the problem here in Mali. Along with inappropriate cultural beliefs and practices, such as thinking that kids don't need to begin eating solid foods until they're nine or ten months old, even though breast milk alone really can't support adequate growth and good health after six months. Breast milk is still necessary for several years, but it's not sufficient by itself. Or the practice of letting the kids themselves decide when and how much they want to eat. If lack of knowledge and inappropriate cultural beliefs and practices are the problem, then nutrition education is the solution. Most of my writings have favored the

second group of factors, arguing that nutrition education is the key
to improving child health.

"But if part of the problem is women's lack of control over their
own bodies, rooted in the position of women within the traditional
social organization, then the solution becomes much more elusive,"
I concluded.

"I'll have to think about this for a while," Moussa answered.

We had reached the river's edge. The Land Rover could go no
further. The deaf pirogue poler and his son, under contract to CARE,
were waiting to pole us across to the other side. Palm fronds rattled
and clacked high above us. We clambered into the boat and fell
silent, bone weary, heart weary. A soft breeze blew across the river,
and gentle waves sloshed against the sides of the pirogue. It was
twilight, that brief interlude when the world that is rural Africa
seems to pause and take a deep breath—when the stinging heat of
day eases, when the blinding sun of day relents, giving way almost
immediately to darkness, when the copper sun sinks to earth and
the first stars of evening dance in the sky overhead.

I roused from my reverie to find the late afternoon sun slanting
in through the window. An entire day had passed. The IV continued
its slow drip into Miranda's arm. "What will I do if Miranda dies?"
I thought, stroking her forehead with the tips of my fingers. "She
won't. Don't think about it. You'll go crazy," I admonished myself.
"But what will I do?" I repeated again to myself. "How can I go back
home? How can I face Steven? What will my family and friends say?
That I sacrificed my daughter on the altar of my career? That I
didn't take good care of her? That I wasn't a good mother? That
I should never have left my family and taken her off to Mali in the
first place? Will Steven ever be able to forgive me?"

"I can't face him," I concluded. "I'll disappear. I'll go away and
live the rest of my life in a remote Bambara village, where no one
can find me. Great idea," I argued sarcastically against myself.
"Deprive your other child of a mother, too, and Steven of his wife
. . . But he won't *want* me back! Not if he blames me for Miranda's
death." The tears welled up again, and I gave in to them, crying
uncontrollably, shaking the bed with my sobs.

Miranda stirred and opened her eyes. She looked around the room
in confusion. "Where am I?" she inquired.

I looked up, daring to hope. "At the Embassy, in the doctor's
office," I explained. I watched her closely. "Do you remember
coming here this morning?"

"Not really," she admitted. "Can I have something to drink?"

"Yes, yes, of course!" I responded gratefully, jumping up, wiping
my face with my arm. "I'll go get you something from Ali Baba's.

I'll be right back."

I raced through the Embassy compound and across the street, returning with two bottles of Orange Crush that she drank thirstily.

"Those were great! I was really thirsty." Color had returned to her cheeks, and her eyes sparkled. "Why were you crying? Were you afraid I was going to die?" she teased.

"Yes! You've been really sick. How do you feel now?" I asked.

"I feel pretty good," she said. "Does that mean the malaria is gone?"

"We'll have to wait and see. They'll do another blood test to make sure, but I think we've turned the corner."

"Huh? Turned the corner?"

"Never mind. Just give me a hug," I said, climbing up on the bed, gathering her in my arms and whispering into her hair. I felt the ghosts of Kay and Mickey slip out the door. "Thank you. Thank you."

"Sure," she giggled. "No problem."

It was time to go home.

14

Postscript, 1993

It is better to light a single candle than sit and curse the darkness.

—Chinese proverb

Peter didn't recognize me when I got off the plane, and it took him about a month to fully accept me again. Today, I doubt that he remembers much about "Mommy and Miranda's trip to Mali." Sometimes I get the distinct impression he thinks we spent the entire six and a half months on the plane. He attends a regular first grade. He is learning to read, and works hard to keep close to his classmates in academic achievement.

Miranda has recovered fully from her chloroquine- and paludrine-resistant malaria. When we left Mali, she weighed only 65 pounds, 30 pounds less than when we arrived. She has made up that loss with pizzas and hamburgers and Blue Bell ice cream. Her brush with death has had no lasting effects, at least physically. I hope that in the years ahead, Miranda will come to realize the formative role that Mali played in her life. I hope that she will remember the material poverty and the spiritual bounty; the heaps of garbage in the capital city and the ineffable beauty of the rural villages; the tears and the laughter. I hope that she will keep all that she saw, all that she heard, all that she felt, in her memory forever. Above all, I hope she will appreciate the benefits that modern technology brings to her life, without forgetting the wonder and value of honest hard labor under the tropical sun. Every day I see evidence that she learned well the lessons Mali had to offer.

I returned to teaching and writing at Texas A&M. I continue to work with Freedom from Hunger on their programs in Dogo arrondissement. Bakary and his staff have formed a new organization, Centre d'Appui Nutritionnel et Economique aux Femmes (CANEF), supported by Freedom from Hunger, to focus solely on Credit with Education activities. I also continue my affiliation with the Academy for Educational Development in its health-care worker training program, and village nutrition communication projects in Mali. Little by little I analyze and publish the results of my Fulbright research in the scholarly anthropological journals. Despite the toll it takes on me emotionally, I can't imagine spending my time and energy on any other topic, anthropological or otherwise. Mali, and her people, continue to hold a fascination for me that I cannot explain.

In August of 1991, Steven and I became the parents of a third child, Alexander Logan Wolfgang Dettwyler, a little carbon copy of Miranda. He has been my constant companion during the writing of this book. I hope that someday he too will experience the wonders and the sorrows of the country that has meant so much to the rest of his family.

Moussa writes that he is fine, and that people are guardedly optimistic about the new government set up after the coup that deposed President Moussa Traore in the spring of 1991. He writes that the new bridge has been completed across the Niger River, and the old one we traversed on foot so many times has been closed for repairs. Moussa also writes that my lovely little friend Ami succumbed to malaria in the fall of 1990. He sends no news of Daouda.

Every morning, I rise before the sun and go outside to retrieve the newspaper. That quiet time, before the kids are awake, is my time to drink coffee, read the newspaper, and prepare for the coming day, which will be filled with the chaos of getting three people out the door to school or work, a baby to nurse, lectures to prepare and give, committee meetings to attend, students to counsel, meals to cook, errands to run, and writing to squeeze in somewhere.

Every morning, before I go back into the house, I turn to the east, toward the rising sun, and spend a few moments giving thanks for all that I have. The very least I can do in honor of all Malian women—who rise before the very same sun to face hours of millet pounding, water hauling, and firewood gathering, as well as an uncertain future for themselves and their children—is to appreciate all that I have. I can only hope that through my work I am able to light a single candle against the darkness that is malnutrition in Africa.

15

Q & A with the Author

The following questions originated in 2008 with students from Tori Saneda's introductory biological anthropology class at Cascadia Community College in Bothell, Washington. I was not able to visit Cascadia but responded by e-mail to questions submitted by students. These are typical of the questions I have received individually from students who have been assigned *Dancing Skeletons*, as well as audience questions when I give lectures at various campuses. These responses have been updated as of summer 2013. Feel free to send me your questions at kathyd@udel.edu.

What made you decide to be an anthropologist, and why did you choose to focus on traditional breastfeeding methods?

When I was in high school, my parents bought a copy of a Time-Life book, *Early Man*, and I was fascinated by the descriptions and visual images of human ancestors, the hominid fossils, etc. I liked biology best in high school (I didn't really understand that anthropology was its own discipline then) and majored in biology the first time I attempted college.

I dropped out of college (the University of California, Davis) the first time, in the fall of 1972. I was young (17, due to having skipped a grade in my early elementary years), and I was overwhelmed by all the work and studying required, because high school had been so easy for me. I was living at home, commuting to school, working almost full-time at a hamburger joint (Mel's Drive-In), and I got sick over Thanksgiving break. I ended up in the hospital and did not return to school.

A few months later, I got a job and moved out of the house, and after a year, while continuing to work full-time—as a civilian file clerk for the Sacramento Army Depot—I began taking night classes at the local junior college, American River College. I took a class from a professor, Dr. Jane Dabaghian, who had been recommended to me as a fantastic teacher by my high school friend, Kerry Whelehan Clifton. That semester, Dr. Dabaghian was teaching "Introduction to Cultural Anthropology" at night school, so that's what I took. She was amazing. The next semester I took the "Introduction to Physical Anthropology" class being offered at night, and we used the Time-Life book, *Early Man*, as one of the textbooks. I loved that class as well. The following year, I tried again going to university full-time at UC Davis. I was still a biology major but liked anthropology, so I kept taking classes in sequence—Intro to Archeology was next. Again, the professor, Dr. Delbert True, was great, so I kept taking classes from him, along with genetics and chemistry and zoology, more cultural and physical anthro courses, etc. Eventually, I just switched my major and earned a BS in anthropology.

When I "discovered" anthropology, it just felt like *home* to me. I understood it; it seemed easy and logical and incredibly interesting, and you could study just about anything and call it anthropology. I was fortunate to have some really, really great teachers, at American River College, at UC Davis, and in graduate school at Indiana University, Bloomington. These were scholars who were willing to discuss and argue and be passionate about things, but who always came back to those fundamental scientific questions of "What evidence do we have? What evidence do we still need? What questions have not yet been asked or not adequately answered?"

One of my professors at UC Davis, Dr. Henry McHenry, encouraged me to go to graduate school and earn a PhD and have a career in academic anthropology. When I was in graduate school, I originally planned to study paleopathology—diseases in ancient human populations as evidenced by the bones left behind. But then I met my husband Steven on the first day of graduate school (almost 36 years ago—yikes!!) and he was heading to Africa for his dissertation research. That sounded much more fun to me than studying skeletons on the fourth floor of Rawles Hall in Bloomington, so I switched my research focus to growth and development among living peoples. We originally had planned to do research among the Nuba of Kordofan Province in the southern Sudan (just east of Darfur). I was going to study the growth and development/nutrition/health of boys who were raised in the cattle camps and spent their childhoods training to be competitive wrestlers, compared to the growth and development, etc., of the boys who stayed in the agricultural villages and spent their childhoods *not* training to be wrestlers.

Suffice it to say that it turned out to be too difficult to get to the southern Sudan, and we ended up with our friends Barbara and Jerry Cashion in Mali, with no specific plans for research. The cultural context of wrestling versus nonwrestling was not relevant in Mali, nor were there major differences in diet between different groups of children. I had learned how to measure kids and I was interested in children's growth and health and more generally in the interactions between human biology and culture. I was nursing my daughter Miranda—she was 15 months old when we first got to Mali. I had participated in the Nestlé boycott back home (Nestlé aggressively marketed their baby formula) and was well aware of the serious negative health consequences of a shift away from breastfeeding to formula use. So I thought perhaps I could cobble together a research project looking at the consequences of the use of formula on children's growth and health in Mali. But then it turned out that practically no one used formula in Mali at the time, which was a very good thing! So instead, I just did a general ethnographic study of infant feeding and growth/health. It was really amazing to be immersed in a culture where everyone breastfed their kids for several years. OK. Enough for the first question!!

How many research topics did you think about before deciding on the one you did?

First, paleopathology of prehistoric Native Americans. Then the wrestling project in Sudan, then formula versus breastfeeding, then breastfeeding in general.

How long did it take you to write this ethnography?

Um, gosh. I don't really remember. I went to Mali a second time in 1989, from June through December. I started work on the book sometime within the next year, and I did a lot of the writing when Alexander was a baby, in 1991 and 1992. Maybe two years total? It went pretty fast. I had written very detailed letters to my husband throughout the 1989 research season, plus I kept a journal, and I'd been telling these stories to students; thus, much of it was already in good shape to be polished as prose. Remember, this was in the days before cell phones, e-mail, and Skype. Once I had the go-ahead from Tom Curtin, my editor at Waveland Press, I churned out chapters relatively quickly.

Have you been back in the field since *Dancing Skeletons* was published? If so, where? Have you revisited many of the children you once measured?

My last research trip to Mali was a very brief trip in the spring of 1990, before *Dancing Skeletons* (*DS*) was written. Once Alex was born, I didn't want to take him to Mali or leave him while he was nursing, and he nursed until he was five-and-a-half-years old. By that time, I was involved in research on evolutionary aspects of breastfeeding and weaning, and working with U.S. mothers who nursed beyond three years. Also, I didn't want my husband to have to take care of all three kids. As the years have gone by, I have not returned to Mali.

Do you keep in touch with any close contacts, such as Moussa, from your journey? If so, do you know if any major changes in lifestyle have occurred in those areas during the time that has passed?

I do not keep in direct contact with Moussa. I'm sure he still doesn't have a phone or Internet access, and no street address to send mail to. Over the years, I have connected him to a number of other anthropologists and health/nutrition researchers who have hired him to be their assistant/guide/translator/research assistant. As far as I know, the women I worked with do not have access to any means of communication—they could not read or write even in Bambara.

In many ways, Mali has done very, very well since the 1980s—at least until 2012. There was a coup in the early 1990s that overthrew the military dictatorship and established democracy. There has been *a lot* of economic development, including lots and lots of tourism money, and an exploding music scene, with a huge concert in the desert outside of Timbuktu every year—until the recent political troubles. I'm sure I would be amazed by all the changes. I expect life out in the villages goes on much as before, although I know that rural Peace Corps volunteers now have cell phones and Internet access. I provide some current information and statistics about maternal/child health in chapter 16, along with a very brief summary of the political unrest.

Seeing so much death, pain, and heartache in Mali, how did you deal with these things? What were your distancing strategies?

Certainly, I used humor—the absurdity of the inequalities I saw was just overwhelming at times. And I did what I could to help, when and where I could, always being aware that what I did might not be the right thing, in the long run. It was not easy.

What was the hardest part about collecting the data and how did you find a way into the culture? It seemed fairly easy from the reader's point of view, but I would imagine it's a lot harder!

Really the only hard parts about collecting the data were the long hours standing on my feet measuring people and having to constantly deal with people who were (rightfully) a little suspicious of just what we were up to. I was imposing on them—keeping them from their work, not really explaining to them why I was doing what I was doing. That was difficult. My original entry into the culture was made easier by the fact that I had my daughter Miranda with me, and she was a nursing baby, and I was studying nursing babies. I think it would have been much more difficult for me to do research on mothering and breastfeeding if I had not already been a mother myself—the women would not have given me much credibility.

And, honestly, I was an amusement to people—a diversion from their routine, someone different, and someone they could teach things to, since I knew nothing about how to behave properly in Bambara society. And I was interested in the women's ideas and views and opinions, something no outsider had ever been particularly interested in. The second time I went back, people were so happy to see me again, and so excited that I had returned, and thrilled to see Miranda again. In the rural areas, I always worked with other organizations (CARE, AMIPJ/Freedom from Hunger) that had already established relationships with the villagers and had projects underway. I don't think it would have been possible to just walk into any rural village and declare that I wanted to measure people and talk to them.

I know that there were some things like prices being higher for whites and the expectation that you wouldn't know anything about the customs or language, but all that aside, was there an issue with your ethnicity and did it prevent some people from allowing you to collect data?

Well, it was certainly a novel experience to be the only white person around (as I was much of the time). People would shout and point and make comments, and the kids would follow me around in packs chanting "Toubabu, toubabu." Also, most Malians automatically assume that all white people are French, and many of them are none too fond of their for-mer colonial masters. So I was treated rudely at first, a number of times, until I established that (1) I wasn't French, and (2) I spoke some Bambara, or at least tried to, something the French would never bother to do. Out in the remoter rural villages, some of the kids and teenagers would run and hide in the fields because they were terrified of the way we looked (we being me, Miranda, Heather, and others). Many of the younger kids in these villages had never seen a white person before and may not have even been told that people with such pale skins existed. So they would run off and hide. And of course, the adults thought it was amusing that the kids were afraid, so they would spin tall tales about us.

In the book you said, "this is my leper" while walking through the city. What does that mean? Why was that something you needed to explain to Heather, your assistant?

Ha. Well, there were so many beggars—lepers on one street corner, mothers of twins on the next block, "Smokin' Joe" outside the American Embassy. If you gave money to everyone, you'd soon be broke. If you gave money out randomly, then you would be hassled by every single person every time you walked by. But if you picked out one designated person—"Your leper"—and always gave money to that person each time you came by, but not to the others, then the others would respect that choice. They wouldn't ask you for money. So for each area where there were lots of beggars, you picked *one* to be *yours*. I can't remember now if Heather wanted to give money to all of them . . . but anyway, that's why I was explaining. Don't give money to just any leper—wait until you see your usual benefactee.

It was the same situation at the market—there were 30 women all sell-ing green beans along one row of the market. If you went to a different one each time, they'd all be hassling you and yelling at you to come to them. So you established a social relationship with one specific green bean seller, and you always bought from her. You made it your "custom" to return to her each time. That is where the word "customer" comes from. And she would be thrilled and give you a good price to keep you coming back, and the other bean sellers would be happy and friendly, but not harass you.

On page 19 of *Dancing Skeletons*, you mentioned the benefits of "moving back and forth between the two worlds of Malian village women and the community of United States expatriates. . . ." How-ever, I would like to know if you agree that there are some advantages to "living like the natives" or—on the flip side—that there are certain disadvantages to not doing so? Why or why not?

The problem with being all by yourself out in the back of beyond some-where—as most anthropological research used to be conducted—is that all too quickly things that at first seemed exotic and weird and interesting become commonplace. If you are immersed in the culture, you just start accepting everything people say and do as normal, typical, "of course," and taken for granted. So you cease to notice the differences—to remember that things didn't always seem so normal and boring.

Moving back and forth between my "Mother Culture" and the Malians kept reminding me of both worlds. And I could talk about my research to other Americans who weren't anthropologists, and their questions and comments would remind me of the outsider perspective that I would otherwise have quickly lost. They would comment on things that seemed perfectly obvious to me, because I had learned why people did them and would not have thought it necessary to explain or write down or comment on. I'm sure that when we were there the first time (1981–83), the fact that we lived in the big white house on the hill placed certain barriers between us and the villagers. They didn't know quite what to think of us. It was easier in the rural villages to live just like they did, sleep on the ground, eat with our hands, etc., and we got to see some things at night that otherwise I would not have been exposed to—like full-moon dancing and partying, and how quickly people went to bed/sleep once the sun went down if there was no moon. So there are advantages and disadvantages to both ways.

Of course today, no matter how remote, most anthropological researchers have access to e-mail, the Internet, and even Skype, so unless you make an effort to be cut off, you are no longer so isolated.

Do you ever look back and wish you would have done something differently while in Mali? If so, what?

There is really only one thing I would do differently. The first time I was there, in the early 1980s, I "intervened" in one family (a family that was not part of my dissertation study), who had a severely malnourished, mentally retarded child. This was before I had had my son Peter, who has Down syndrome. This boy was about three years of age, could not stand or walk or talk, and was subsisting solely on his mother's milk. I bought and made homemade formula for his mother to give him, as her milk supply was dwindling and he was losing weight. He got somewhat better on the formula and even started to eat solid food and was able to walk a little with assistance. However, his mother decided to wean him at that point, and soon after being weaned he died because of the lack of breast milk. I felt afterward that I should never have intervened in the first place—that I gave the family false hope that he would recover. It might have been better if he had simply died earlier, on his own, without my interference.

Did being in Mali impact your way of living when you returned to the U.S.?

Oh definitely. I was already fairly unmaterialistic before I went to Mali but became even antimaterialistic after I returned. I was already fairly devoted to family and friends before I went to Mali but became even more so, especially valuing extended family more. Certainly my mothering practices were already leaning toward what is today called "Attachment Parenting" but became even more so from my experiences in Mali. I was profoundly affected by the realization that babies don't cry when they are held all the time and nursed whenever they want. And that babies don't have to be in a quiet environment to sleep. And that it is possible to do all sorts of work while also taking care of an infant or toddler, especially if you put the child on your back. When Alex was little, I used to put him in a backpack while I was cooking dinner. It kept him safe and out of the way. He could see what was going on, and I could talk to him and give him attention even while I was getting dinner ready. I don't know if that influenced his interest in cooking, but he has become an accomplished chef.

What was the most disturbing belief of some of the [Malian] people toward their health? Was it that they believed that more food, especially the more nutritious food should go to the adults because the children didn't "deserve" it? Or was it that *Schistosoma* and peeing blood was so common that it had become a rite of passage for young boys? Or female circumcision?

I'd have to say that none of the Malian beliefs were "disturbing" to me. They were interesting, fascinating, curious, thought-provoking, but not disturbing. I am much more disturbed by the common U.S. belief that formula is OK for kids, and that it doesn't matter if children are breastfed or not. Right up there also is the common U.S. belief that children should sleep alone, and that it is normal and natural for children to cry a lot. And of course, breast augmentation surgery—mammary mutilation—I find to be really sad, and quite appalling.

Would you recommend other people going to Africa to do what you did, or perhaps do you think it was too emotionally draining?

Of course people should travel and have adventures and wonderful, life-changing experiences!! You only have one life to live, and it flies by all too quickly. My time in Mali was emotionally draining, but it was also enlightening and wonderful and . . . words fail me. Of course, everyone should travel—to other parts of their home country and to as many other parts of the world as they can.

What is the pervasive view of homosexuality in Bambara (Malian) culture? Overall, do they believe it exists? Do they view it predominantly in a positive/neutral/negative light?

I didn't really do any research on this topic, or talk to people about it much. And I haven't been there since 1990, and Mali is a big country, with lots of different people in it. Having said all that, some people certainly know that homosexuality exists, and some people certainly think it is kind of strange. Other people said, when the topic came up somehow, that they had never heard of two men having sex with one another and would ask me, "Exactly how does that work?" Same with two women.

On the other hand, remember that physical affection and emotional affection are different than sexual lust. In Mali, men had very close friendships with other men, including brothers and other relatives, as well as unrelated friends. They could hold hands, put their arms around each other, etc., without there being any sexual connotation.

I would say that many Malian men get the majority of their emotional needs met through their relationships with other men, but these relationships are not sexual. Same for the women—women stick together, sisters, mother/daughter pairs, co-wives, friends, neighbors, etc. They have very strong emotional friendships and get much of their emotional support from other women. Again, this is not sexual. The U.S. view of homosexuality as a dichotomous variable (you're either homosexual or heterosexual) is very limited and limiting. Sexual orientation is a continuum, as Alfred Kinsey demonstrated back in the 1940s and 1950s. The U.S. view that physical affection *must* be sexual really gets in the way of any fruitful discussion of these matters cross-culturally.

Has U.S. culture's sexual fascination with women's breasts filtered into the Bambara culture at all? Have the women there ever begun to wonder if there can be a sexual reaction from the breasts?

Again, the same caveats as above—I haven't done any research on this. I would be very surprised if Malians have incorporated any notions of the Western sexualization of breasts into their worldview. Even the way this question is worded is a little odd. There really isn't a "sexual reaction" from *anyone's* breasts, except the one that is learned. Sexual pleasure is mostly in one's brain. That's why a stranger caressing you against your will does not provide sexual pleasure. It's why having the gynecologist do a breast exam to check for cancerous lumps is not enjoyable. It's also why you can learn to get "sexual pleasure" from almost anything—from someone sucking on your toes (!!), or biting your earlobe, or rubbing your forearm. Many longtime couples develop secret signals for indicating sexual interest, and just having your partner give that signal can elicit all sorts of arousal— even if it is something otherwise innocuous like reaching over and pinching your little finger in a dark movie theater.

Having said all that, certainly there are some other places around the world where the Hooters' view of breasts as sexual attractants for males has gained a foothold. Korea comes immediately to mind—women there have started to wear padded bras, get breast implants, etc., as men there soak up the notion that bigger breasts are sexier. Across the Middle East, the pop culture phenomenon of singers and actresses with big (fake) breasts has become common, and some women in these regions are now getting breast implants.

Did you find any more children "who never grow up"? Was any further explanation of their condition made (either by inference or further information)?

I never came across any more discussion of this issue, although I did ask. Most people were not willing to talk about it. It was considered somewhat shameful and embarrassing, and people didn't like to talk about the whole situation. Several times in CARE villages in the Macina region in northern Mali, people would bring out children with kwashiorkor only when we specifically asked about them, and sometimes the neighbors were surprised that these kids existed, because they had never seen them before.

Did you notice any food allergies in the children in Mali such as lactose intolerance?

Well, first of all, lactose intolerance isn't a food allergy. Most people in the world cease to produce lactase, the enzyme that digests lactose (milk sugar) in mid- to late-childhood. After that time, if they drink milk, they can't digest it, so the bacteria in their gut eat it up and produce a lot of gas and diarrhea and nausea and bloating. That isn't the same as an allergy, where your body reacts to something in the environment as though it were a foreign, toxic, substance. I never noticed anyone with any kind of an allergy in Mali, but then again, I wasn't studying that. These are all really good questions, and someone should go study these issues, in Mali or elsewhere!!

Has the CARE organization gone on to supplement their program of rebuilding villages with fresh water and immunizations to also include a nutrition course, so the children they are saving can live to adulthood?

I really haven't kept in contact with the CARE folks. I know they still have programs in Mali, and right after I was there in 1989–90, they did incorporate nutrition projects into their village health programs. But I'm sure the programs have continued to evolve and change over the years.

Have the malnutrition rates in Mali and its neighboring populations gone down at all after your visits?

There have been several nutrition surveys and KAP (knowledge, attitudes, practices) surveys done in the regions where I worked, both by CARE and AMIPJ/Freedom from Hunger, showing that the information was getting across. As to significant changes in practice, and long-term effects on malnutrition, I don't really know. My work in Mali was "rediscovered" in the mid- to late-1990s by the folks from Novartis, a multinational company based in Switzerland that does a lot of development work in Mali and other West African countries. I know that John Scheuring of Novartis (whom I knew from when we were there the first time in the early 1980s) was using my research to augment the programs Novartis was working on to improve child health and survival. They focused on improving the nutritional value of the plants people grew, planting mango and baobab trees that happened to have higher than usual levels of Vitamins A and C, teaching people to malt the millet grain before making it into porridge for the kids to increase protein intake, etc. In chapter 16, I provide some general statistics for Mali, showing gradually improving nutritional status for children and lower death rates for infants and children. I hope my work contributed in some small way to these improved conditions.

Has there been any further explanation of the "Kafoune" look; has it been linked to a genetic predisposition, the same kind of malnutrition (missing the same groups of foods), or an unknown mix of both?

No, that's still an open question, waiting for someone to do research on. There are lots of researchers who work on cranio-facial measurements as indicators of genetic and developmental abnormalities, but no one is looking at this issue of "almost starving to death as a child, but surviving"—at least not as far as I am aware.

Did you ever fulfill your dreams of developing a "culturally appropriate nutrition education program"? And if so, where have you put these into action and what results have you seen from the program?

The folks from CARE, Freedom from Hunger, and the Academy for Educational Development, along with Novartis, mentioned above, have all used my research as the basis for nutrition education development materials and programs, in Mali and in other countries in West Africa. There are too many other variables involved to know what, if any, impact my specific work has had in the long run.

In the book you worried about the effects of your recommendations to the parents, and that the recommendations could possibly result in harm. Did the mothers of these children see the recommendations as possibly harmful?

Sometimes mothers would protest or argue against my suggestions. And sometimes they were probably right. Other times, I'm sure, people just smiled and nodded, and then concluded after I left that I was ignorant and silly.

Are "neighborhood needles" common? Why are syringes not sold with the prescriptions?

Neighborhood needles are common throughout the world, including any area in the U.S. where illegal drugs are used. Syringes are expensive. You could buy a new syringe with each prescription in Mali, but since most people couldn't even afford the prescription, they certainly couldn't afford a new needle each time. A number of needle exchange programs have been introduced in the U.S.'s fight against drug addiction, to try to slow the rate of transmission of HIV, Hepatitis B, and other blood-borne diseases.

The children in Mali, who were almost all malnourished, were thought to look normal by adults in their communities. What do they think about the weight of American children? What do they think about their ages correlating to height?

Most Malians didn't have any idea what American kids looked like. The few American kids in Mali were mostly thin by American standards, because of the lack of high-calorie junk food (no pizzas, no ice cream, no candy, etc.) and the lack of TV, video games, etc. Since most people didn't know the ages of other people's kids, they had no perspective from which to judge if a child was tall for her age, or not. I did have a few people who found it difficult to believe that Miranda at age nine (in 1989) was the same child I'd had with me in 1981–83—primarily because she was so much taller than the kids her age who had been in my dissertation sample. They thought this must be a different child, an older child. She was plump when we went to Mali in 1989, about 95 pounds, but skinny when we came home—about 65 pounds. Probably half of the weight loss was from the factors I mentioned above (different diet, lots and lots and lots of walking) and half from her bout of malaria. In Mali, the most malnourished children don't survive, so those who do survive often grow up to be fairly tall as adults. There were many women taller than me in Mali, and I was 5 feet 8 inches back then. Alas, I'm a little shorter these days.

Certainly when I first got back to the U.S. in December of 1989, I was amazed and disgusted by all the fat kids I saw everywhere, and by the incredible amount of food many Americans waste. But, as always, you soon get used to what you see every day.

Was the site of female circumcision prone to infection? If so, were the reasons environmental or other things like clothing?

Female circumcision certainly can lead to infection because of the use of nonsterile instruments for the cutting and the fact that the genitals are always warm and moist, perfect breeding conditions for bacteria. Also, Mali is very dusty during the dry season, so it is easy for wounds to become infected. Sometimes the cloths used to cover or pack the area weren't the cleanest and weren't changed often enough. People didn't have sterile dressings to use.

Now that several years have passed since both the publication of *Dancing Skeletons* **and your two initial research ventures into Mali, what do you believe is the** *most* **significant cause of malnutrition and what would your recommended plan of action be?**

I think that lack of information/knowledge is the most significant factor and that nutrition education programs have the best chance of improving conditions for children. But it is also critical to provide immunizations against all the usual childhood diseases and to support the overall economy so that people aren't faced with difficult choices about where to spend what little money they have. As with many complex problems, there are numerous contributing factors, and any combination of several may lead to a similar outcome. In Mali, you have many contributing factors, including lack of information/knowledge, poverty, drought, high-carbohydrate/low-protein staples, lots of diseases, not always clean water supplies, little access to medical care (whether traditional or Western), and on and on and on.

In many ways, it is analogous to the situation in the United States, where we have many factors that contribute to violence and aggression in children and adults. I use a wonderful book when I teach my class "Anthropology and Human Nature." It's called *Ghosts from the Nursery: Tracing the Roots of Violence*, by Robin Karr-Morse and Meredith S. Wiley (1998). They systematically go through all the adverse environmental factors that contribute to violence, beginning in the womb with the mother's use/abuse of alcohol, tobacco, and legal and illegal drugs, and exposure to maternal stress hormones if she is being abused herself. Use of drugs during labor and delivery—to ease the mother's pain—has a number of serious consequences for the child, including difficulty with breastfeeding. Other difficulties during childbirth, separation of mother and baby after birth, lack of breastfeeding, lack of physical touch, being forced to sleep alone—all of these can contribute to a later predisposition to aggression and violence. Additionally, there may be physical and emotional abuse, especially head injury, neglect, malnutrition, being a witness to violence in the home, exposure to drugs and alcohol, mental illness in the parents, absence of the father, chronic poverty, and on and on and on. Any one or two or even three of these factors might not result in long-term serious outcomes for the child. But they add up, just as any particular case of malnutrition in a child in Mali might be the result of a combination of numerous factors. This relationship, between multiple causes and similar outcomes, is known as *overdetermination*. It makes it difficult to come up with any simple solution that will be effective and sustainable. We still need to keep trying, though. The ongoing ACE study, begun in the 1990s by the CDC and Kaiser Permanente, is trying to tease out some of these relationships with respect to "Adverse Childhood Experiences" and later physical and emotional well-being (ACES 2013). See http://www.cdc.gov/ace/about.htm for more information.

When do girls typically get married in Mali? Is it as soon as they leave their mother's house?

When I was there, in the villages where I worked, all the girls stayed at home with their parents until they were married, regardless of their age at marriage. They didn't experience living on their own as single women. Most got married in their late teens. Recent statistics show about half of all girls aged 15–19 years are already married.

How are widows treated in Mali?

I don't really know. I know that sometimes, if they were young enough, they were taken in by one of their husband's brothers. Other times they were remarried to someone else. If they were past child-bearing years they might not remarry but would stay with their husband's family and their children.

When did Malian habits move from "traditional" to modern (as in the case of nursing)?

I'm not sure I understand the question. There is no clearcut distinction between traditional and modern in any culture. I don't know exactly when people stopped nursing their kids for five, six, or seven years and switched to weaning at two years. I don't even know how widespread the belief/practice was of nursing for only two years. I do know that some of the mothers in my dissertation sample, say those who were 20 to 50 in the early 1980s, could remember having been nursed until they were five or six, or their younger siblings having nursed that long. But I didn't find any children still being nursed to that age in Mali in the 1980s. In the U.S., yes, but not in Mali.

You mentioned that there was little to no discussion in Mali about politics and religion. What are the reasons for that silence and what were the current events that made you unable to talk about common issues of that nature?

I suspect you misinterpreted an offhand comment I made. Certainly I didn't talk to people about politics and religion, but that was only because I didn't have the vocabulary, not because there were any taboos about those topics. My Bambara knowledge was limited to the topics of my research— different types of diarrhea, vomiting, fever, appetite, health, foods, etc. I talked to women pretty much only about my research topics. Remember, my time was also limited. I could chat at length about the color and consistency of an infant's diarrhea but didn't have the language fluency to ask a woman whether or not she still held some traditional animist beliefs, or what her position was on Tuareg political concerns.

As an American, do you get more respect than the average married, adult Malian woman?

Respect from whom? Certainly Malian women, like most West African women, are held in extremely high regard by their children and have a lot of power in their families and their societies in general, at least when it comes to women's issues. I was anomalous not because I was a woman but because I was a white woman, so people often weren't sure how to treat me or deal with me. Most of their experience with "toubabs" was with white men, so some people were a little perplexed about what to think of me.

Do you plan on bringing any of your children to a foreign country with you for fieldwork in the future, or are you a little apprehensive after Miranda's malaria scare?

My kids are all grown up now. I didn't want to take Alex to the field while he was little (see above). He's never been to Mali, alas. And now I am semi-retired and don't plan on doing any more field research.

How old are your children now and what are they doing?

Miranda is now 33. She went to Randolph-Macon Woman's College in Virginia for her undergraduate degree in physics and then earned an MA in physics from UT Brownsville. She got married in 2005 and has lived in Germany, Ireland, Austria, and now Wales. She has gone back to school to become an architect. She has two children.

Peter is 28 years old. He lives at home with us and is a constant source of amusement and love and silliness. He talks a lot more than he used to, and he spends his days at a program run by Easter Seals, where he has a number of friends. He is a fan of the Eagles (the singing group, not the football team) and the White Stripes and enjoys watching *American Idol* and *The Daily Show* with Jon Stewart (he calls him "The Funny Guy"). His favorite foods are hamburgers, fries, and chocolate milkshakes from McDonald's, pizza, and ice cream.

Alexander, who was an infant when I wrote *Dancing Skeletons*, is now 22 years old. In May of 2013 he graduated from Indiana University of Pennsylvania with a BA in Anthropology and moved to Pittsburgh. In September of 2012, he married his lovely biochemist wife Shenin, who works for the University of Pittsburgh doing something to mice involving neurodevelopment (following a stint working in a lab messing with *Drosophila* genes).

My husband and best friend, Steven, is the Director of Community Mental Health, Substance Abuse, and Gambling Addiction Programs for the State of Delaware. He has a PhD in Cultural Anthropology and finds it useful in everything he does as an administrator working with multiple, different stakeholders, including patients, doctors, families, judges, policemen, hospital administrators, etc. Together, we keep the home fires burning.

In 1999, I was diagnosed with breast cancer, and made the decision to leave my position at Texas A&M University and move to Delaware, where we have extended family. I've been cancer-free since treatment, and have subsequently worked on a variety of projects. I taught at Millersville University in Pennsylvania for two years and have been teaching part-time at the University of Delaware beginning in 2005. I continue to lecture at breastfeeding/lactation conferences and at universities. From 2009 through 2012 I held a second job working in the wee hours of the morning baking sweets from scratch at a local bakery. I spend a lot of time at the local bark park with my standard poodles, Truman and Ulysses, where I toil alone at a never-ending task—trying to free the local, native trees from the invasive vines that are killing them. In 2011, I completed an introductory cultural anthropology textbook, *Cultural Anthropology & Human Experience: The Feast of Life,* also published by Waveland Press. My current research and writing project, begun in 2012, involves creating a research database from five hardbound, hand-written ledgers containing admissions information and clinical notes for patients at the Delaware State (Mental) Hospital, dating from 1894 to 1916. At that time, the hospital served as a sanctuary not only for those with mental illnesses of various sorts, but also for those with developmental disabilities, traumatic brain injuries, seizure disorders, age-related senility, syphilis, and alcohol and drug addictions. The ledgers hold many fascinating stories, as well as some truly heartbreaking ones. I hope to bring back to light some of these long-forgotten lives.

16

Update on Mali, 2013

As part of updating *Dancing Skeletons* for this 20th anniversary edition, I wanted to bring students up to date on what has happened in Mali since I was last there in 1990, particularly with respect to maternal/child health, demography, education, female genital mutilation (FGM), and development projects. Due to the widely reported Tuareg insurgency that erupted in northern Mali in 2012, it also seemed necessary to provide some background on political events in Mali. Thus, this additional new chapter begins with some statistics about health, demography, and so on.

In order to put the Malian data in a broader context, I chose to compare it to similar data for the United States, and for Japan. I chose Japan because it has better indicators than the United States for many variables, and serves to underscore the idea that the U.S. does not have the best outcomes for all measurements of success and development.

As I was comparing the three countries, it occurred to me that many of these measurements reflect a misleading Western bias. Why is literacy important as a measure of a country's development, but multilingualism is not? Why is the percentage of women in Mali undergoing female genital mutilation of concern in terms of women's health, but the very high rate of breast augmentation surgery (female mammary mutilation) and female genital "cosmetic" surgery in the US is not? Why is it problematic for teenage girls in Mali to get married, but not a problem for teenage girls in the U.S. to have children outside of marriage? Is Western-style education intrinsically superior to traditional forms of learning, which focus on practical skills? Thus, in the sections that follow, in addition to offering the comparative data, I explore the broader cultural context of these data and encourage students to think critically about how the lives of people around the world often are measured and judged according to peculiarly Western standards.

The second section of the chapter provides an update on several important development projects in Mali, including the ongoing work of Freedom from Hunger. The final section provides a brief history of politics and forms of government in Mali, some context for the 2012 Tuareg insurgency in the north, and a report on the outcome of the 2013 elections that restored democracy to the people of Mali.

Comparative Statistics

Except where otherwise indicated, all of the statistics discussed below come from online "Country Statistics" provided by UNICEF as of June 2013 (http://www.unicef.org/statistics/index_countrystats.html).

TABLE 1   Basic Indicators for Health

Basic Indicators for Health	Mali	U.S.	Japan
Contraceptive prevalence (%) 2007–2012	8	79	54
Antenatal care (%) 2007–2012, ($\geq$ 1 visit)	70	—	—
Antenatal care (%) 2007–2012, ($\geq$ 4 visits)	35	—	—
Delivery care (%) 2007–2012, Skilled attendant at birth	49	—	—
Delivery care (%) 2007–2012, Institutional delivery	45	—	100
Delivery care (%) 2007–2012, C-section	2	31	—
Maternal mortality ratio, 2010, Adjusted (per 100,000 live births)	540	21	5
Maternal mortality ratio, 2010, Lifetime risk of maternal death (1 in:__)	28	2,400	12,200
Low birth weight (%) 2007–2011 (less than 5.5 lbs. or 2500 grams)	19	8	8
Early initiation of breastfeeding (%), 2007–2011 (within one hour of birth)	46	—	—
Exclusive breastfeeding <6 months (%), 2007–2011 (nothing other than breast milk)	38	16.3 (CDC)	—
Introduction of solid, semi-solid or soft foods 6–8 months (%), 2007–2011	25	—	—
Breastfeeding at age 2 years (%), 2007–2011 *U.S. data at 18 months, from the CDC in 2009	56	9*	—
Neonatal mortality rate (per 1,000 live births) in 2011 (birth to 28 days)	49	4	1
Under 1 year mortality rate (Infant Mortality Rate, per 1,000 live births) • In 1990 • In 2011	132 98	9 6	5 2
Under 5 years mortality rate (Childhood Mortality Rate, per 1,000 live births) • In 1990 • In 2011 • Males/females in 2011	257 176 182/169	11 8 8/7	6 3 4/3

Basic Indicators for Health	Mali	U.S.	Japan
Life expectancy at birth in 2011	51	79	83
Underweight (%) 2007–2011, moderate & severe (weight for age)	27	1	—
Stunting (%) 2007–2011, moderate & severe (height for age)	38	3	—
Wasting (%) 2007–2011, moderate & severe (weight for height)	15	0	—
Overweight (%) 2007–2011, moderate & severe (weight for height, BMI $\geq$ 25)	—	8	—
Vitamin A supplementation full coverage (%) 2011	96	—	—
Iodized salt consumption (%) 2007–2011	79	—	—

Discussion of Table 1, Basic Indicators for Health

Contraceptive Use

It is not surprising that the rates of contraceptive use are so low in Mali, as people generally still want to have many children, especially the men, and many options that are available in developed countries are not as easy to find in Mali. Additionally, women still rely on lactational amenorrhea to space out their births.

Antenatal Care (Pregnancy and Labor) and Delivery

UNICEF does not collect or report statistics for the U.S. or Japan for these indicators. In Mali, 70% of women see a health care professional at least once during their pregnancy, but pregnancy is considered a normal part of life, not a medical issue. "Skilled attendants" are present at 49% of the births in Mali, with 45% of all births taking place in an institutional setting—a hospital or regional/local birthing center. According to the World Health Organization (2013):

> A *skilled birth attendant* is an accredited health professional—such as a midwife, doctor or nurse—who has been educated and trained to proficiency in the skills needed to manage normal (uncomplicated) pregnancies, childbirth and the immediate postnatal period, and in the identification, management and referral of complications in women and newborns. Traditional birth attendants, trained or not, are excluded from the category of skilled attendant at delivery.

In the Malian context, some traditional birth attendants are very knowledgeable and skilled and may know how to do things that skilled birth attendants may not know. For example, a traditional birth attendant in Mali likely knows how to monitor the fetus' health without electronic fetal monitors, how to manually manipulate a badly positioned fetus from outside the mother's body to facilitate delivery (external version), and how to maximize the size of the birth canal by having the mother on all fours or in the squatting position.

Cesarean Section

Because we are both bipedal and large-brained at birth, humans face what is known as an *obstetrical dilemma*—how to balance the needs of the mother for efficient bipedalism with the tight fit of the fetus/newborn's head through the birth canal. Throughout human evolution and prehistory, and continuing up to modern times, some women died during childbirth because the fetus' head was too large to pass through the mother's bony pelvis. Additionally, some fetuses are in a breech position (feet, buttocks, or knees presenting first) or are lying crosswise to the birth canal. Some of these malpositioned children cannot be born vaginally, and baby or mother, or both, may die under such circumstances. Thus, Cesarean-section births, where the fetus is surgically removed from the mother's uterus, can be a life-saving option, when done properly. According to the World Health Organization, for the best maternal/child outcomes, a country's C-section rate should be between 10 and 15%. "Countries with *C-section rates below 10% were considered to show underuse*, while countries with *rates above 15% were considered to show overuse*" (Gibbons et al. 2010).

Thus, Mali's 2% C-section rate, as reported by UNICEF, reflects an underuse of C-section procedures, which might account for some of the high maternal mortality in Mali. Underuse of C-sections is likely due to a combination of factors. First, in many regions of Mali, mothers, birth attendants, and even physicians, may not be able to diagnose conditions that would call for a C-section, or they don't make the decision to seek care in a timely manner. Second, there may be delays in reaching care. Even when it is recognized that a C-section is necessary, the mother may be far from a medical facility that can provide such surgery safely.

At the same time, the U.S. rate of C-sections is 31%—a rate that is much higher than WHO's 10–15% recommendations (Gibbons et al. 2010). Again, the overuse of C-sections is likely due to a combination of factors. First, many hospitals and physicians in the U.S. are worried about malpractice lawsuits and therefore perform a C-section at the first sign of anything unusual during the labor. Second, many U.S. physicians don't know how to safely deliver when it involves a fetus in a breech position, a vaginal birth after a previous Cesarean, or when there are twins or triplets, so they always perform C-sections in such cases. Third, C-sections are preferred by some women who fear the pain of vaginal childbirth or are concerned about stretching out their vaginas.

Maternal Mortality Ratio

The maternal mortality ratio for Mali is disconcertingly high—540 deaths per 100,000 live births. Childbirth-related maternal deaths in developing countries such as Mali can be attributed to both direct and indirect causes. Direct causes are estimated to be responsible for 75–80% of all maternal mortality and include eclampsia/high blood pressure, postpartum hemorrhage, infection/sepsis, unsafe abortion, and prolonged/obstructed labor (the mother literally dies of blood loss and exhaustion). Indirect causes account for 20–25% of maternal deaths and include anemia from malaria, anemia from other causes (hookworm, Vitamin A deficiency, etc.), HIV/AIDS, different forms of malnutrition, hepatitis, and diabetes.

The maternal mortality rate in the U.S. is much lower than in Mali, at 21 deaths per 100,000 live births, but the rate for Japan is much lower still, at only 5 deaths per 100,000 live births. The United States has experienced a recent increase in the maternal mortality rate, especially among specific groups such as African American women, older women, and women who are obese, have cardiovascular disease, or have diabetes. Between 28 and 50% of such deaths are thought to be preventable through such basic practices as adequately controlling blood pressure in hypertensive women, adequately diagnosing and treating pulmonary edema in women with pre-eclampsia, paying closer attention to vital signs following a Cesarean section, and controlling hemorrhages following a Cesarean section (Joint Commission 2010).

Low Birth Weight

The percentage of low birth weight babies in Mali is 19%, much higher than the 8% reported for the U.S. and Japan. This is attributable in large part to maternal malnutrition and maternal malaria during pregnancy. Fraternal twinning is also much more common in West Africa than either the U.S. or Japan, and twins are often premature or have low birth weights, although this probably doesn't account for very much of the difference.

Breastfeeding

Data on rates of breastfeeding at various ages are collected because breastfeeding is such an essential and critical part of child health in all populations. Unfortunately, the data are not always collected using the same definitions or the same time frames, making comparisons difficult. UNICEF reports that 46% of babies in Mali are breastfed for the first time within one hour of birth (considered the standard/optimal practice), but there are no comparable data for the U.S. or Japan. *Exclusive breast-feeding*—nothing other than breast milk—to the recommended age of 6 months, is enjoyed by 38% of the Malian babies but only by 16.3% of U.S. children. Again, there are no data for Japan. In Mali, 56% of the children are still breastfeeding at two years of age, the *minimum* age recommended by both the World Health Organization and the American Academy of Family Physicians. UNICEF doesn't provide data for the U.S., and the Centers for Disease Control, which collects breastfeeding data for the U.S., only measures duration up to 18 months. The most recent data, from 2009, showed only 9% of U.S. children still being breastfed at 18 months, well below the recommended minimum age.

Mortality Rates in Children

Mortality rates for children of all ages are high in Mali. For the *neonatal period*, the first 28 days of life, the rate for Mali in 2011 was 49 deaths per 1,000 live births. In the U.S., the neonatal mortality rate was 4 deaths per 1,000 live births, and in Japan it was only 1 death per 1,000 live births. The main causes of neonatal mortality in Mali are malaria, tetanus, gastrointestinal illness, and respiratory infections. Additionally, there are a number of congenital physical defects that are incompatible with life (like Peter's duodenal atresia) but are easily repaired through basic surgery. Most of these children in Mali probably die without being diagnosed.

There are many different government agencies and NGOs (nongovernmental organizations) working in Mali to reduce both maternal and neonatal mortality through a variety of programs.

Infant mortality is measured as deaths from birth to one year of age, per 1,000 live births and incorporates neonatal mortality. The data for all three countries show a marked decrease in infant mortality between 1990 and 2011, from 132 to 98 for Mali over that time period. This is still a very high infant mortality rate compared to the U.S. and Japan but does indicate that conditions are improving in Mali. Based on my experiences in the 1980s, I suspect that many of the postneonatal infant deaths in Mali are due to diseases that can be prevented through vaccination programs, including chicken pox, measles, mumps, rubella, tetanus, and diphtheria. As immunization programs continue to expand in Mali and coverage increases, the infant mortality rate should drop even further. Other likely contributors to the postneonatal infant mortality rate are gastrointestinal and respiratory infections.

Childhood mortality is measured as deaths from birth to five years of age, per 1,000 live births and incorporates infant mortality. Again, the data show marked improvements in conditions for children in Mali between 1990 and 2011, a drop from 257 to 176. To put this in a larger context, when I was doing my initial research in the early 1980s, the rural childhood mortality rate for Mali was close to 500—almost half of all children in rural villages were dying before the age of 5 years. Improvements in access to health care, both prevention and treatment, cleaner water supplies, and better child feeding practices have all contributed to more children surviving in Mali beyond the age of 5 years. However, the childhood mortality rate of 176 deaths per 1,000 live births is still ridiculously high compared to the rate for the U.S. of only 8 deaths, or the rate for Japan of only 3 deaths—especially considering that the two leading causes of death for children ages 1–4 years in the U.S. in 2010 were (1) accidents (unintentional injuries) and (2) congenital malformations, deformations, and chromosomal abnormalities. At the same time, a number of other African countries have seen recent increases in childhood mortality due to HIV/AIDS. As is typical throughout time and in all populations, males have slightly higher childhood mortality rates than females.

Life Expectancy at Birth

Life expectancy at birth directly reflects the number of infants and children who die in a population. Thus, given Mali's still relatively high infant and childhood mortality, it is not surprising that the life expectancy at birth is only 51 years, compared to 79 years for the U.S. and 83 years for Japan. A life expectancy of 51 years does not mean that no one lives beyond their 40s or 50s. Rather, lots of children die, dragging down the average age of death. A child in Mali who survives his or her first 5 years has an amazingly strong immune system and a life expectancy of 65 years (World Life Expectancy 2010). Without access to such modern health care technologies as blood transfusions, intravenous lines for drugs and feeding, surgery, antibiotics, and cancer chemotherapy, not very many people in Mali survive beyond the age of 80 years.

Growth Variables

UNICEF provides data for Mali and the U.S. for percentage of children who are moderately or severely *underweight* (low weight for age), *stunted* (low height for age), or *wasted* (low weight for height), and for the U.S. alone for the category of moderately and severely overweight (BMI $\geq$ 25). According to these data, 27% of Malian children are underweight (compared to only 1% for the U.S.), 38% are stunted (compared to 3% for the U.S.), and 15% are wasted (0% for the U.S. in this category). At the other end of the malnutrition spectrum, 8% of children in the U.S. are considered to be moderately or severely overweight, while no data are provided for Malian children. I did encounter one child who was overweight during more than 2 years of research in Mali, but clearly obesity is not the problem for children in Mali that it is for children in the U.S. To put the Malian data in longer-term perspective, there has been a slow but fairly steady improvement in nutritional status for children in Mali over the past 20 years. There have been so many different programs, from a variety of organizations, that it isn't possible to say how much, if any, of this improvement can be attributed directly or indirectly to my work. In a later section, I highlight some of the ongoing projects to improve the survival, nutrition, and health of children in Mali.

Vitamin A and Iodine Supplementation

Vitamin A deficiency was one of the targets of my research with CARE in rural villages in northern Mali in 1989 and 1990. Both children and, especially, pregnant women were found to be suffering from Vitamin A deficiency. CARE and other projects conducted a variety of programs to provide Vitamin A and education about the importance of Vitamin A-rich foods to villages around the country. As of 2011, UNICEF reports that 96% of the population has access to adequate sources of Vitamin A. Having sufficient Vitamin A helps people cope with a variety of gastrointestinal and respiratory illnesses; the high rate of coverage in Mali today is no doubt contributing to improved health for all.

During my work in rural villages in southern Mali in 1989 I encountered a very high rate of goiters, due to iodine deficiency. At the time, there was little being done to solve this problem, but according to UNICEF, by 2011, 79% of the population was consuming iodized salt. Because almost everyone uses salt for preparing food, adding iodine to salt sources has long been considered a simple and effective way to supplement the diet. I suspect I would see far fewer goiters if I were to return to Mali today. Vitamin A and iodine deficiencies are not considered significant dietary issues in the U.S. or Japan, and UNICEF does not provide data for either country.

A New Health Issue for Malian Children

Medical anthropologist Carolyn Sargent travelled to Mali in 2011 to do some consulting work. Upon her return, I asked her if there were any new health concerns affecting children in Mali. In addition to citing worries over the presence of members of "Al Qaeda in the Islamic Maghreb" in northern Mali, she said that respiratory illnesses among children in Bamako have been on the rise in recent years. Two main factors are thought to be responsible—the increase in air pollution as more cars and trucks take to the roads in the capital, and the increasing use of charcoal as a source of fuel for cooking, instead of the traditional wood (Sargent 2011).

TABLE 2   Demographic & Social Indicators

Demographic & Social Indicators	Mali	U.S.	Japan
Population (thousands) in 2011, total	15,840	313,085	126,497
Percent of population under 18 years in 2011	54%	24%	16%
Percent of population under 5 years in 2011	19%	7%	4%
Population annual growth rate (%), 1990–2011	3	1	0
Population annual growth rate (%), 2011–2030 [predicted]	3	1	0
Crude death rate, 1970/1990/2011	30/21/14	9/9/8	7/7/9
Crude birth rate, 1970/1990/2011	49/49/46	16/16/14	19/10/8
Total fertility rate 1970/1990/2011	7/7/6	2/2/2	2/2/1
Urbanized population (%), 2011	35	82	91
GNI per capita (U.S.$) 2011	610	48,450	45,180
Total adult literacy rate (%) 2007–2011	31	—	—
Primary school net enrollment ratio (%) 2008–2011	66	96	100

Discussion of Table 2, Demographic & Social Indicators

Population Size

In 2011, Mali's population was approaching 16 million people and growing at a rate of about 3% per year, as it has since 1990. Both the U.S. and Japan have much larger populations, but the U.S. population is only growing at a rate of 1%, while Japan's population is holding steady with a 0% growth rate since 1990, and the same is predicted for the future. Of greater significance than absolute numbers of people, however, is the age structure of the population. As can be seen from the table, in 2011, just over half of Mali's population was *under 18 years of age*, with 19% *under 5 years of age*. This is a fairly typical population structure for a developing country where infant and childhood mortality rates are still relatively high and where few people live beyond the age of 80. In contrast, the U.S. has only 24% of the population under 18, and Japan has even less, with 16%. For those under 5, the figures are 7% for the U.S. and 4% for Japan. These are typical population structures for a developed country where few infants and children die and where many people live beyond the age of 80. Indeed, Japan's life expectancy at birth is 83 years, and many people have expressed concern that the dearth of children and young workers will create hardships for the society as a whole. The government is worried that Japanese women are marrying later or not at all and choosing to have no children or only one child. A number of government policies and programs have been developed to encourage higher levels of childbearing, including subsidized day care. At the same time, in developing countries, the focus remains on helping women get equal access to education and employment and access to contraceptives so they can choose if and when to have children.

Death and Birth Rates and Fertility Levels

The data for these variables are fairly self-explanatory. The *crude death rate* is the number of deaths occurring in a given year, per 1,000 people. Mali's crude death rate of 30 in 1970 is the highest, but Mali also shows sharp declines, to 21 in 1990 and 14 in 2011. The U.S. death rate over the same time frame has stayed the same or dropped slightly, from 9 in 1970 to 8 in 2011. In Japan, the death rate has actually risen, from 7 in 1990 to 9 in 2011, probably due to the increasingly older population structure. At the same time that the death rate has been falling in Mali, the *crude birth rate* has barely changed. The crude birth rate is the number of births occurring in a given year, per 1,000 people. Mali's birth rate has declined only slightly, from 49 in 1970 and 1990, to 46 in 2011. This is fairly typical of a society in the early stages of the *demographic transition*, where death rates fall first, to be followed some years later by a change in reproductive behavior, to lower birth rates as well. It suggests that Mali's overall population will continue to grow for the foreseeable future. In the U.S., the crude birth rate has dropped from 16 in 1970 and 1990 to 14 in 2011, a minor decrease. Over the same time period, Japan has experienced a rapid drop in its birth rate, from 19 in 1970 to 10 in 1990 to only 8 in 2011.

The *total fertility rate* reflects the typical number of children born to each woman. For Mali, the rate has declined from 7 to 6 over the time period reflected here. It has stayed steady at 2 for the U.S., and for Japan it has declined from 2 to 1. A total fertility rate of 2.1 is considered necessary for replacement of the current population. It is hard to know if the data from Mali accurately reflect total births, especially from rural villages. During my research, I found that women were very reluctant to talk about miscarriages, stillbirths, neonatal deaths, and even the deaths of older children. If Malian women in 2011 are having an average of 6 children, most of whom survive, that would be a dramatic change from earlier generations where many more children were born, and many died.

Urban versus Rural Population Distribution

The data on urbanization reflect the fact that most Malians still live in rural agricultural villages (or live as nomadic pastoralists, or riverside fisherfolk), with only 35% of the population living in urban areas in 2011. The migration from rural to urban life has long been the focus of many anthropological studies around the world. The U.S. has experienced a rapid rise in urban living, with 82% of the population defined as urban in 2011, and Japan is almost completely urban at 91%. Although urban areas may offer more opportunities for Western-style education and jobs outside the subsistence agricultural sector, they also have disadvantages, including the need for a job to earn money to pay for housing and food, more crowding, and higher crime rates. The lure of the "bright lights, big city" has drawn many, mostly younger adults, away from the rural lifestyle that was traditionally practiced for hundreds (or thousands) of years.

GNI per Capita (US $)

The GNI per capita is the value of a country's total income in a year, divided by its population. It reflects the average income of a country's citizens and can give you some idea of the general standard of living. However, the GNI value can also be very misleading, both in terms of conditions within a country and for between-country comparisons. In 2011, the GNI for Malians was US $610 per year, compared to a staggering US $48,450 for the U.S. and US $45,180 for Japan.

Within countries, income is seldom evenly distributed—often a small minority of the population controls the majority of the wealth. In the U.S., the top 1% of income earners controls 24% of the income, and income inequality has been rising sharply since reaching a low in the 1970s. In Mali, a significant proportion of the population remains mostly outside the money economy, thus the GNI per capita doesn't really provide much information, either for within or between-country comparisons. Certainly, in Mali, people living in urban areas and working for salary or wages control most of the monetary income. However, in Mali, and in the U.S. and other countries, the cost of living can vary dramatically from one region to another. In the U.S. in 2013, a household income of $50,000 per year will provide a solid middle- to upper-middle-class living in some regions (the South, the rural Midwest) but would not be sufficient in the larger cities of either the East or West Coast (Boston, New York City, Los Angeles, San Francisco).

At the same time, in rural Mali, most people are subsistence farmers, spending most of their time and energy growing crops, herding cattle, or fishing to provide food for themselves. They can build their own houses from mud brick and thatch, so they don't have to pay rent or mortgages. Without electricity or gas, there is no electric or gas bill, no need for electric appliances such as washing machines and vacuum cleaners. Without the Internet and television, there is no cable bill. Without cars, there are no car loans and no need to purchase gasoline or pay for insurance or car repairs. In Mali, few people still grow cotton and weave the cloth for their own clothes, but they usually have only a few sets of clothing. A Westerner might view rural Malians as "dirt poor." Conversely, they can also be viewed as being *free from* the shallow materialism of the West and the *tyranny* of feeling obliged to spend money on the latest status symbols (computers, iPhones, televisions, cars, clothes, vacations, etc.). In his book *Nuer Journeys, Nuer Lives: Sudanese Refugees in Minnesota* (2007), anthropologist Jon Holtzman discusses the incredible frustrations of Sudanese immigrants to the U.S., who are unused to having to earn money to pay for their basic needs for shelter and food, and unused to having to travel long distances by car or bus in order to get to work. The 2012 Mali country report by Bertelsmann Stiftung, BTI (http://www. bti-project.de/fileadmin/Inhalte/reports/2012/pdf/BTI%202012%20

Mali.pdf) provides a detailed analysis of the recent economic situation in Mali and a better understanding of what it means to live in a country where the GNI is only US $610 per year.

Literacy and School Enrollment

The percentage of the population who can read and the percentage of children enrolled in Western-style schools are often used as indicators of development. This reflects a Western emphasis on written materials and formal schooling where students sit in classrooms and listen to teachers blather on and on, often far removed from the practical application (if any) of the material they are learning. Thus, while the figures for Mali for recent years—an adult literacy rate of 31% and primary school enrollment rate of 66%—appear low, their interpretation requires some analysis of the cultural context.

The adult literacy rate is defined as the proportion of adults over the age of 15 years who can read and write. The UNICEF literacy data for Mali probably refer to literacy in French, the language of the colonial-era government and still the language of most Malian public schools. Bambara, the primary spoken language of Mali, has been a written language only since the late 1980s, and it is unclear if contemporary public school students learn to read and write in Bambara as well as French. More than two-thirds of Malians are classified as being "illiterate," yet some of them can read French, but not write it, and some can read and write in Bambara or other languages. Additionally, most Malians are able to speak several languages: Bambara—either as their native tongue or in its use as a *lingua franca* across West Africa—French, English, and one or more of the other national languages of Mali such as Fula, Songhai, Bozo, Dogon, Tamasheq, and Senoufo. If, instead of literacy, a measure of how many languages an adult could speak were used as an index of development, many Western countries, especially the United States, would score very low.

UNICEF doesn't provide data for literacy rates in the U.S. and Japan, but other sources say that both countries have a literacy rate of greater than 97%. Again, this can be somewhat misleading, as different studies define literacy in different ways. Numerous studies have shown that a typical U.S. high school *graduate* reads at the 5th to 7th grade level. Likewise, there are many studies showing that college students often arrive on campus without the basic literacy and math skills they need to succeed and are required to take noncredit remedial courses. For all of these reasons, it is unclear what a literacy rate of 31% for Mali, compared to the more than 97% reported for the U.S. and Japan, really means in terms of people's everyday lives.

A similar problem arises when trying to interpret the comparative data on school enrollment. There are many ways to learn information, critical thinking, and practical skills other than formal, Western-style classroom education. Traditionally, in much of the world, children learned what they needed to know and be able to do by observation and practice, either informally or formally in arrangements such as apprenticeships. In Mali, most rural children in farming communities know most of what they need to be successful adults by the time they are teenagers, if not before. They have vast knowledge of practical skills and ample opportunity to practice and refine their abilities. Girls learn how to grow crops, process foods, cook, haul water, chop firewood, and take care of children. Some specialize in herbal medical knowledge or bone-setting (first-aid type) skills. Others become ceramic or textile artists (Frank 2007). Boys also learn how to grow crops, and some learn, from an early age, how to work leather or metal or wood, how to weave, how to dance, and how to be hunters and leaders. Just like measuring development by how many languages a person can speak, if we used the ability to carry out the daily tasks of adulthood by the time you are 15 years old, Malians would score very high, while teenagers in the U.S. and Japan would score very low. It is not at all clear how to make reasonable comparisons between a female Malian teen's ability to grow, harvest, process, and cook food and otherwise provide for a family, and a U.S. teen's ability to explain the causes of the Civil War, do algebra, identify John Steinbeck, or share photos of grumpy cats. (Note: Years from now, if anyone is still reading this book, they'll be wondering what in the world people were thinking in 2013 when they used the power of computers and Internet technology to share photos of grumpy cats.)

TABLE 3   Protection for Women & Children

Protection for Women & Children	Mali	U.S.	Japan
Child labor (%) 2002–2011	21		
Child marriage (%) 2002–2011, married by 15 years	15		
Child marriage (%) 2002–2011, married by 18 years	55		
Female genital mutilation/cutting (%) 2002–2011, prevalence, adult women	89		
Female genital mutilation/cutting (%) 2002–2011, prevalence, daughters	75		
Support for female genital mutilation/cutting (%) 2002–2011	73		
Support for justified wife-beating, (%) 2002–2011, among women	87		

Discussion of Table 3, Protection for Women & Children

Child Labor

Before discussing the data on child labor, UNICEF's definition must be explained. To quote directly and completely from their website:

> Child labour—Percentage of children aged 5 to 14 years of age involved in child labour activities at the moment of the survey. A child is considered to be involved in child labour activities under the following classification: (a) children 5 to 11 years of age that during the week

preceding the survey did at least one hour of economic activity or at least 28 hours of domestic work, and (b) children 12 to 14 years of age that during the week preceding the survey did at least 14 hours of economic activity or at least 42 hours of economic activity and domestic work combined.

Once again, we see the influence of Western cultural beliefs about childhood and the value of different types of work on measures of development. A full deconstruction of these assumptions is beyond the scope of this commentary, so I'll limit myself to a few comments to spur critical thinking and discussion of these issues. Presumably, UNICEF considers child labor to be a "bad thing." Children should be sitting in the classroom or playing and having fun, not working to help support themselves and their families. It is unclear to me how one can compare an hour of harvesting onions to an hour of soccer practice, or an hour of washing clothes to an hour of playing video games. Even more of a conundrum/enigma is the equating of one hour of "economic activity" to 28 hours of domestic work. I can only presume that this reflects the devaluing of traditionally female labor involved in the running of a household. How does one hour a week at a job—say, a 10-year-old child in the U.S. delivering newspapers or dog-walking, at minimum wage—become the equivalent of 28 hours of helping with washing dishes, cooking, cleaning, laundry, vacuuming, and other domestic chores? That's four hours per day of domestic work, every single day, versus one hour of "economic activity."

In Mali, children are expected to help with both domestic and productive labor as soon as, and to the extent that, they are able. Young girls, especially, are expected to take over some of their mother's domestic and child-care responsibilities from a very early age. It is not uncommon to see the six-year-old in charge of the one-year-old while the mother does heavier labor in the fields or around the house, or sells items in the local market. It is not necessarily a good thing that many children in the U.S. are excused from any responsibility for even *knowing how to contribute to the upkeep of a household*—let alone actually contributing. Many U.S. college freshmen show up on campus not knowing how to cook, how to do laundry, how to keep their dorm room floor clean, how to manage their money, and so on. Note that I am not giving my stamp of approval to child labor in dangerous sweatshops, where children sit at machines or on assembly lines, or labor in rock quarries or coal mines and work 12- to 14-hour days without breaks and without adequate food and water. UNICEF does not, apparently, gather data on this type of child labor. But when they state that 21% of children in Mali are involved in child labor, the reader needs to know that most or all of this labor is not of the sweatshop or coal mine variety. And even though they don't provide data for the U.S. or Japan, some children in these countries do provide at least some productive or domestic labor to their families.

Child Marriage

UNICEF measures child marriage—which it presumably disapproves of, or views as a measure of backwardness and underdevelopment—in two ways: by the percentage of women married by the time they are 15 years of age, and by the percentage of women married by the time they are 18 years of age. They provide data only for Mali, and the percentages are 15 and 55, respectively. That means slightly more than half of all women are married by the age of 18 years; thus the median age of first marriage must be somewhat less than 18 years. It is understandable that such a measure might be used as an indicator of women's rights and status. In many contexts, early marriage is considered unfavorable for women's educational and economic opportunities and accomplishments. Additionally, early marriage often leads to early childbearing, and mothers in their teens are more likely to suffer complications during labor and delivery and give birth to low birth weight infants. If they are married to much older men with more sexual experience, they also face higher risks of sexually transmitted diseases. But in cultural contexts where the main role of women is to become wives and mothers, and few members of either sex go to college or work at salaried jobs, the implication that it is a bad thing for 55% of all Malian women to be married by age 18 seems a little ambiguous in terms of its impact on women.

If we look to other sources for comparable data for the U.S. and Japan, some interesting information turns up. In the U.S., data on median age at first marriage is available, by sex, for the years from 1890 to 2010 (Elliott et al. 2012). For men, the median age was 26.5 years in 1890 and declined fairly steadily for several decades, then declined more steeply in the 1940s to a low of 24 years of age, where it remained from 1950 to 1970. At that point, the median age of first marriage for men began to rise again, steadily at first, and then more steeply beginning in 2000, to 28.4 years in 2010—above the 1890 median age of 26.5 years. For women, the median age in 1890 was 23.6 years and declined fairly steadily for several decades, then declined more steeply in the 1940s to a low of 20.5 years of age. It began to rise again, several decades before the men, steadily at first, and then more steeply beginning in 2000, to 26.8 years in 2010—above the 1890 median age of 23.6 years.

In the U.S., the past several decades have seen a steady rise in the percentage of births that are to unmarried women. In 1940, less than 5% of all U.S. births were to unmarried women; the figure for 2010 is 40.8%. Of those births to unmarried women, 23% were to teenagers (data from 2007, Ventura 2009). Or, to look at the data from a different perspective, 93% of all births to girls aged 15 to 17 years were nonmarital; 82% of all births to girls aged 18–19 were nonmarital. Thus, it appears that while "child marriages" are very uncommon in the U.S.—one source suggests only 1.5% of all girls in the U.S. are married by age 18—plenty of teenagers are having children. Unmarried teenage childbearing, it seems to me, is just as detrimental to a young woman's chances of completing her education and working outside the home in the U.S. as marriage is in Mali.

The situation is dramatically different for Japan. Data from 2003 show that, at that time, Japanese men and women had the highest median age at first marriage in the world (Kawamura 2009). The median age for marriage for men was 29.4 years, while the median age for women was 27.6 years—approximately one year older than women cited in the U.S. data from 2010. In Japan, women still tend to have children only if they are married—only 1–2% of all births in Japan have been "out of wedlock" over the past 40 years. Traditional gender roles that assign almost all of the child-care responsibilities and domestic labor to women make marriage and family difficult or incompatible with employment for women outside the home and make marriage less attractive to young women who are pursuing an education and a career.

Thus, if the goal is to optimize women's opportunities to pursue education and careers by postponing marriage and childbearing, then Mali is doing a relatively poor job because many women marry early, while the U.S. is doing a relatively poor job because many teenagers are having children. Japan seems to be "doing it right"—but at the same time, the low birth rate in Japan is itself a cause for concern, as discussed above.

Female Genital Mutilation/Cutting

As discussed earlier in this book, female genital mutilation(FGM)/cutting is a long-standing tradition in Mali, where most girls have clitoridectomies as infants or young girls. In 2002, the Malian government launched a national program (Programme National de Lutte contre la Pratique de l'Excision) to discourage FGM, but it has had little effect in the last decade. UNICEF's data from 2002–2011 shows an overwhelming majority of females in Mali have been circumcised—89% of adult women and 75% of their daughters. Overall, 73% of Malians surveyed expressed support for FGM as a requirement for social acceptance and as a proper expression of womanhood.

UNICEF does not provide data on FGM/cutting for the U.S. or Japan, but that doesn't mean it isn't occurring. Occasionally one hears of a case in the U.S. where an immigrant family is criticized or even arrested for pursuing traditional forms of female circumcision for their daughters, but this is extremely rare. At the same time, various forms of FGM/cutting exist in the U.S., and some types are increasing in prevalence. Until the 1990s, it was quite common in the United States for women to have their natural vaginal opening enlarged during labor and delivery through a surgical incision called an episiotomy. Theoretically, this allowed more room for the baby's head as it emerged from the birth canal. After delivery, in many cases, the mother's vagina would be sewn up so that it was tighter than it was before giving birth. This was done for her husband's sexual pleasure, often without the woman's knowledge or consent.

Episiotomies have fallen out of favor in the U.S. in recent decades, but clitoral mutilation and vaginoplasty not related to childbirth are becoming more and more common. Women are encouraged to have their labia trimmed (to improve their appearance), to have the hood of their clitoris removed (supposedly to increase their own pleasure and shorten the time to orgasm), and to have their vaginal openings tightened up (to increase their partner's pleasure). For more information on how this is advertised and promoted as being "good for women," see http://www.clitoralunhooding. com/clitoral-unhooding.html.

In addition to the growing popularity of FGM in the U.S., female mammary mutilation (breast augmentation and related surgeries) and other types of plastic surgery to "enhance beauty" continue to flourish. From the American Society for Aesthetic Plastic Surgery comes this report in 2013:

> Breast augmentation has regained its status in 2012 as the leading surgical procedure in the United States after slipping back into second position in 2011. This is no surprise; today's low cut and scooped out tops demand attractive cleavage. Also, the return of silicone gel implants to the market in 2006 may be a driving force in breast augmentation increase. Women have traditionally favored silicone because of its more natural look and feel. There were 369,928 breast augmentations performed in 2012 compared with 316,848 in 2011. (ASAPS 2013)

In the U.S. in 2012, 1.7 million cosmetic surgical procedures were performed—up from 1.1 million in 2011. A full 90% of all such procedures were done to women. Breast augmentation was the most popular, followed by liposuction (fat removal), abdominoplasty (tummies), blepharoplasty (eyelids), and rhinoplasty (noses).

Some people will argue that, in contrast to FGM in places like Mali, most, if not all, of these U.S. surgeries were the product of an adult woman's own free choice. But the concept of "free choice" is itself problematic when the cultural context is one of enormous societal, family, peer, and self-imposed pressure to somehow achieve one's culture's unnatural ideals of beauty and slenderness (but with large perky breasts). It would be enlightening for UNICEF to start including data from the International Society of Aesthetic Plastic Surgery, which reports data on how many women, in countries around the world, surgically alter their bodies to meet their society's standards for beauty and male sexual gratification. Not surprisingly, data from 2011 show that the United States leads the world in cosmetic plastic surgeries, followed closely by Brazil, China, and Japan (ISAPS 2011).

Support for Justified Wife-Beating

This final statistic, about the fact that 87% of Malian women support "justified wife beating," also needs to be put in context. Since I actually used the example of "wife beating in Mali" in my introductory cultural anthropology textbook to illustrate the difference between cultural beliefs and social structure, I'm simply going to excerpt parts of that section here:

> Cultural beliefs and the social structures that are built on them do not always agree completely. Social structure refers to the institutions, the traditions, the organization of social life, that arise out of cultural beliefs, but then take on a somewhat independent existence. New members born into the population have to deal with the social structure they find in place, whether or not they agree with the underlying cultural beliefs. In addition, the way the society is organized may affect exactly how cultural beliefs actually turn into observable behaviors.
>
> A comparison of domestic violence (one spouse physically abusing the other) will serve as a specific example. During my research among the Bambara of Mali (West Africa) in the 1980s, the prevailing sentiment in the community was that a man had the right to physically discipline his wife. If she did something he had forbidden, failed to

do something she was supposed to, or showed disrespect to him, he was allowed to hit her. That was considered perfectly reasonable, a man's right. The prevailing sentiment in the United States at the time (and still today) was that domestic violence was absolutely wrong, not justifiable under any circumstances, and punishable by the criminal justice system. Any person who beat their spouse was viewed with disdain, and every year many people were sent to prison on these charges.

Given the stated cultural beliefs in these two different contexts, you might expect to find that domestic violence was much more common in Mali than in the United States. But you would be wrong. In Mali, although physical punishment was seen as an appropriate and justifiable response to misbehavior, the reality is that life in Mali is very much lived in public. Most adult men live with their parents, their brothers, their own wife (or wives) and children, and their brothers' wives and children. Most daily activities take place outside, in the central courtyard of the compound. If you want to hit your wife, fine, but you have to do it in front of any number of other adults and children, including your own parents and your brothers. Other family members would generally not intervene if a man hit his wife once, or even twice, but they would certainly stop him if there was even a remote possibility that he would seriously hurt the woman. She could appeal to the other adults in the compound for help, or simply run outside into the street while his brothers restrained him. More often, a man would control his own behavior, because he didn't want to be seen as someone who flew off the handle and let his emotions get the best of him. Thus, although it was permitted for men to hit their wives, it very seldom happened.

In the U.S., although the cultural beliefs say that violence is wrong, the reality is that most married adults live by themselves, with no other adults around to hear or observe or intervene in their behavior. People live in separate houses, where the neighbors can't hear, or in apartment buildings where the neighbors are prone to mind their own business and not call the police for fear of turning the man's wrath on whoever reported the violence. Because domestic violence is stigmatized, women are more likely to suffer in silence and not to tell anyone of the abuse, thus perpetuating the cycle. Perpetrators may convince their wives or girlfriends that it is their own fault they are being hit, saying: "It's not OK for a man to hit a woman, but damn, you leave me no choice!" With no one around to witness the violence, to stand up for the woman, or to restrain the man, the woman may suffer serious injury, including black eyes, broken bones, miscarriage, and even death.

Thus, even though Malian cultural beliefs allow a man to physically discipline his wife, the public nature of domestic life means that there is practically no serious domestic violence—no broken bones, no deaths, no slow starvation, no eroding away of one's sense of self through chronic emotional abuse. Although American beliefs discourage physical discipline, the private nature of domestic life means that men can get away with seriously injuring or even killing their wives, while the neighbors are not aware that anything bad is happening inside the house. (Dettwyler 2011:7–8, edited)

Clearly, at the time the UNICEF survey was conducted (2002–2011), most women in Mali still felt that men were justified in beating their wife or wives if provoked. It is almost certainly the case, however, that actual domestic violence is both more common and more severe in the United States than it is in Mali. Unfortunately, it is nearly impossible to find comparable statistics on rates of domestic violence for countries around the world, and for different time periods. A high proportion of incidents of domestic violence go unreported in all countries. In addition, surveys often ask the question in such a way as to render the information useless. For example, they ask if a person has ever (even once, even many years ago) been assaulted by a domestic partner. Thus, a single hit from a drunken date is equated to systematic, ongoing, deliberate beatings from a spouse. Likewise, a bruised arm from being grabbed during an argument is equated to being raped and beaten until you are in a coma. Finally, the data are collected in different ways with each survey, making it meaningless to compare statistics from the 1990s, say, with those from the 2010s. Unlike statistics on undernutrition or school attendance, there are no standards for collecting data and reporting on levels of domestic violence.

Development Programs

Many different government agencies and nongovernmental organizations (NGOs) continue to work in Mali to try to improve the lives of the people in a sustainable manner. As the statistics discussed earlier show, there has been slow but fairly steady progress since my first research visit in the early 1980s. Mortality rates are dropping, especially for newborns, infants, and children; maternal mortality is lower; life expectancy is increasing; and rates of malnutrition are lower. Mothers now have much greater access to immunizations and other types of primary health care for themselves and their children. A number of creative programs have been established to help women gain greater access to education and to their own sources of income, as well as to increase the nutritional value of traditional foods. In this section, I briefly describe several recent and current health and nutrition projects taking place in Mali.

Freedom from Hunger

Freedom from Hunger (FFH) continues to play a major role in development efforts in Mali. They launched their signature *Credit with Education* program in 1989 with 50 women in Mali (part of the research I conducted in Dogo) and 50 women in Thailand. Today, the program serves more than 1.6 million people in 17 countries across Africa, Asia, and Latin America.

There is compelling evidence that FFH's *Credit with Education* program has made significant improvement in the lives of women and children in the countries where it is implemented, including gains in child nutritional status. For a summary, see Chris Dunford's 2013 blog update at *The Evidence Project: What We're Learning About Microfinance and World Hunger*, "Impact on Child Nutrition Status," posted June 13, 2013 (Dunford 2013).

Dr. Dunford worked for Freedom from Hunger from 1984 to 2012. He was the cocreator of the *Credit with Education* methodology and was the president of FFH in 1991–2011. He currently works as an independent consultant. Other relevant publications include MkNelly and Watson (2003) and the Oxfam America report (Oxfam 2013).

A new program began in 2009 to extend the microfinance and money management lessons of *Credit with Education* to the next generation. The new program, *Advancing Integrated Microfinance for Youth* (AIM Youth), is part of a collaboration with The MasterCard Foundation. According to the FFH website:

> In West Africa, *AIM Youth* will reach 22,000 young people in Mali. Malian youth tend to live in rural areas, where potable water and electricity are rare. Freedom from Hunger's local partners, Nyèsigiso and Kondo Jigima (federations of credit unions) and Tonus and CAEB (NGOs) are adding their own resources and local expertise to support the outreach effort. In Mali, a tradition of early marriage means that many adolescent girls are married and pregnant by the age of 19. Two-thirds of these young women and half the young men are illiterate. Because poverty and chronic hunger are so widespread, sound money management practices and the discipline of saving help *AIM Youth* participants to build and protect their assets.

The Freedom from Hunger website at https://www.freedomfromhunger. org/mali provides background and current updates on all of their projects. A portion of the proceeds from the sale of *Dancing Skeletons* is donated to FFH every year, and readers are encouraged to donate on their own.

Novartis—Early 1980s to 2000

Another major participant in health care development in Mali is Novartis, a company based in Basel, Switzerland. Novartis was formed in 1996 by the merger of two other Swiss companies, Ciba-Geigy and Sandoz. Novartis focuses on health care research, development, and implementation, including new medicines, eye care, generic pharmaceuticals, preventive vaccines, and research on improving nutrition. Part of Novartis' mission of corporate responsibility is their Foundation for Sustainable Development, "a non-profit based organization that . . . contributes to global development with a human face through various projects and programs, dialog and networking activities, and think-tank work."

From the early 1980s until his retirement in 2005, John F. Scheuring was one of the primary researchers working to improve the nutritional value of agricultural crops and weaning foods in Mali. At different times he worked for ICRISAT (the International Crop Research Institute for the Semi-Arid Tropics), Novartis, and then Syngenta. At Novartis he was the scientific advisor to their Foundation for Sustainable Development.

As part of his work in Mali with Novartis, Dr. Scheuring participated in several projects to help improve the nutritional status of infants and young children, all involving locally available technologies. One project focused on teaching mothers to incorporate protein from cowpeas into the traditional millet porridge they feed their children as one of their first foods other than breast milk. A second project involved malting (germination of the grain seed) to help increase the caloric density of such porridges. The third project, with the Novartis "Sight and Life" program, involved identifying better sources of Vitamins A and C for Malian diets. Leaves from wild baobab trees are often sun-dried, pounded into powder, and used in the daily sauce. The researchers discovered that baobab trees with smaller leaves provided more beta carotene than trees with larger leaves. When the smaller-leafed trees are harvested preferentially, and those leaves are then dried in the shade, rather than in direct sunlight, the provitamin A (beta carotene) content is much higher. A series of radio broadcasts were developed and aired to encourage rural villagers to focus on choosing trees with smaller leaves and drying them in the shade (Scheuring et al. 1999). Another important finding of this research was that market samples of baobab leaf powder had much lower levels of beta carotene than would be expected. It turned out that sellers often "cut" the baobab leaf powder with bulky, non-nutritive fillers, rendering the powder less nutritious. People were urged to find and harvest leaves directly from wild trees and process the leaves themselves, rather than purchasing baobab leaf powder in the markets.

In addition to eating baobab leaves, Malians make various food products from the fruit of the baobab tree, which can be a significant source of Vitamin C. Scheuring and colleagues discovered that, due to genetic variation, baobab trees differed significantly in the amount of Vitamin C typically found in their fruit. But how to ensure that all rural villagers had access to baobab trees with high levels of Vitamin C in their fruit? "Branches from the trees with the highest vitamin C content have been grafted onto an orchard of young baobab trees on the Cinzana Research Station in the Ségou region of Mali. This 'vitamin C' orchard may serve as important graft stock for Sahelian vitamin C orchards of the future (Sidibé et al. 1996, 1998)" (Scheuring et al. 1999).

Novartis—2000 to 2013

In recent years, Novartis has focused their development-related efforts in Mali on improving access to primary health care through addressing seven of the eight Millennium Development Goals:

> In September 2000, building upon a decade of major United Nations conferences and summits, world leaders came together at United Nations Headquarters in New York to adopt the *United Nations Millennium Declaration*, committing their nations to a new global partnership to reduce extreme poverty and setting out a series of time-bound targets—with a deadline of 2015—that have become known as the Millennium Development Goals. The eight Millennium Development Goals (MDGs)—which range from halving extreme poverty rates to halting the spread of HIV/AIDS and providing universal primary education, all by the target date of 2015—form a blueprint agreed to by all the world's countries and all the world's leading development institutions. They have galvanized unprecedented efforts to meet the needs of the world's poorest. (http://www.un.org/millenniumgoals/)

TABLE 4 How Novartis projects in Mali in 2013 address seven of the Millennium Development Goals

Millennium Development Goal	Novartis projects in Mali (as part of "Access to Primary Healthcare Services in Rural Mali")
1 ERADICATE EXTREME POVERTY AND HUNGER	Income-generating activities for rural communities, such as jatropha [plant] cultivation, poultry and milk production; income-generating activities for women's groups; and measures against malnutrition in children
3 PROMOTE GENDER EQUALITY AND EMPOWER WOMEN	Loans for women's groups; training women as village health workers to conduct health education campaigns
4 REDUCE CHILD MORTALITY	Child vaccination, village-based preventive and curative services; quality of care improvement (incl. child health); health insurance protection; and measures against malnutrition in children
5 IMPROVE MATERNAL HEALTH	Quality of care improvement (incl. maternal health); health insurance protection; prenatal consultation; and village-based preventive and curative services
6 COMBAT HIV/AIDS, MALARIA AND OTHER DISEASES	Improvement of access to healthcare; health insurance protection; and village-based preventive and curative services
7 ENSURE ENVIRONMENTAL SUSTAINABILITY	Installation of incinerators in health centers; contribution to carbon sequestration and reforestation through jatropha plantations
8 GLOBAL PARTNERSHIP FOR DEVELOPMENT	Collaboration with regional and district authorities for health and social development, Union Technique de la Mutualité Malienne (UTM) and the University of Geneva

Further information about the Novartis Foundation for Sustainable Development in general can be found here: http://www.novartisfoundation.org/. The 2012 report on Mali, "The Novartis Foundation for Sustainable Development in Mali: Improving Access to Primary Healthcare," can be found here: http://www.novartisfoundation.org/platform/apps/Publication/getfmfile. asp?id=616&el=4698&se=9117041&doc=259&dse=3 and more information is available here: http://www.novartisfoundation.org/page/content/index. asp?MenuID=578&ID=1762&Menu=3&Item=44.23.

Syngenta Foundation 2006–2012

In 2000, Novartis spun off their agricultural-related activities (Novartis Agribusiness), and it merged with Zeneca Agrochemicals to form Syngenta. Shortly thereafter, Syngenta stopped all of their direct nutrition-related work in Mali (Scheuring 2013), but they continue to carry out a number of development projects in the country.

In 2006, the Syngenta Foundation initiated the PRECAD Project (Projet de Renforcement des Capacités pour une Agriculture Durable), which ran until 2012. The initial focus was research on sorghum, cowpea, and millet. In 2011–2012, the focus shifted from research to enterprise development. The objective of the project was to improve farmer's productivity in pearl millet-based farming systems and, through training developed in collaboration with the farmers themselves, develop sustainable cooperative enterprises. Through such activities, the ultimate goal was to increase production, increase income, improve standards of living, and enhance food security.

The past 30 years of work by Syngenta and its predecessors in Mali were documented in a 2011 report, "When the Granaries Are Full" (Ferroni and Gabathuler 2011, in French). An English-language summary is also available online as "Syngenta Foundation: 30 years' experience in Mali" (Syngenta Foundation 2012).

CANEF

AMIPJ/CANEF was the Malian NGO that I worked with in Dogo Arrondissement in 1989, under a partnership with Freedom from Hunger. For a number of years, CANEF continued its work in microfinance, helping women in rural villages borrow money, start small income-producing projects, and repay their loans. In the mid-1990s, Freedom from Hunger severed its ties with CANEF, citing difficulties with the transparency of their practices and records. In 2013, the only information I could find online consisted of several posts (in French) accusing Bakary Traoré, the founder and CEO of CANEF, of illegal activities, including allegations that he embezzled money from CANEF and reports that the organization had shut its doors, leaving thousands of savings participants in the lurch. If these claims are true, they are very disheartening.

The Political Situation

During the colonial period, from 1890 to 1960, Mali was part of French West Africa (French Sudan). Like many other modern nation-states, the country's borders were drawn somewhat arbitrarily by Europeans, without any consideration of the people who lived in the region. Thus, Mali's population is made up of people from many different ethnic/cultural heritages, while, at the same time, some ethnic/cultural groups such as the Bambara, the Tuareg, and the Fulani live in a number of different countries, not just in Mali. In Mali, this has resulted in ongoing strife, especially between the Tuareg population of northern Mali and the government in Bamako.

The Tuareg of Mali are nomadic pastoralists who occupy the northern two-thirds of the country, which consists of parts of the Sahara Desert and the Sahel, just south of the Sahara; some sedentary groups live full-time at oases. In addition to milk (from their herds of goats and camels), millet, and dates form the staples of their diet. Originally animists, some Tuareg converted to Christianity as it spread across North Africa, and then to Islam, when it was brought to the region by traders. By the 16th century, most Tuareg identified themselves as Muslims. This northern region of

Mali is sparsely settled, and, until the advent of cell phones, communication with the rest of the country was difficult and sporadic. Politicians running the country from Bamako paid little attention to the concerns of the Tuareg and other groups living far from the capital. Since independence from France in 1960, there have been periodic stirrings for some form of independence or autonomy for the northern regions, but they were of little consequence. A brief history of Malian government leadership will set the stage for a further discussion of the situation at the present time.

The first president after independence was Modibo Keita, who ruled until 1968, when he was overthrown in a bloodless military coup led by Moussa Traoré. Traoré was the president through the 1980s and the political situation was fairly stable and quiet during the times I was there conducting research, with a single-party political system. By 1989–90, however, there was growing unrest among the general population who suspected Traoré and his wife of corruption and of siphoning money out of the country. In 1991, the movement to establish a true multiparty democracy erupted into four days of antigovernment protests. A group of military officers, led by Amadou Toumani Touré, arrested President Traoré and took over the government. A new constitution was written and adopted in 1992, and Alpha Oumar Konaré became the first democratically elected president of Mali. Konaré served two five-year terms (1992–2002), and was followed by Amadou Toumani Touré, elected in 2002, who also served two terms (2002–2012).

In 2012, rather more serious political strife began in the northern part of the country, with a more organized and better armed Tuareg force once again raising the issue of autonomy. In the current conflict, there are several different factions of Tuareg "rebels." The main faction is the National Movement for the Liberation of Azawad (MNLA), where *Azawad* refers to the region of northern Mali that the Tuareg would like to establish as an independent, autonomous state or country. The MNLA includes a number of Tuareg who served as mercenaries for Muammar Gaddafi of Libya. After Gaddafi was killed in 2011, many of his Tuareg backers returned to Mali, bringing weapons, training, and experience in warfare. Their return reinvigorated the Tuareg independence movement, which began anew with attacks on several towns in northern Mali in January 2012.

Various Tuareg factions have been supported by other groups, including Al Qaeda in the Islamic Maghreb (AQIM). AQIM is an Islamist political group whose primary goal is to overthrow the government of Algeria (and perhaps Tunisia) and create an Algerian Islamic state with *sharia* law. It is unclear just how large, and how organized, AQIM really is, and to what extent it has the backing of other Al Qaeda groups. There have also been reports of conflicts between some members of AQIM and MNLA. Other splinter groups have formed and then disbanded over the past two years.

In March 2012, members of the Malian military, angry over the government's handling of the Tuareg rebellion in the north, overthrew the democratically elected president. This coup elicited immediate condemnation and severe economic sanctions from the international community, including a termination of all U.S. assistance to the Government of Mali. When the dust settled at the end of March, the north was firmly under the control of the Tuareg. A transitional government was established in August 2012, led by parliament speaker Dioncounda Traoré, with Cheik Modibo Diarra serving as prime minister.

In January 2013, at the request of the Malian government in Bamako, the French joined the fray on behalf of Mali and the international community, launching an air-based military attack designed to push the rebel forces back to the north. The rebels retreated and were eventually driven north of Timbuktu. One ongoing concern about conditions in northern Mali is the issue of protecting and preserving thousands of ancient brittle religious and historical manuscripts housed in Timbuktu. The following excerpt from *TIME* briefly explains the issues (Walt 2013):

> One week after Islamic militants fled Timbuktu under French bombing strikes, preservationists are deeply uncertain about how to continue protecting the city's priceless ancient documents—a conundrum that cuts to the heart of how treasures are safeguarded through political upheaval in places where locals have little trust in government. When French and African forces rumbled into northern Mali's ancient capital 10 days ago, Timbuktu's mayor, who had little direct information, told journalists erroneously that the jihadists had destroyed "all the important documents" and that Malians needed to "kill all the rebels." In fact, Timbuktu's residents and preservationists had told *TIME* early last year that they had rescued tens of thousands of manuscripts before the militants seized northern Mali. They agreed to talk on the condition that *TIME* kept their secret until the jihadists had been defeated. The operation was conducted by Timbuktu's old families, which have looked after the city's 300,000 or so ancient documents for centuries. The residents left behind just a few hundred manuscripts in Timbuktu's only publicly run collection, the Ahmed Baba Institute, in order to conceal the fact that they'd hidden the bulk of them elsewhere; it was those that were destroyed last month.

American Fulbright scholar and professional photographer Alexandra Huddleston worked in Timbuktu for several years just prior to the recent troubles, documenting the long-standing traditions of Islamic scholarship through her photographs. Her work, including a short video and information about her book *333 Saints: A Life of Scholarship Under Threat*, can be seen here: http://333saints.wordpress.com/.

The latest news from Mali is heartening. Democratic elections were held on July 28, 2013, with a run-off held on August 11, 2013. In the first round, Ibrahim Boubacar Keïta was the resounding favorite, with 39 percent of the vote, compared to Soumaïla Cissé's 19 percent. In the run-off election, Keïta earned a clear victory with 78 percent of the vote. While the country's recent political struggles had threatened to compromise the progress made over the past several decades, the return of a democratically elected government and the subsequent resumption of aid from the United States and other countries should help improve conditions for all Malians in the years to come.

To keep up with the latest news from Mali, access Journal of Mali (Mali in one click) at http://www.journaldumali.com/ or Maliweb.net (virtual Mali) at http://www.maliweb.net/.

Bibliography

ACE Study. 2013. Centers for Disease Control. http://www.cdc.gov/ace/about.htm. Accessed August 29, 2013.

ASAPS—American Society for Aesthetic Plastic Surgery. 2013. Most popular cosmetic surgery procedures in 2012. March 12, 2013. http://www.surgery.org/consumers/plastic-surgery-news-briefs/popular-cosmetic-surgery-procedures-2012-1049714. Accessed June 18, 2013.

Atwood, Margaret. 1986. *The handmaid's tale*. Boston: Houghton Mifflin.

Bertelsmann Stiftung, BTI. 2012. *Mali country report*. Gütersloh: Bertelsmann Stiftung, 2012. http://www.bti-project.de/fileadmin/Inhalte/reports/2012/pdf/BTI%202012%20Mali.pdf. Accessed June 26, 2013.

Beston, Henry. 1977. *The outermost house*. New York: Penguin Books.

Biebuyck, Daniel, and Kahombo C. Mateene. 1971. *The Mwindo epic*. Berkeley: University of California Press.

Bird, Charles. 1972. Heroic songs of the Mande hunters. In Richard M. Dorson, ed. *African folklore*. Bloomington: Indiana University Press.

Bohannan, Paul. 1992. *We, the alien: An introduction to cultural anthropology*. Long Grove, IL: Waveland Press.

Cannon, Poppy. 1964. Revolution in the kitchen. *Saturday Review* 47. October 24.

Cashion, Barbara Warren. 1988. *Creation of a local growth standard based on well-nourished Malian children, and its application to a village sample of unknown age*. Ph.D. diss., Indiana University, Bloomington. Ann Arbor: UMI.

Cassidy, Claire M. 1987. World-view conflict and toddler malnutrition. In Nancy Scheper-Hughes, ed. *Child survival: Anthropological perspectives on the treatment and maltreatment of children*. Dordrecht/Boston: D. Reidel.

Chilson, Peter. 2013. *We never knew exactly where: Dispatches from the lost country of Mali*. Publisher: Foreign Policy and the Pulitzer Center. http://www.foreignpolicy.com/ebooks/we_never_knew_exactly_where. Accessed June 26, 2013.

Cruickshank, Robert, Kenneth L. Standard, and Hugh B. L. Russell. 1976. *Epidemiology and community health in warm climate countries*. New York: Churchill Livingstone.

Dettwyler, Katherine A. 1985. *Breastfeeding, weaning, and other infant feeding practices in Mali and their effects on growth and development*. Ph.D. diss., Indiana University, Bloomington. Ann Arbor: UMI.

Dettwyler, Katherine A. 1991. Can paleopathology provide evidence for "compassion"? *American Journal of Physical Anthropology* 84:375–384.

Dettwyler, Katherine A. 1991. Growth status of children in rural Mali: Implications for nutrition education programs. *American Journal of Human Biology* 3:447–462.

Dettwyler, Katherine A. 1992. Nutritional status of adults in rural Mali. *American Journal of Physical Anthropology* 88:309–321.

Dettwyler, Katherine A. 2011. *Cultural anthropology and human experience: The feast of life.* Long Grove, IL: Waveland Press.

Dettwyler, Katherine A., and Claudia Fishman. 1990. *Field research in Macina for Vitamin A communications.* Washington, DC: Nutrition Communication Project, Academy for Educational Development.

Dettwyler, Steven P. 1985. *Senoufo migrants in Bamako: Changing agricultural production strategies and household organization in an urban environment.* Ph.D. diss., Indiana University, Bloomington. Ann Arbor: UMI.

Dunford, Chris. 2013. Impact on child nutrition status. *The evidence project: What we're learning about microfinance and world hunger.* http://microfinanceandworldhunger.org/wordpress/2013/06/impact-on-child-nutrition-status/. Accessed June 26, 2013.

Elliott, Diana B., Kristy Krivickas, Matthew W. Brault, and Rose M. Kreider. 2012. Historical marriage trends from 1890–2010: A focus on race differences. *SEHSD Working Paper Number 2012-12.* United States Census Bureau, Center for Economic Studies. http://www.census.gov/hhes/socdemo/marriage/data/acs/ElliottetalPAA2012paper.pdf. Accessed June 26, 2013.

Evans-Pritchard, E. E. 1937. *Witchcraft, oracles, and magic among the Azande.* Oxford: Oxford University Press.

Evans-Pritchard, E. E. 1940. *The Nuer: A description of the modes of livelihood and political institutions of a Nilotic people.* Oxford: Oxford University Press.

Farley, John. 1991. *Bilharzia: A history of imperial tropical medicine.* New York: Cambridge University Press.

Ferroni, Sonia, and Ernst Gabathuler. 2011. Quand les greniers se remplissent. Centre for Development and Environment, Universität, Bern. http://www.cde.unibe.ch/CDE/pdf/F_Fullversion_low_Quand_les_greniers_se_remplissent.pdf. Accessed June 26, 2013.

Frank, Barbara E. 2007 Marks of identity: Potters of the Folona (Mali) and their "mothers." *African Arts,* Spring 2007, Vol. 40, No. 1, pages 30–41.

Geertz, Clifford. 1973. *The interpretation of cultures.* New York: Basic Books, Inc.

Gibbons, Luz, José M. Belizán, Jeremy A. Lauer, Ana P. Betrán, Mario Merialdi, and Fernando Althabe. 2010. The global numbers and costs of additionally needed and unnecessary cesarean sections performed per year: Overuse as a barrier to universal coverage. *World Health Report, Background Paper, 30.* http://www.who.int/healthsystems/topics/financing/healthreport/30C-sectioncosts.pdf. Accessed June 13, 2013.

Groce, Nora. 1985. *Everyone here spoke sign language: Hereditary deafness on Martha's Vineyard.* Cambridge: Harvard University Press.

Harris, Eddy L. 1992. *Native stranger: A black American's journey into the heart of Africa.* New York: Simon & Schuster.

Holtzman, Jon D. 2008. *Nuer journeys, Nuer lives: Sudanese refugees in Minnesota,* 2nd ed. New York: Allyn & Bacon.

Hoving, Thomas. 1981. *King of the confessors.* New York: Simon & Schuster. (Source of the quote by Montaigne).

Howell, Nancy. 1990. *Surviving fieldwork: A report of the advisory panel on health and safety in fieldwork.* Washington, DC: American Anthropological Association. Special Publication No. 26.

Imperato, Pascal James. 1977. *African folk medicine: Practices and beliefs of the Bambara and other peoples.* Baltimore: York Press.

ISAPS—International Society for Aesthetic Plastic Surgery. 2011. ISAPS International survey on aesthetic/cosmetic procedures performed in 2011. http://www.isaps.org/files/html-contents/Downloads/ISAPS%20Results%20-%20Procedures%20in%202011.pdf. Accessed June 18, 2013.

Joint Commission. 2010. Preventing maternal death. *Sentinel Event Alert, Issue #44.* January 26, 2010. http://www.jointcommission.org/assets/1/18/sea_44.pdf. Accessed June 13, 2013.

Karp, Ivan. 1978. *Fields of change among the Iteso of Kenya.* Boston: Routledge and Kegan Paul.

Karr-Morse, Robin, and Meredith S. Wiley. 1998. *Ghosts from the nursery: Tracing the roots of violence.* New York: Grove/Atlantic.

Kawamura, Sayaka. 2009. What is behind the delayed marriage in Japan? Do women postpone marriage because they are traditional or because they are egalitarian? http://paa2009.princeton.edu/papers/90537. Accessed June 26, 2013.

Kushner, Harold S. 1981. *When bad things happen to good people.* New York: Shocken Books.

Mali's conflict, the Sahel's crisis (World Politics Review Special Reports). *World Politics Review* (January 21, 2013). http://www.worldpoliticsreview.com/articles/12454/special-report-malis-conflict-the-sahels-crisis. Accessed June 26, 2013.

McKenna, James J. 1986. An anthropological perspective on the Sudden Infant Death Syndrome (SIDS): The role of parental breathing cues and speech breathing adaptations. *Medical Anthropology* 10(1):9–91.

McLean, Scilla, and Efua Graham. 1985. *Female circumcision, excision and infibulation: The facts and proposals for change.* London: Minority Rights Group Report No. 47. Second revised edition.

McNaughton, Patrick R. 1979. *Secret sculptures of Komo: Art and power in Bamana (Bambara) initiation associations.* Philadelphia: Institute for the Study of Human Issues. Working Papers in the Traditional Arts, No. 4.

Mead, Margaret. 1928. *Coming of age in Samoa; A psychological study of primitive youth for Western civilisation.* New York: W. Morrow.

MkNelly, Barbara, and April Watson. 2003. *Credit with education.* Impact Review No. 3: Children's Nutritional Status, October 2003. Freedom from Hunger. https://www.freedomfromhunger.org/sites/default/files/childrens_nutritional_status.pdf. Accessed June 26, 2013.

Olson, Emelie A. 1981. Socioeconomic and psychocultural contexts of child abuse and neglect in Turkey. In Jill Korbin, ed. *Child abuse and neglect: Cross-cultural perspectives.* Berkeley: University of California Press.

Oxfam 2013. *Saving for change: Financial inclusion and resilience for the world's poorest people.* Revised Report Summary, May 2013. http://www.oxfamamerica.org/files/oxfam-america-sfc-ipa-bara-toplines.pdf. Accessed June 26, 2013.

Parry, E. H. O. 1976. *Principles of medicine in Africa.* Oxford: Oxford University Press.

Rothman, Barbara Katz. 1986. *The tentative pregnancy: Prenatal diagnosis and the meaning of parenthood.* New York: Viking Press.

Sargent, Carolyn. 2011. Personal communication.

Scheper-Hughes, Nancy. 1987. Culture, scarcity, and maternal thinking: Mother love and child death in northeast Brazil. In Nancy Scheper-Hughes, ed. *Child survival: Anthropological perspectives on the treatment and maltreatment of children.* Dordrecht/Boston: D. Reidel.

Scheper-Hughes, Nancy. 1992. *Death without weeping: The violence of everyday life in Brazil.* Berkeley: University of California Press.

Scheuring, J. F., M. Sidibé, and M. Frigg. 1999. Malian agronomic research identifies local baobab tree as source of vitamin A and vitamin C. *Sight and Life,* Newsletter 1, 1999. http://www.mightybaobab.com/scientific-papers/MalianAgronomicResearchIdentifiesBaobabAsSourceOfVitaminC.pdf. Accessed June 26, 2013.

Scheuring, John F. 2013. Personal communication.

Schneider, Harold K. 1974. *Economic man: The anthropology of economics.* New York: Free Press.

Sheer, Jessica, and Nora Groce. 1988. Impairment as a human constant: Cross-cultural and historical perspectives on variation. *Journal of Social Issues* 44(1):23–37.

Shriver, Lionel. 1987. *The female of the species.* New York: Penguin Books.

Stephenson, Lani S., and Celia Holland. 1987. *The impact of helminth injections on human nutrition: Schistosomes and soil-transmitted helminths.* London: Taylor & Francis.

Stoller, Paul, and Cheryl Olkes. 1987. *In sorcery's shadow: A memoir of apprenticeship among the Songhay of Niger.* Chicago: University of Chicago Press.

Syngenta Foundation. 2012. Syngenta Foundation: 30 years' experience in Mali. http://www.syngentafoundation.org/_temp/30_years_in_Mali_e.pdf. Accessed June 26, 2013.

Trevathan, Wenda. 1987. *Human birth: An evolutionary perspective.* New York: Aldine de Gruyter.

UNICEF Definitions. http://www.unicef.org/infobycountry/stats_popup9.html. Accessed June 17, 2013.

Ventura, Stephanie J. 2009. Changing patterns of nonmarital childbearing in the United States. *National Center for Health Statistics/CDC Data Brief No. 18,* May 2009. http://www.cdc.gov/nchs/data/databriefs/db18.pdf. Accessed June 26, 2013.

Walt, Vivienne. 2013. Timbuktu's ancient libraries: Saved by locals, endangered by a government. *TIME* Magazine, February 4, 2013. http://world.time.com/2013/02/04/timbuktus-ancient-libraries-saved-by-locals-endangered-by-a-government/. Accessed June 20, 2013.

World Health Organization. 2013. Health services coverage statistics. Definition of "skilled birth attendant." http://www.who.int/healthinfo/statistics/indbirthswithskilledhealthpersonnel/en/. Accessed June 13, 2013.

World Life Expectancy. 2010. http://www.worldlifeexpectancy.com/. Accessed June 26, 2013.

Acknowledgments

Many friends, relatives, and organizations helped make my research in Mali, and this book, possible. In terms of financial support, I am greatly indebted to the following organizations that have helped fund my research in Mali: the Graduate School of Indiana University, Bloomington; Sigma Xi, the Scientific Research Society; the Pottenger Foundation for Anthropological Research; the Fulbright Scholar Program; the College of Liberal Arts and the Department of Anthropology at Texas A&M University; the Academy for Educational Development; and Freedom from Hunger. For personal support, I thank Ivan Karp, who introduced me to African ethnography and the works of E. E. Evans-Pritchard; Paul L. Jamison, who guided my research efforts and has always believed in me; Barbara and Gerry Cashion, who first introduced me to Mali; Moussa Diarra, my research collaborator and good friend, who contributed above and beyond the call of duty; Rookia Diakite, who provided many excellent meals; the staff of AMIPJ/CANEF—Bakary Traoré, Falaye Doumbia, Tiedo Ba, Saran Sidibe, and Abibatou Niare—and Kathleen Stack from Freedom from Hunger, all of whom facilitated the research in Dogo; Heather Mari Katz, my undergraduate research assistant, who unflaggingly recorded the anthropometric data and never complained about the rigorous field conditions; Claudia Parvanta of the Academy for Educational Development, who has helped turn my research into health promotion programs in Mali and other West African countries; Neil Woodruff, the U.S.A.I.D. health officer who provided critical logistical and emotional support during the first month of research in Mali; and Thomas T. Kane and Sue Hammerton, who provided friendship and support during later stages of the fieldwork.

With specific reference to the writing of this book, I am indebted first of all to Jane Kepp of the School of American Research Press. Jane's enthusiasm for the early chapters of the manuscript and insightful suggestions for restructuring the narrative are greatly appreciated. Her ideas about what makes for interesting reading permeate the text. Tom Curtin, at Waveland Press, has been an enthusiastic supporter from the beginning, providing inspiration as well as gentle cajoling to finish the book. Thanks Tom!! Lee Cronk and Bruce Dickson, my congenial colleagues at Texas A&M, provided encouragement and support during the writing, including graciously relinquishing the research computer when I needed to use it. The cover art for the original edition (now appearing on the title page) is based on a drawing I got at a street fair in Bloomington, Indiana, in the late 1970s. Phyllis Rash Hughes is the artist, and the drawing introduced me to her trademark "dancing skeletons," a different version of which sits on my desk. Wanda Giles provided meticulous, and much appreciated, copy-editing, as well as insightful comments on how the book affected her. "Spellcheck" can never replace an excellent copy-editor! Jim Lyle and the staff at Texas A&M's Photographic Services turned my color slides into black-and-white prints. Cathryn Clement, of Texas A&M's International Agricultural Program, provided the maps. Joanna Casey provided me with the source of the quotation by Lionel Shriver. My sister, Diana Dulaney, provided a keen editorial eye during the early draft stages. Melissa Cuthbert took loving care of Alexander so that I could work on the computer at home. To all of these people, my sincere gratitude.

Saving the best for last, four people deserve particular mention. My sons Peter and Alexander constantly remind me of what is truly important in life. My daughter, Miranda, serves that purpose as well. She also acted as my research assistant and general factotum in Mali and deserves a special thanks for "hanging out" without complaint during the field research. I could not have gone to the field without her, and I apologize for the suffering she endured in Mali on her mother's behalf. She is a great kid, and I admire her courage and her generosity. My husband and best friend, Steven, waited at home and lovingly served as both mother and father to Peter for six long months. This selfless act of faith and love can never be repaid.

Of course, I owe my biggest debt of gratitude to the women and children of Mali who allowed me to participate in, observe, and record their lives. I hope I have done them justice.

For this 20th Anniversary Edition of *Dancing Skeletons*, I extend my appreciation to the many students who have written, asking questions or telling me how much the book meant to them. As always, I want to thank the wonderful folks at Waveland Press, and especially Tom Curtin and Jeni Ogilvie, editors *extraordinaire*. They have put up with my many eccentricities with grace and humor.